T0407139

ABOLISH CRIMINOLOGY

Abolish Criminology presents critical scholarship on criminology and criminal justice ideologies and practices, alongside emerging freedom-driven visions and practices for new world formations.

The book introduces readers to a detailed history and analysis of crime as a concept and its colonizing trajectories into existence and enforcement. These significant contexts buried within peculiar academic histories and classroom practices are often overlooked or unknown outside academic and public discussions, causing the impact of racializing-gendering-sexualizing histories to extend and grow through criminology's creation of crime, extending how the concept is weaponized and enforced through the criminal legal system. It offers written, visual, and poetic teachings from the perspectives of students, professors, imprisoned and formerly imprisoned persons, and artists. This allows readers to engage in multi-sensory, inter-disciplinary, and multi-perspective teachings on criminology's often discussed but seldom interrogated mythologies on violence and danger, and their wide-reaching enforcements through the criminal legal system's research, theories, agencies, and dominant cultures.

Abolish Criminology serves the needs of undergraduate and graduate students and educators in the social sciences, arts, and humanities. It will also appeal to scholars, researchers, policy makers, activists, community organizers, social movement builders, and various reading groups in the general public who are grappling with increased critical public discourse on policing and criminal legal reform or abolition.

Viviane Saleh-Hanna is Full Professor of Crime and Justice Studies and Director of Black Studies at the University of Massachusetts, Dartmouth. Her scholarship centers wholistic justice, abolition, anti-colonialism, Black feminist hauntology, structurally abusive relationships, and freedom dreams inspired by Octavia E. Butler, Toni Morrison, and new world formations of Afrofuturism.

Jason M. Williams is Associate Professor of Justice Studies at Montclair State University. He's an activist scholar specializing in racial and gender disparity, and mistreatment within the criminal legal system; a nationally recognized and quoted qualitative criminologist with publications on re-entry, policing, and social control; and is engaged in community-grounded research.

Michael J. Coyle is Professor in the Department of Political Science and Criminal Justice, California State University, Chico. He is the author of *Talking Criminal Justice: Language and the Just Society* (Routledge, 2013) and the forthcoming *Seeing Crime: Penal Abolition as the End of Utopian Criminal Justice*.

Routledge Studies in Penal Abolition and Transformative Justice Series

Michael J. Coyle and David Scott

The *Routledge Studies in Penal Abolition and Transformative Justice* book series provides the leading publishing location for literature that both reflects key abolitionist thought and helps to set the agenda for local and global abolitionist ideas and interventions. It fosters research that works toward the systemic and systematic dismantling of penal structures and processes, and toward social living that is grounded in relationships that consider the needs of all. This international book series seeks contributions from all around the world (east, north, south, and west) that both engages and furthers abolitionist and transformative practice, study, politics and theory. It welcomes work that examines abolition and transformative justice empirically, theoretically, historically, culturally, spatially, or rhetorically, as well as books that are situated within or at the interstices of critiques of ableism, capitalism, hetero-normativity, militarism, patriarchy, state power, racism, settler colonialism, and xenophobia.

www.routledge.com/Routledge-Studies-in-Penal-Abolition-and-Transformative-Justice/book-series/PATJ#:~:text=About%20the%20Series,global%20abolitionist%20ideas%20and%20interventions.

Building Abolition
Decarceration and Social Justice
Kelly Struthers Montford and Chloë Taylor

Contesting Carceral Logic
Michael J. Coyle and Mechthild Nagel

Ludic Ubuntu Ethics
Decolonizing Justice
Mechthild Nagel

Abolish Criminology
Edited by Viviane Saleh-Hanna, Jason M. Williams, and Michael J. Coyle

ABOLISH CRIMINOLOGY

Edited by Viviane Saleh-Hanna, Jason M. Williams, and Michael J. Coyle

Routledge
Taylor & Francis Group

LONDON AND NEW YORK

Cover artwork: Dara Kwayera Imani Bayer. Photograph of artwork by
Samson Awoson

First published 2024
by Routledge
4 Park Square, Milton Park, Abingdon, Oxon OX14 4RN

and by Routledge
605 Third Avenue, New York, NY 10158

Routledge is an imprint of the Taylor & Francis Group, an informa business

British Library Cataloguing-in-Publication Data
A catalogue record for this book is available from the British Library

Library of Congress Cataloging-in-Publication Data
Names: Saleh-Hanna, Viviane, 1976– editor. | Williams, Jason M.,
    1986– editor. | Coyle, Michael J., editor.
Title: Abolish criminology / edited by Viviane Saleh-Hanna, Jason M.
    Williams and Michael J. Coyle.
Description: Abingdon, Oxon ; New York, NY : Routledge, 2022. |
    Series: Routledge studies in penal abolitionism and transformative
    justice | Includes bibliographical references and index.
Identifiers: LCCN 2022056467 (print) | LCCN 2022056468 (ebook) |
    ISBN 9780367419905 (hardback) | ISBN 9780367521332 (paperback) |
    ISBN 9780367817114 (ebook)
Subjects: LCSH: Critical criminology. | Criminal justice, Administration
    of—Moral and ethical aspects.
Classification: LCC HV6019 .A26 2022 (print) | LCC HV6019 (ebook) |
    DDC 364—dc23/eng/20221128
LC record available at https://lccn.loc.gov/2022056467
LC ebook record available at https://lccn.loc.gov/2022056468

ISBN: 978-0-367-41990-5 (hbk)
ISBN: 978-0-367-52133-2 (pbk)
ISBN: 978-0-367-81711-4 (ebk)

DOI: 10.4324/9780367817114

Typeset in Bembo
by Apex CoVantage, LLC

We dedicate this book to future generations who shall inherit a world without prisons, policing, courts, crime, and criminology – may they all be born free.

CONTENTS

FIGURES

CONTRIBUTORS

Viviane Saleh-Hanna is Full Professor of Crime and Justice Studies and Director of Black Studies at the University of Massachusetts, Dartmouth. Her scholarship centers wholistic justice, abolition, anti-colonialism, Black feminist hauntology, structurally abusive relationships, and freedom dreams inspired by Octavia E. Butler, Toni Morrison, and new world formations of Afrofuturism.

Jason M. Williams is Associate Professor of Justice Studies at Montclair State University. He's an activist scholar specializing in racial and gender disparity, and mistreatment within the criminal legal system. He's a nationally recognized and quoted qualitative criminologist with publications on re-entry, policing, and social control, and is engaged in community-grounded research.

Michael J. Coyle, PhD, is Professor, Department of Political Science and Criminal Justice, California State University, Chico. He is the author of *Talking Criminal Justice: Language and the Just Society* (Routledge, 2013) and the forthcoming *Seeing Crime: Penal Abolition as the End of Utopian Criminal Justice.*

Christopher Bickel is Associate Professor of Sociology and Criminology and Justice Studies, California State University, San Marcos. He is currently director of the Continuation to College Program in San Diego County, California, which encourages at-promise youth to attend colleges and universities.

Michelle Brown is a critical criminologist and visual scholar at the University of Tennessee, working to decarcerate the Appalachian South, with loved ones living inside and working for the prison state. Her work focuses upon countervisual practices and strategies – how we unsee and unbecome prisons, police, and empires in order to build freedom.

Tatiana Lopes DosSantos is a Cabo Verdean woman based in Rhode Island. She earned a Bachelor of Arts degree in Crime and Justice Studies from the University of Massachusetts, Dartmouth and was the recipient of her department's Harriet Tubman Award for Intersectional Scholarship. Since graduating, she has focused on creating poetry and music. Tatiana has a passion for liberation that pours into her work.

Charlemya Erasme (she/her/hers) is a Haitian American who cares deeply about system-level change and alleviating suffering. Charlemya's journey is constantly evolving. Family, faith, and curiosity guide her. She holds two degrees from the University of Massachusetts, Dartmouth: a Bachelor of Science in Biology and Master of Science in STEM Education with a science concentration.

Erin Katherine Krafft is Associate Professor of Crime and Justice Studies and Director of the Urban Studies Program at the University of Massachusetts, Dartmouth. Her research centers transnational feminisms, particularly those of the US, Soviet Russia, and contemporary Russia, as well as practices of collaborative and anti-oppressive education.

Martin J. Leyva is a formerly incarcerated Chicano scholar and a doctoral student at UC San Diego. He earned a Master of Arts in Sociological Practice from California State University, San Marcos. He has led training on Best Practices for Working with Formerly Incarcerated Individuals, Emotional Intelligence, and Spiritual Self Care and Healing.

Vanessa Lynn Lovelace is Assistant Professor of Crime and Justice Studies at the University of Massachusetts, Dartmouth. Her research and teaching centers abolitionisms, and anti-oppressive feminist theories and methods. In particular, her work unpacks how narratives of freedom become mapped on/in the land.

Toniqua Mikell is Assistant Professor of Crime and Justice Studies at the University of Massachusetts, Dartmouth. She is an intersectional criminologist who employs Black feminism, queer criminology, and critical race theory to understand the social control of Black women and femme-identifying individuals within carceral states.

Ryan Phillips is Assistant Professor in the Department of Criminal Justice and Criminology at Marshall University. He earned his PhD in Criminology and Criminal Justice at Old Dominion University, and his MS and BS at Eastern Kentucky University. His primary areas of study are Marxist criminology and critical prison studies, with a specific focus on ideology.

Brian Pitman is Assistant Professor in sociology at the University of Maine, primarily concentrating his research and teaching in criminology and criminal justice. He received his PhD from Old Dominion University in 2019, his MA from the University of North Carolina, Wilmington, and his BS from the University of North Carolina, Pembroke.

Xuan Santos is a formerly incarcerated and award-winning Associate Professor of Sociology, Criminology and Justice Studies at California State University, San Marcos. He is the cofounder and Executive Director of Project Rebound (CSUSM chapter). He works with undocumented, formerly incarcerated, and students and community members who have been affected by the criminal legal system.

Holly Sims-Bruno has Bachelor and Master of Science degrees in Criminal Justice from Eastern Kentucky University and a PhD in Criminal Justice from Indiana University in Bloomington. She is currently an adjunct instructor for the Department of Criminal Justice at the University of Indianapolis.

Oscar F. Soto is a formerly incarcerated Xicano Marxist activist-scholar. He is a PhD candidate in Sociology and Black Studies at the University of California, Santa Barbara. In addition, he is a lecturer at California State University, San Marcos, and UC Santa Barbara.

Derrick Washington is a 36-year-young Black man currently challenging an armed robbery homicide conviction while in a maximum security prison in Massachusetts. While in prison, Washington founded the organization Emancipation Initiative, which advocates for ending sentences of life without parole and restoring universal incarcerated suffrage in Massachusetts. This work has been featured in The Atlantic and The Boston Globe. He was also involved in work with Harvard University students on a campaign to divest Harvard from prisons.

Stephen T. Young is Associate Professor in Criminal Justice and Criminology at Marshall University in Huntington, West Virginia. He earned his PhD in Criminology and Criminal Justice at Old Dominion University, and his MS and BA from Marshall University. His primary area of concentration is critical rural criminology.

ABOLISH CRIMINOLOGY

Viviane Saleh-Hanna, Jason M. Williams, and Michael J. Coyle

Criminology Is the Head of the Snake: Abolitionist Lessons from Frederick Douglass

Work on this book began before the murder of George Floyd by police officers in Minneapolis, before the COVID-19 pandemic sent the whole world into quarantined lockdowns, and before The Movement for Black Lives gained worldwide prominence with demands to defund the police and end criminal legal violence specifically, and anti-Black racism structurally within the United States and around the world. For the first time in the life of the criminal legal system, abolition gained prominence within widespread public discourses. And while much of that mainstream dialogue was misinformed and lacked the critical lens that abolitionists have spent decades developing, the significance of a growing public discourse about the abolition of the criminal legal system – or at the very least, the abolition of the police – cannot be overlooked.

The seeds for contemporary movements to abolish the criminal legal system were planted many years ago, gaining prominence through the prison abolitionist and then penal abolitionist movements of ICOPA (the International Conference on Penal Abolition) starting in the 1980s in Canada and traveling to Europe, central America, the U.S., Australia, New Zealand, west Africa, the Caribbean, and south America (Saleh-Hanna 2008; Delisle et al. 2015) and expanding significantly in the 1990s through the work of Black, Indigenous, and queer abolitionist feminists who formed and grew Critical Resistance in the U.S. (Sudbury 2009; Davis and Rodriguez 2000).

It is crucial to understand contemporary abolitionist movements as a creation and extension of the work of historic abolitionists like Frederick Douglass (1865), who warned us about the limitations of the Thirteenth Amendment to abolish slavery

DOI: 10.4324/9780367817114-1

(but not enslavement) in the United States. Shortly after it was passed Douglass said, "the work of abolitionists is not done" for slavery has taken on many names to progress its profit-driven violence: "You and I and all of us had better wait and see what new form this old monster will assume, in what new skin this old snake will come forth next" (85). Many of the seeds planted and nurtured by historic abolitionists against enslavement and colonialism have been tended to by prison and penal abolitionist communities, activists, organizers, artists, and scholars (imprisoned, formerly imprisoned, allied, and kin). These seeds began to sprout in directions acutely focused on policing and carceral violence in 2020, breaking ground to find a moment of sustained light within dominant white cultures for the first time. That moment has been a long time coming.

The authors whose work collectively create this book lives within the "before and after" worlds of the last few years. They offer a collection of understandings that have long been held within abolitionist enclaves and that continue to liberate our notions of justice from criminology's imprisoning landscapes. Abolitionists within the academy have known this to be necessary, because the theories and ideas developed within the obscure corridors of criminology's academic halls are so dominant that they flow seamlessly within popular colonial cultures, forming the storylines of crime TV and newscasts, indoctrinating a colonial worldview that dangerously naturalizes and embodies white supremacist assumptions about humanity, society, and the role of law – and these in turn create criminology's dangerous impression that we cannot live, cannot be safe, and cannot exist without the criminal legal system's oversight and colonial law's power. When criminology's theories and ideologies are turned into "storylines" in the news and within entertainment venues, people begin to assume criminology's imaginations and musings are factual and rational descriptions and explanations as opposed to a more accurate context: the writings and debates of mainly white men who have almost always stood on the side of white supremacy through an undercurrent of support for racialized enslavement, segregation, imprisonment, impoverishment, heteropatriarchy, genderism, ableism, and colonialism.

The purpose of this book has always been to provide an accessible and critical context of the dominant schools of thought that shape criminology's discourse. The goal is to reach the heart of the matter of justice on our way to the head of that monster that Frederick Douglass warned about. Please know that the head of the monster, at this time, is criminology. The abolition of criminology's thought patterns and behaviors is a crucial part of the multi-faceted and necessary work of abolition. This book offers a start for that conversation through a collection of writings and artwork by abolitionist scholars, students, organizers, artists, and imprisoned or formerly imprisoned voices, who are best positioned to reflect on the inner workings of criminology and criminal justice in the academy, as well as a larger analysis of how western universities colonize thought and perpetuate injustice. This book also offers chapters that highlight abolitionist thought and research on justice that transcends and overshadows the mediocre patterns and sterilizing writings of criminology's white gaze (Saleh-Hanna 2017b).

Abolish Criminology reflects a collective effort to contribute to a more accessible and critical conversation about criminology by putting together a host of voices with a shared view pointing towards freedom from the criminal legal system's behaviors and thinking patterns. While the troubled attitudes and behaviors of this discipline are offered through many of the chapters, at the outset, the reader should be prepared for a rigorous historical and theoretical analysis that places criminology and criminal justice within their most accurate contexts, building on the works of many who have worked to locate criminology and academic criminal justice disciplines within colonialism (Agozino 2003, 2010; Saleh-Hanna 2008, 2017b; Chartrand 2014; Tauri and Porou 2014; Comack 2012; Dobchuk-Land 2017; Coyle and Schept 2017), white supremacy and heteropatriarchy (Childs 2015; Saleh-Hanna 2015; Saleh-Hanna 2017b; Williams and Battle 2017; James 1996), and racial capitalism (Davis 2003; Gilmore 2007; Blackmon 2009; Oshinsky 1996; Robinson 1983; Williams 1944).

Though criminology and academic criminal justice emanate from such a context, criminologists still widely set this history aside and profess to be engaged in a scientific, value-neutral, and objective search for solutions to the problem of "crime." While the transgressions and harms of social living are ubiquitous and in need of addressing (Coyle 2018), and while a utopian interpretation of the criminalizing system dominates public discourse (Coyle Forthcoming), the chapters comprising this volume highlight: that the criminal legal system (law, police, courts, prisons, probation, and all branches of rehabilitation professed by positivists) and its theories (criminology and academic criminal justice) are causatively driven by a white supremacist, heteropatriarchal, impoverishing, colonizing, and punitive model of thought. Consequently, our call to abolish criminology is not a denial of harms, violence, and transgressions, but a denial of criminology's model that requires us to close our eyes to so much pain and suffering while insisting that the historic roots and expanding foundations of this system do not still maintain its edifice.

The broader context of the current moment makes the publication of this book all the more urgent. While the documented history of policing throughout Turtle Island originates from patrols to capture enslaved Africans and extends the conquests of Indigenous lands and genocide against Indigenous peoples (Williams 2021; Maynard 2017; Bell and Schreiner 2018) in criminology, the problems of policing and imprisonment are rewritten and framed as concerns for "equal application of the law," "fair treatment under the law," and "excessive use of force" as if force is not, by nature, excessive (Saleh-Hanna 2017a). The line of continuation is diminished and disappeared through criminology as criminologists debate a rhetoric of reform, rehabilitation, and better police training versus more laws, harsher punishments, and building a larger and more armed police force. With the advent of new technology (hand-held camcorders on a balcony in Los Angeles capturing the Los Angeles Police Department brutalizing Rodney King expands to become cell phones with cameras in people's pockets all over the world) coupled with social media platforms providing opportunities to post and reach unprecedented numbers of people, the colonizing and enslaving roots of the criminal legal system emerge from behind the screen and mirrors of criminology's theories, and western science's house of cards comes tumbling down. As recorded police encounters going viral unmask a "driving while Black," "walking while Black," and "breathing while Black" reality, a global Black Lives Matter movement re-emerges from locked down pandemic homes to protest and put forth organized responses, once again, in the summer of 2020, after having taken to the streets after Michael Brown was murdered in Ferguson in 2014, and after rising up when Trayvon Martin's killer was set free in 2013, after taking to the streets to march across conquered lands countless times between now and Emmet Till's open casket funeral in 1955 (Williams 2017; Saleh-Hanna 2017a).

The Movement for Black Lives has created pathways into a larger public space through which we can engage questions that have been pressing for centuries: why are the entities we are directed to call for help during our most vulnerable moments the same entities given the power to arrest, interrogate, and violate us? The institutionalized nature of this contradiction produces a deeply abusive system of power that many know and have experienced intimately within abusive interpersonal settings (Saleh-Hanna 2017a). In fact, why is the criminal legal system or any entity of white colonial law situated in a position to shape, define, and answer genuine community questions of what we are to do about racism, heterosexism, genderism, houselessness, disability, a wide spectrum of health and wellness needs, and what Gilmore (2020) calls the state's organized abandonment of communities? While much has happened within the immediate days, months, and years following the 2020 uprisings (and too much has not happened while the system's backlash to defund the police continues to fund them more), the carefully developed critique of those on the ground in the U.S. within the belly of the colonial beast, such as All of Us or None, Audre Lorde Project, Black Lives Matter, Black and Pink, Critical Resistance, Cops Off Campus Coalition, Generation Five, No More Prisons, Philly Stands Up, The Red Nation, and so many more within and beyond the U.S. continue to birth pathways towards freedom. As new realities arise, such as the COVID-19 pandemic whose more than half a billion confirmed cases and more than six million deaths have disproportionately affected Black, Indigenous, and colonized communities (World 2022), the tentacles of white supremacy meet new resistance.

With every extension of colonial violence through racially motivated and almost exclusively cis male gendered mass shootings, the continuation of incarceration, policing, and the ongoing struggle for the majority of the world's population to regain footing upon liberated lands, the fight against criminology's conquests and colonialism's grip upon our conceptions, imaginations, and expectations of justice grow more and more urgent.

In offering this book we illustrate how widely naturalized renditions of criminology's colonizing theories and assumptions about justice continue to constitute key stumbling blocks to freedom driven abolitionism. To address these obstacles the chapters in this book present an abolitionist analysis of academic criminology and criminal justice theories and epistemologies alongside critical ethnographies of both western academic and criminal legal settings. To inspire readers to think about the worlds we can create beyond the limiting narratives and binaries of criminology we also introduce samples of resurgent knowledges and understandings. These rewrite our expectations and definitions of justice and refocus our lens for justice away from the fear-driving mythologies that criminologists have written about us and towards the freedom we know is long overdue.

An Overview of the Book

Abolish Criminology is made up of 13 chapters, the last of which is a poem. In the first chapter, *A Call for Wild Seed Justice*, Viviane Saleh-Hanna reflects on Dara Kwayera Imani Bayer's abolitionist cover artwork and Octavia E. Butler's revolutionary stories and reflections to offer a Wild Seed vision for new world formations full of unpredicted pathways to justice and freedom. Saleh-Hanna's chapter on Wild Seed Justice produced the framework that helped us organize this book and articulate the relationships that exist between the chapters. It is a framework that was inspired by Imani's cover art and an organizing process that emerged after all the chapters were confirmed. In the second chapter, *Unwanted: Epistemic Erasure of Black Radical Possibility in Criminology*, Jason M. Williams provides a critical assessment of criminology's epistemic violence through an autoethnographic method and Black radical critique of the discipline. In this chapter Williams introduces a Black radical epistemic framework that has long been stifled due to criminology's white supremacist and oppressive nature. He briefly introduces his experiences in the field as a case study to unpack the power dynamics inherent in the cultivation of criminological knowledge. In the third chapter, *The History of Criminology Is a History of White Supremacy*, Saleh-Hanna draws a clear map of criminology's longstanding and specific relationship with white power in the United States. She provides students and educators in criminology with anti-colonial tools to deconstruct the contradictions and mythologies of criminology's fake opposites and incomplete histories. In the fourth chapter, *The History of Criminal Justice as the Academic Arm of State Violence*, Brian Pitman, Stephen T. Young, and Ryan Phillips trace positivism's scientific racism of criminal justice in the academy. They illustrate how criminology and academic criminal justice function as an international tool of white supremacy through its centralization and professionalization of the criminal legal system's violence.

Collectively, these chapters introduce the historic and practiced contexts of academic criminology and criminal justice, starting inside western academic settings and growing exponentially as the ripple effects of this field reverberate outward into the world through dominant cultures, institutions, and the criminal legal system's colonizing and enslaving agencies. The analysis offered in these chapters is a Wild Seed analysis that counters and challenges criminology's dominant narratives, untelling the storylines of colonialism's domesticated and conquered reframings of justice.

In the fifth chapter, *The White Racialized Center of Criminology*, Holly Sims-Bruno traces how whiteness became the standard disposition for all people and how white supremacy forms the core of orthodox criminology. In the sixth chapter, *Evolving Standards*, Derrick Washington shares his lived experiences with arrest and imprisonment to illustrate how dignity-depriving social conditions simultaneously racialize, gender, and criminalize behavior. His framing for the abolition of criminology requires us to understand that the field systemically obscures the inter-relationality and codependence of racism, socioeconomics, punishment, and criminalized behavior. In the seventh chapter, *Trans Black Women Deserve Better: Expanding Queer Criminology to Unpack Trans Misogynoir in the Field of Criminology*, Toniqua Mikell introduces an intersectional abolitionist lens to distinguish how current queer criminology paradigms create a reality where white cisgender gay men monopolize public understandings of queerness and being, resulting in research and policy that further marginalizes and perpetuates the criminalization of this system's most violated and exploited communities. Mikell's chapter helps us understand how and why Black trans women embody and keep alive that which carceral systems of heteropatriarchal white supremacy are driven to consume and oppress. In the eighth chapter, *Barrio Criminology: Chicanx and Latinx Prison Abolition*, Xuan Santos, Oscar F. Soto, Martin J. Leyva and Christopher Bickel share their stories of perseverance and resistance as system impacted scholars to explain how U.S. institutions work to maintain a "white, homogeneous, nationalistic identity" by forcing Indigenous Chicanx and Latinx persons into second-class citizenship through the prison industrial complex and its expansions within immigration detention centers. Their analysis of how housing, imprisoning, educational, and policing institutions are interwoven offers an unwavering foundation for us to understand the large and intersecting parameters of criminolgy and abolition.

Cumulatively, these four chapters trace and document how criminology's academic theories institutionalize white power cultures within carceral systems of punishment that serve and protect whiteness – not just as an identity but as a position of power that is possible only through the continued colonization and carceral exploitation of Black, Indigenous, and intersectional queer peoples, communities, lands, and nations. These chapters embody Wild Seed wisdoms and understandings that repeat and echo anti-colonialism against all colonizing odds.

In the ninth chapter, *Biology and Criminology Entangled: Education as a Meeting Point*, Charlemya Erasme reflects on her experiences in an undergraduate natural science program to delineate how both criminology and biology (often framed as "objective") use overlapping narratives of human genetic difference to uphold overlapping oppressive values of "superior" and "inferior" humans. Within Erasme's autoethnography of western natural science classrooms, we stumble upon Lombroso – not as a historic, scientific figure, but as a living idea and lens that frames and orders race within natural science disciplines in a public university setting. In the tenth chapter, *Abolish the Courthouse: Uncovering the Space of "Justice" in a Black Feminist Criminal Trial*, Vanessa Lynn Lovelace employs a Black postcolonial feminist analysis to examine, through a case study of Assata Shakur's courtroom trial, how the often overlooked and under-critiqued sites of courthouses and courtrooms are imagined at the periphery of criminal legal violence when in practice, they sit at the center of a mythology that forces us to imagine colonial violence as civilized, logical, and ordered. Within Lovelace's research on the courthouse we meet colonizing courtroom architectures in the form of "well-designed security" and rituals of secrecy and enclosure that function to bridge policing with imprisonment. In the eleventh chapter, *Marxist Criminology Abolishes Lombroso, Marxist Criminology Abolishes Itself*, Erin Katherine Krafft breaks theoretical ground in criminology by offering an overlooked and understudied Russian context to assess critical and [white] radical criminology's dominant Marxist ideologies. She traces the impact of Marxist criminology on the Russian state, and introduces its effect on academic criminology and social control in Russia. In the twelfth chapter, *Abolition Now: Counter-Images and Visual Criminology*, Michelle Brown underscores the visual meaning behind abolitionist discourses, the racialization of criminality, and the prison industrial complex. Brown's chapter introduces us to a form of abolitionism that locates and interrupts dominant criminology's visual manifestations in the world.

Together these chapters offer insight and opportunities for us to reflect upon the places and senses we are socialized to turn away from or overlook in our critiques of criminology and the criminal legal system's behaviors and impact. The analysis that flows through these chapters allows us to look with new eyes and seek new answers through larger questions – this is abolitionism's work towards new world formations. These chapters share and illustrate the power that lies within anti-colonial ways of knowing (Absolon, 2022), and the critiques and unlearning what can occur when we turn to spaces and understandings colonization has taught us to overlook, naturalize, or take for granted.

The chapters that comprise this book are a beautiful representation of Wild Seed research: they illustrate the power of context and vision, and the teachings we have been building as we undo this system's grasp on justice. The last chapter and last word, for now, on the matter of abolishing criminology comes in the form of the rose that grew from concrete – a poem that was written by a Tatiana Lopes DosSantos while she was sitting in Saleh-Hanna's History of Criminology course described in Chapter 3. *Civil Lies* is a love letter to DosSantos's Indigenous African motherland, a love expressed within the grief of what colonization takes away by force. Within this poem, we can read a despair that many in Diaspora feel, and when DosSantos denounces the intergenerational losses incurred through this system's relay race of white supremacist institutions across time, we are affirmed and uplifted to expect and demand more. Exorcising the repressive and violent denials of Black life in Africa's Diaspora, DosSantos declares,

for each of these atrocities in hell, they will rot.

Collectively, this book provides readers the room to think about why abolition is a way forward and the space to think about what justice can be and do in a world we want to live in. Our hope is to raise consciousness about the many issues that students, scholars, organizers, artists, and believers in justice have been thinking about, questioning, building, and deconstructing. In particular, with this book, we hope to introduce criminology as the violent and domineering presence it is, and to introduce a more specific discourse that places the abolition of criminology within larger movements to abolish the criminal legal system and its many systems of carceral control. Abolition Now.

References

Absolon, K.E. (2022). *Kaandossiwin: How We Come to Know: Indigenous Re-search Methodologies*. Blackpoint, Nova Scotia: Fernwood Publishing.

Agozino, B. 2003. *Counter-Colonial Criminology: A Critique of Imperialist Reason*. London: Pluto Press.

Agozino, B. 2010. "What Is Criminology? A Control-Freak Discipline!" *African Journal of Criminology & Justice Studies* 4(1) (June): i–xx.

Bell, C. and K. Schreiner. 2018. "The International Relations of Police Power in Settler Colonialism: The 'Civilizing' Mission of Canada's Mounties." *International Journal* 73(1): 111–128.

Blackmon, D.A. 2009. *Slavery by Another Name: The Re-Enslavement of Black Americans from the Civil War to World War II*. New York: First Anchor Books.

Chartrand, V. 2014. "Penal and Colonial Politics Over Life: Women and Penal Release Schemes in NSW, Australia." *Settler Colonial Studies* 14(3), 301–320.

Childs, D. 2015. *Slaves of the State: Black Incarceration from the Chain Gang to the Penitentiary*. Minneapolis: University of Minnesota Press.

Comack, E. 2012. *Racialized Policing: Aboriginal People's Encounters with the Police*. Winnipeg: Fernwood Books Ltd.

Coyle, M.J. Forthcoming. *Seeing Crime: Penal Abolition as the End of Utopian Criminal Justice*. Berkeley: University of California Press.

Coyle, M.J. 2018. "Transgression and Standard Theories: Contributions Toward Penal Abolition." *Critical Criminology* 26(3): 325–339.

Coyle, M.J. and J. Schept. 2017. "Penal Abolition and the State: Colonial, Racial and Gender Violences." *Contemporary Justice Review* 20(4): 399–403.

Davis, A.Y. 2003. *Are Prisons Obsolete?* New York: Seven Stories Press.

Davis, A.Y. and D. Rodriguez. 2000. "The Challenge of Prison Abolition: A Conversation". *Social Justice, 27*(3(81)): 212–218.

Delisle, C., M. Basualdo, A. Ilea and A. Hughes. 2015. "The International Conference on Penal Abolition (ICOPA)." *Champ Pénal/Penal Field* 12. https://doi.org/10.4000/champ penal.9146 (accessed September 19, 2022).

Dobchuk-Land, B. 2017. "Resisting 'Progressive' Carceral Expansion: Lessons for Abolitionists from Anti-Colonial Resistance." *Contemporary Justice Review* 20(4): 404–418.

Douglass, F. 1865. "In What New Skin Will the Old Snake Come Forth?" An Address Delivered in New York, New York, on 10 May 1865. In John W. Blassingame and John R. McKivigan (eds.), *The Frederick Douglass Papers*. New Haven, CT: Yale University Press, 1991.

Gilmore, R.W. 2007. *Golden Gulag: Prisons, Surplus, Crisis, and Opposition in Globalizing California*. Berkeley: University of California Press.

Gilmore, R.W. 2020. Radio Interview on *Democracy Now!* May 5, 2020.

Oshinsky, D.M. 1996. *Worse Than Slavery: Parchman Farm and the Ordeal of Jim Crow Justice*. New York: Free Press.

James, J. 1996. *Resisting State Violence: Radicalism, Gender, and Race in U.S. Culture*. Minneapolis, MN: University of Minnesota Press.

Maynard, R. 2017. *Policing Black Lives: State Violence in Canada from Slavery to the Present*. Blackpoint, Nova Scotia: Fernwood Publishing.

Robinson, C.J. 1983. *Black Marxism: The Making of the Black Radical Tradition*. London: Zed Press.

Saleh-Hanna, V. 2008. *Colonial Systems of Control: Criminal Justice in Nigeria*. Ottawa: University of Ottawa Press.

Saleh-Hanna, V. 2015. "Black Feminist Hauntology: Rememory the Ghosts of Abolition?" *Champ pénal/Penal Field* 13. Available at: http://journals.openedition.org/champpenal/9168.

Saleh-Hanna, V. 2017a. "An Abolitionist Theory on Crime: Ending the Abusive Relationship with Racist-Imperialist-Patriarchy [R.I.P.]." *The Contemporary Justice Review* 20(4): 419–441.

Saleh-Hanna, V. 2017b. "Reversing Criminology's White Gaze: As Lombroso's Disembodied Head Peers Through a Glass Jar in a Museum Foreshadowed by Sara Baartman's Ghost." In J.Z. Wilson, S. Hodgkinson, J. Piche and K. Walby (eds.), *The Palgrave Handbook on Prison Tourism* (pp. 689–711). Hampshire, UK: Palgrave Macmillan.

Sudbury, J. 2009. "Maroon Abolitionists: Black Gender-Oppressed Activists in the Anti-Prison Movement in the U.S. and Canada." *Meridians: Feminism, Race, Transnationalism* 9(1): 1–29.

Tauri, J.M. and N. Porou. 2014. "Criminal Justice in Contemporary Settler Colonialism." *African Journal of Criminology and Justice Studies* 8(1): 20–37.

Williams, E. 1944. *Capitalism and Slavery*. Chapel Hill, NC: University of North Carolina Press.

Williams, J.M. 2021. "US Policing as Racialized Violence and Control: A Qualitative Assessment of Black Narratives from Ferguson, Missouri." *Journal of Ethnicity in Criminal Justice* 19(3–4): 267–290.

Williams, J.M. 2017. "Race and Justice Outcomes: Contextualizing Racial Discrimination and Ferguson." *Ralph Bunche Journal of Public Affairs* 6(1). Available at: https://digitalscholarship.tsu.edu/rbjpa/vol6/iss1/5.

Williams, J.M. and N.T. Battle. 2017. "African Americans and Punishment for Crime: A Critique of Mainstream and Neoliberal Discourses." *Journal of Offender Rehabilitation* 56(8): 552–566.

World Health Organization. 2022. "Coronavirus (COVID-19) Dashboard." Available at: https://covid19.who.int/ (accessed June 15, 2022).

Criminology's Violent Ideologies Rippling Across Place and Time

1

A CALL FOR WILD SEED JUSTICE

Viviane Saleh-Hanna

Dara Kwayera Imani Bayer's artwork for the cover of this book moved me to write a piece I have mulled over for some years. This is a chapter inspired by Octavia E. Butler's Parables (1993, 1998) and her Patternist series (1976, 1977, 1978, 1980, 1984), with special focus on symbolism and lessons from Earthseed (1993, 1998) and Wild Seed (1980). While Butler's Earthseed philosophies laid out in *The Parable of the Sower* (1993) and *The Parable of the Talents* (1998) constitute her most cited works (because Earthseed offers powerful medicine), it is an intersectional reading of Butler's Earthseed wisdoms and Wild Seed lessons that nourish me most along this journey to locate and name the layering and nuanced dimensions of criminology's violence.

Wild Seed (1980) is the name Octavia E. Butler gave the prequel she wrote to the Patternist series. *Wild Seed* gives us the origin story of the central character Anyanwu. Within Anyanwu's life narratives, Butler introduces Wild Seed as an abolitionist concept and strategy that Imani painted into the cover art for this book. In this chapter, I start with reflections on criminology inspired by Imani's cover art, paving and inspiring pathways towards a discussion of Octavia E. Butler's Earthseed teachings and Wild Seed pathways to articulate a call for Wild Seed Justice: an abolitionist framework meant to liberate us from the limiting, harmful imaginations and expectations of justice that colonialism, criminology, and the criminal legal system enforce.

> In order to rise
> From its own ashes
> A phoenix
> First
> Must
> Burn
> (Parable of the Sower, by Octavia E. Butler (1993: 154)

DOI: 10.4324/9780367817114-3

Dara Kwayera Imani Bayer

> Imani means "faith" in Swahili and, as the seventh principle of Kwanzaa, is considered an essential value in the ongoing struggle for liberation and justice. Within the context of Black history, I see faith as the divine belief that self, family, community, and society can positively transform and exist in alignment with the highest expression of humanity.
>
> (Dara Kwayera Imani Bayer, 2016a, 2016b)

Imani – planted in the middle of Dara Kwayera Imani Bayer's full name is the seed through which so many of her artistic creations are born. For this reason and with her permission, I refer to her in my writing as Imani instead of Bayer as prescribed by standard academic practices.

When we asked Imani to paint a cover for *Abolish Criminology* I knew her artistic vision and talent would offer us more than cover art. Within Imani's art, I have always met freedom dreams and a spirit of knowledge and resistance that stands – unwavering – against colonialism and its many mechanisms of captivity, enslavement, and imprisonment. Imani Arts[1] offers us a deep and layered understanding of that which binds us and that which we must dream and dare to imagine to be able to get free. In so many ways and from a wide spectrum of land, space, and time relationships, Imani inspires us to consider how our lives are an immediate extension of our planet, and to reflect upon the relationships that exist between creation, humanity, time, land, water, cosmos, and the intergenerational violations of colonialism's white power systems of conquest. The cover art that Imani created for *Abolish Criminology* allows us to consider these dimensions with a very specific focus on white power's criminology (Saleh-Hanna, 2017b) and our place as human beings within the inhuman landscapes of carceral systems.

To visualize and create the cover art, Imani reviewed the book's table of contents and chapter abstracts. She read a few completed chapters and spent time browsing through images of mainstream criminology's book covers. From these encounters with each of us who contributed to the making of this book, and with a visual understanding of dominant criminology's public-facing aesthetics, Imani offers a powerful image full of visual statements and wisdoms for us to decipher, reflect upon, and access.

In Imani's cover art we meet criminology's desolate landscapes, branded by a European blueprint of a slave ship, framed by a skyline of industrial wastelands that pollute the air and poison the lands and waters we need for life. That skyline and its stormy clouds sit at the surface of colonization's abuse and exploitations against Black and Indigenous lands, waters, skies, humanity, and ways of life. Deconstructing carceralist "CSI" [lab-coat TV cop] narratives within criminology, Imani painted a digital fingerprint upon these lands, marking criminology's journey from slavery into the digital age, reminding us to never forget the roots and realities of criminology's violence (Saleh-Hanna, 2017a). The faces of past and future humans breathe life into this landscape – emerging from the grass roots with wild seeds[2] to sow. The land is depicted as a human body, both a womb holding future lives facing a birth canal, and legs open with descendants emerged to birth new worlds. In Imani's painting we can literally see ourselves as the land, and the land as an extension of us. From this understanding, the slave ship (representing historic imprisonments) and digital fingerprint (representing modern systems of enslavement) are branded upon the land, branded upon the bodies of Black, Indigenous, colonized ancestors and descendants, branded upon collective social bodies and humanity's consciousness. Imani's cover art brings the vastness of carceral violence into sight, allowing us to see the layered and entangling natures of colonial conquest and the harms these brand (literally burned into the land and into enslaved-colonized human flesh) and brand (copyrighting, institutionalizing, branding justice as belonging only to colonial laws, criminology's theories, and the criminal legal system) and brand (commercialized and industrialized to be sold as crime TV within cop shows and mockumentaries that supplement and expand the reaches of traditional colonial journalism's corporate crime-reporting schemes) and brand.

The spreading of dandelion seeds is particularly striking within the context of criminology, for these bright yellow medicinal plants embody all that the suburbs hate. These are the very places that criminology (particularly the Chicago School of Thought and so many sociological positivists) claim to be 'safest', naming them a destination for those who want to achieve secure, crime-free lives – these suburbs are famously provoked and goaded by the bright yellow of the dandelion flower, its wild seeds spreading year after year to produce ecosystems snuffed out by sterile green lawns in colonial suburbs and vast golf courses consuming water in the midst of drought conditions so that rich white men can have soft landings for their small white balls. Fed by the wind to move through the ebbs and flows of creation, wild seeds land in places they are not supposed to land, blooming wherever they are needed to bloom, shining yellow and disrupting the cookie-cutter lawns of sterlized, occupied lands. Above all else, dandelion seeds spreading across green lawns represent white-settler inabilities to control the land and their failure to flex colonial manpower over its beauty. In so many ways, the chapters in this book are Wild Seeds blowing through to disrupt colonized academic landscapes that sterilize and seek to continue the conquest of justice.

In criminology's arena, as you breeze through traditional, classical, positivist, and even critical criminology's barren landscapes, you will encounter the box in which justice has been contained and domesticated. You will encounter the paradigms in which justice suffocates so that the violent logic of legality can grow – boxing justice into state power, disfiguring accountability into punishment, minimizing humanity into a caricatured image of that which those in power must rehabilitate or threaten, and imprisoning colonized communities further into domains for surveillance and exploitation. In so many ways, Imani's cover embodies and puts into visual formation the significance of the works shared in *Abolish Criminology* and the power of what Octavia E. Butler offered to us when she created Anyanwu's character as the embodiment of Wild Seed powers. The Wild Seed knowledges shared in this book have, against all odds, been grown outside of criminology's walls and beyond the paradigms of criminology's conquests. These chapters, like so many anticolonial writings and wisdoms, form abolitionist roots within the world-altering formations of anticolonialist thought. To abolish criminology's thought patterns and carceralist cultures is to plant seeds, that form roots, that can and will birth new worlds where freedom is real and justice is tangible in our day-to-day lives.

Octavia E. Butler

"SO DO YOU REALLY believe that in the future we're going to have the kind of trouble you write about in your books?" a student asked me as I was signing books after a talk. The young man was referring to the troubles I'd described in *Parable of the Sower* and *Parable of the Talents*, novels that take place in a near future of increasing drug addiction and illiteracy, marked by the popularity of prisons and the unpopularity of public schools, the vast and growing gap between the rich and everyone else, and the whole nasty family of problems brought on by global warming.

"I didn't make up the problems," I pointed out. "All I did was look around at the problems we're neglecting now and give them about 30 years to grow into full-fledged disasters."

(Butler, 2000)

Octavia Estelle Butler wrote the Parables in the mid-1990s and the interview she mentions above took place at the turn of the 21st century. Two decades later, here we are, existing within with so many pieces of the future world she described. In fact, we got here a few years sooner than she anticipated. For those who are unfamiliar with Butler's novels, here is brief summary of what that student was asking and how much the response to his question is *yes*, those are precisely the problems we are facing now: in so many ways we have arrived at the future Butler warned about.

The Parable of the Sower (1993) and *The Parable of the Talents* (1998) tell the story of a community trying to survive a hyper privatized and militarized world. It is set on the western coast of the United States in the year 2032. In that world, a demagogue dictator came to power under a campaign to 'Make America Great Again' – Butler got this from Ronald Reagan's 1980 campaign slogan (yes, Trump stole that too along with so many leftist critiques of the media and grassroots language to describe oppression) though the demagogue she describes is less like Reagan and more like Trump – the lesson here being that one created paths for the other to emerge.

"SO DO YOU REALLY believe that in the future we're going to have the kind of trouble you write about in your books?" a student asked me as I was signing books after a talk.

Twenty years after a student asked this question, we find ourselves living within the shadows of the world she described. At this time (as in the Parables), western corporations and colonial governments are scaling back almost all checks and balances on industrial toxins that pollute and destroy land-water-air resources. The natural resources we need to stay alive have been privatized in manners similar to the future world Butler described. In the Parables, water was a scarce commodity, and in the United States, Flint, Michigan's struggle and losses due to toxic public waters and the lack of access to publicly sourced water in Jackson Mississippi (Gerlak et al., 2022) are mirrored. Access to clean drinking water is necessary for life, and these struggles over water (as an extension of the land that has been stolen) are the start, not the end, of what is to come. In the Parables, as in our current lives, economic inflation collides with privatizing systems of governance, causing more and more of us to have access to fewer and fewer resources outside the grasps and exploitative reach of corporations, and the few scraps they throw towards those whose labor they exploit. The mass exploitations described in the Parables were amplified by the demagogue politician who weaponized western religion's dogmas and heteropatri-archal, racist tropes to shield and institute fascist policies that operate on a platform of open corruption. Ultimately, the Parables are about a community trying to escape in order to survive a system that has tipped their world into apocalyptic days – not because the Bible predicted an end of the world but because Bible-thumping fascists brought them there.

> Sooner or later the generation that says "we're living in our last days" really will be. But not because somebody strikes us from heaven. We'll do it to ourselves. And, to the future.
>
> *(Butler, 2010: 9)*

The Parable of the Sower (1993) starts inside a small community living behind a walled-off cul-de-sac owned by the corporation that exploits almost all areas of their lives. Lauren Olamina, a young Black woman, leads her community out of that cul-de-sac. She is armed with Earthseed philosophies that she created to sur-vive and counter the disarming and subduing effects of her father's church and her community's culture of trying to survive by submitting to authority and turning a terrorized blind eye to power's corruption. Lauren's Earthseed philosophies include the central belief that:

> All that you touch
> You Change.
>
> All that you Change
> Changes you.
>
> The only lasting truth
> Is Change.
>
> God
> Is Change.
>
> (Butler, *Parable of the Sower*, 1993: 3)

Butler's Earthseed philosophies on change reframe and amplify the spirit of what Thomas Mathiesen teaches in his writings about the "unfinished" nature of abolition. Reflecting on this in *The Politics of Abolition* (1974), Mathiesen wrote that "any attempt to change the existing order into something completely finished, a fully formed entity, is destined to fail: in the process of finishing lies a return to the by-gone" (1974: 13). As a result, Mathiesen suggests we anchor our work of changing the world into the sketches stage of being, and to do what is possible to stay there by resisting the pressure to transform into a finished shape – for it is in the process of reaching the end or achieving 'the finished' that requires all growth to stop, allowing dogma the opportunity to settle in and institutionalize new or repeated renditions of old systems of oppression and power: *the only lasting truth is change*, because it is in the very process of changing and adapting to the needs of humanity in balanced relation to, or in justice with, the needs of the planet – and by extension, the needs of humanity – that we locate freedom and enter into the unending portals of abolitionism: "the only lasting truth is change."

Mathiesen asks us to consider how to start the sketch (the birth of new social movements, the start of new ideas) and how to resist the enormous political pressures that will arise as our sketches and the worlds we are creating begin to gain legitimacy and power in mainstream spaces. This is precisely the moment abolitionists were facing when the Black Lives Matter movement went global during the COVID-19 pandemic and the demands to abolish or defund the police went viral in the aftermath of George Floyd's murder. Mathiesen suggests that the key to both of these questions – of starting new sketches and of resisting the pressure to finish the picture – is abolition. He said, "*Abolition* runs like a red thread" through both, "Abolition is the point of departure" (13).

All that you touch you change.
All that you change changes you.

If abolition is the red thread running through the sketches of new world formations, then carceralism is the white thread that runs through all the institutions of colonialism and conquest. Locating pressure points that can unravel such threads is the work of creating new worlds – and realizing when your own threads begin to mimic those unraveling before your eyes is just as important.

In the next section, I explore how the red thread described by Mathiesen and Butler's Earthseed understandings move with the world and adapt to the needs of humanity and the planet, and are fed and nurtured by Butler's Wild Seed powers to form new visions and pathways to freedom. These teachings are particularly important in the aftermath of the 2020 uprisings that have been followed by an increase (not decline) in U.S. police budgets and U.S. police murder of racialized people – as white power works to avenge the moments and demands for freedom birthed after George Floyd's murder went viral (Manthey, Esposito and Hernandez, 2022; The Official Mapping Police Violence Database, https://mappingpoliceviolence.org/).

Wild Seed

> Anyanwu had too much power. In spite of Doro's fascination with her, his first instinct was to kill her. He was not in the habit of keeping alive people he could not control absolutely.
>
> (Butler, *Wild Seed*, 1980: 97)

In the Patternist series (starting with *Mind of My Mind* written in 1977) Butler introduces us to Doro, a body snatcher who achieves immortality by consuming the soul of his target, or anyone who is near him in the moments he faces death. When we first meet Doro in *Mind of My Mind* we are not yet sure what he is – we only know of his powers and his abusive control over the people he 'breeds'. In *Wild Seed* we learn that Doro started out human and learned early in life that he possessed the power to snatch people's souls and inhabit their bodies. This is a power mimicked in the land theft and occupation processes of colonization and white settlerism, the body theft and occupation processes of enslavement and imprisonment, and the justice theft and occupation processes of the criminal legal system. Over the course of his life, Doro, like colonization and its destructive, death-making systems of power, took over countless lives to keep himself going and in-control across many generations. Doro embodied many terrible things, but most significant in my reading of the Patternist series: he is a eugenicist trolling the planet, capturing and breeding people whom, he could sense, had special powers that he could exploit. We can read his body as carceral systems of colonial conquest and his mind as the academic landscapes of criminology. The people he (Doro) and they (criminologists) prey upon were already disenfranchised by vicious systems of colonial conquest. Doro referred to the survivors of his violence as 'his seeds' and built entire communities to 'breed' them into human weapons he could use at will. This is parallel to how criminology and criminologists hunt down, exploit, interrogate, punish, try to 'rehabilitate', control, and weaponize criminalized communities, cultures, and people (both inside prisons and beyond) to expand carceral state power.

Doro was a parasite, a monster who experimented on humans to exploit their abilities and centralize their powers for his own use. I read Lombroso's research specifically and all of criminology in general within Doro's character. In more ways than we can count, Doro's character is the embodiment of carceral white supremacy. He was born out of Butler's deep insights into the cultures and practices of colonialism, enslavement, imprisonment, and the common white threads of carceral exploitation that bind them and us together. In Doro's story we locate threatening systems of colonial governance that rely on deterrence (the threat of violence) to control access to our own thoughts, not to speak of the freedoms we are denied, and the immense threats of violence we face in our day-to-day lives within the borders and power of the criminal legal system. Doro embodies positivism's risk assessments, neighborhood surveillances, human experimentations, and obsessive interrogation with intent to exploit the bodies, spaces, cultures, homes, families, talents, potentials, and ways of life of the oppressed. Doro intersects positivism seamlessly with classical criminology's carceral logics of deterrence. His breeding and manipulations reek of positivism's rehabilitation schemas, while his use of surveillance to fulfill a promise to violate those who do not fall in line with his ways and expectations is a classical criminologist's idealized vision of control. Doro embodies criminology's goals and behaviors through the criminal legal system's narratives, intentions, and ways of exerting control.

> You didn't cheat him. You didn't steal from him or lie to him. You didn't disobey him. He'd find you out, then he'd kill you. How could you fight that? He wasn't telepathic, but I had never seen anyone get a lie past him. And I had never seen anyone escape him. He did have some kind of tracking sense. He locked in on people. Anybody he'd met once, he could find again. He thought about them, and he knew which way to go to get them. Once he was close to them, they didn't have a chance.
>
> *(Butler, 1977: 27)*

Yet, in *Wild Seed* (1980) it is not Doro, but Anyanwu – the Wild Seed – who takes center stage. The story begins in 1690. Anyanwu was living a quiet life within Igbo-land's Onitsha in the eastern territories of Nigeria's countryside. She was born with abilities that allowed her to detect and heal any ailments or illnesses within her body and the bodies of those she encountered. Anyanwu embodies our planet: she is relational and holds within herself all that is needed for a good life and well being. She is centuries old and has experienced many cycles of love and loss across a beautiful and lonely life full of communities, family, and lovers. She faces great love and loss as she continues to love and outlive generation after generation of her kin and chosen communities.

Anyanwu, like our planet, is also a shape shifter whose body reads, stores, and reproduces the memory of all flesh and vegetation she interacts with or consumes. Throughout *Wild Seed* Anyanwu lives within her body as female, as male, and as a variety of mammals and avians (birds). In her mammal and avian forms, she was most free, for Doro's carceral senses could not locate or track her. In her avian form Anyanwu flew in the air as a bird, and as a mammal she swam in the ocean as a dolphin, and roamed the forest as a wolf or large dog. Born outside Doro's grid and breeding projects, Anyanwu had powers beyond Doro's comprehension and control. She was not 'his' seed – she was Wild Seed.

When Doro 'discovers' Anyanwu in 1690, she is hiding from European slavers who were starting to encroach upon her territories. Doro convinces her (in proper carceral fashion through threat and unbalancing persuasions) that her only refuge from being sold into chattel slavery is through escape on his ship across the Atlantic. In her reluctant acceptance of Doro as the least evil of many evils she was facing, we can read the many pathways into reluctant acceptance that colonial systems of power pave to entrap and pull us into their folds (Saleh-Hanna, 2008). During her journey out of her homeland, Anyanwu witnesses chattel enslavement, land theft, and white settler occupations of Turtle Island. Over the years she meets, births, and cares after many of Doro's victims. There are times when her discourse with Doro is peaceful and times when it is turbulent. At one point, Anyanwu realizes that peaceful coexistence with Doro's violence is nothing more and nothing less than a survival mechanism. She begins to disengage in whatever ways she can and finds herself having to reckon with the affection and familiarity she had developed for him over the years – in the same ways abolitionists strive to disengage and reckon with the dependencies, familiarities, and relationships we have willingly or reluctantly formed with colonizing institutions, cultures, and economies.

Butler's use of Wild Seed as *a state of existence* for Anyanwu inspires me because it is a beautiful and messy story of resistance. Both chattel slavery and the eras of imprisonment we live in now exist alongside Doro's enslavements and eugenicist experiments in the Patternist series. When Butler placed Doro's violence and Anyanwu's power within the world we know, alongside and in direct interaction with institutions we are familiar with and oppressed by, she created a parallel and a mirror through which we can study our trajectories within (through Doro) *as well as beyond* (through Anyanwu) the carceral exploitations and entrapments of white power.

Throughout Butler's Patternist series, and as Wild Seed unfolds as an abolitionist philosophy personified within Anyanwu's character, the tensions between fierce femme powers and toxic masculinist carceralism collide into meaningful expressions and warnings against gender binaries, against systemic violence, against the structurally abusive nature of colonialism (Saleh-Hanna, 2015, 2017a). In their interactions we hear Doro's threats and coercions, Anyanwu's considerations and attempts to 'keep the peace', and eventually her shape-shifted exit out of Doro's tangled webs, followed by a return to him that had me screaming at the book. *Wild Seed* is not a western fairytale where the kidnapper is reframed into a knight in shining armor. *Wild Seed* is the nuanced story of slavery's imprisonments, and the many ways that these systems seduce and entrap us within structurally abusive relationships (Saleh-Hanna, 2017a), consuming us and blurring the boundaries (Cohen, 1985) of where they end and where we begin. Wild Seed is an abolitionist, anti-colonial, freedom-driven story of large and small deaths, survivals, and triumphs met along the abolitionist road to freedom.

Wild Seed Lessons Along the Way

I started writing *Colonial Systems of Control* (2008) while living in Nigeria after I finished my master's degree in criminology in Canada. I finished writing the book while completing my doctoral degree in criminal justice in the United States. The bulk of my writing on colonialism happened in Nigeria and during my journeys throughout west and north Africa. As I journey further into the articulation of north African identity at the intersections of Black and Indigenous, I have started to reflect and share more about my time in XHMI (pronounced Keemi – meaning Land of the Black Soil – colonized into the Arab Republic of Egypt) during those years. In this section I break silence and share one of those previously untold stories as one example of Wild Seed justice.

Early in this century, I have a distinct memory of leaning against the rails of a ship on the Nile in Upper ХНМІ and weeping as I took in the grand, majestic truth of the massive temple we were approaching. The multiplying dimensions of loss caused by colonization were so loud in these explicit moments of grief – spiritual, geographic, demographic, legal, political, economic – all of it, cumulative and vast, without proper words to be expressed. I tried:

> I use the term 'penal colonialism' in reference to contemporary conditions when discussing criminal justice in Nigeria. In addition, I prefer to rely on terms such as "economic colonialism," "political colonialism," "educational colonialism," "cultural colonialism," "geographical colonialism," "spiritual colonialism," and "psychological colonialism" when discussing other areas of colonial oppression. The violent reality is that colonialism has infiltrated and dominated entire social structures in Africa [and the world over]. In dealing with this violence we must first articulate it in its entirety.
>
> *(Saleh-Hanna, 2008: 21)*

About a week after my trip on the Nile into Upper ХНМІ, I was sitting inside an Egyptian prison waiting room getting ready to meet Nigerian prisoners held captive there. I learned about their imprisonment while speaking with a woman who was on the same ship I was on during my journey along the Nile. She was an international human rights worker who overheard me speaking with my mother and sisters about my work with prisoners in Nigeria. She shared that she was in touch with Nigerian prisoners held inside an Egyptian prison and asked if I would be willing to meet with them and return to Nigeria with letters and prison-made gifts for their families. I said I was. This was such an unexpected moment of connection and work. What were the odds she would be on the same ship *and* would overhear the specific conversation I was having? I share this to ask you to consider how Wild Seed moments like this add meaning and bring us closer to the magic of collective resistance. When I reflect on the work that emerged from that unlikely crossing of paths I amplify the sketches of brief moments and sensations that undermine and counter, disband and fertilize the sterilizing and controlled nature of prisons and carceral violence. Stumbling upon an unexpected journey of pan-African family reunification was so crucial in a world that is built upon the predictable and overwhelming repetitions of carceral ruptures and separations. So many abolitionists have spoken about unexpected moments and connections like this one along the way. I hope more of us start to publicly share these moments as abolitionist work progresses: the Wild Seed nature of abolitionism must be embraced so that we can avoid the mundane and predetermined flows of vanguardism and worn-out clichés. But we must also expect and prepare for these Wild Seed moments to bring forth new struggles and growing pains. "All that you touch you change. All that you change changes you" (Butler, 1993).

Sitting inside an Egyptian prison's waiting room, I felt the heaviness of all we had lost, have been forced to carry and denied as Indigenous, Black, north African NІpЄМѝХНМІ (the Indigenous name of Egyptians with **NIρЄΜΝ** - pronounced NiRemen - meaning 'people' and **ΧΗΜΙ** – pronounced Keemi – meaning 'Black soil'). So clearly visible – out in the open – within that (and all) prison(s), between the same barking orders of prison guards echoing across, and beneath the grief-filled chatter of families that idles through all prison waiting rooms filled with adults, youths, children, and babies waiting to see their imprisoned loved ones, sat our cumulative loss: of our north Africaness and the many spectrums of Blackness buried within multiple Arab, Ottoman, and European conquests; our thousands-of-years-old, beautiful, dynamic, queer, mystic, cosmic spiritualities imprisoned inside museums and Egyptology's colonizing tropes, outlawed by heteropatriarchy's institutions; our fluid and intersectional relationships with the river Nile and surrounding desert trapped within the binaries of dogma and orthodoxy; our music and spoken tongue, our beloved **ΜЄΤρЄΜΝΧΗΜΙ** [pronounced MetRemen-Keemi – meaning language of the people of the Black soil] transitioned into Coptic letters (Greek and Demotic letters applied to our ancestral language) and hidden within the beautiful folds of **ΧΗΜΙ**'s creolized spoken Arabic, resurfacing in the ways we speak to our babies and uttered openly yet vastly mispronounced in liturgical worship; our collective histories and familial destinies sat trapped in that prison waiting room, waiting.

The heaviness of the loss of **ΧΗΜΙ** was particularly heavy that day, as I became acutely aware of the fact that the prison was more familiar to me than the **NIρЄΜΝΧΗΜΙ** setting I was in. The deep familiarity I had developed with prisons through my work as an abolitionist was juxtaposed against the fact that Egypt and Egyptians were less familiar to me than the prison that duplicates itself across oceans and conquered time. We were also sitting in a waiting room accented with the pain and struggles of estrangement and loneliness. I could not help but feel the weight of estrangement from my own north African homelands and found myself feeling a loneliness I did not realize I held buried so deep within my heart and soul. I held it together while inside that prison but wept on Cairo's public transportation all the way back to my teta's apartment in Heliopolis. So many people offered tissues and comfort along the way. I could not explain nor stop my tears and eventually, people just let me be.

I traveled from **ΧΗΜΙ** back to Nigeria with letters and gifts for the families of the Nigerian prisoners I met that day. More than a decade prior, they were on layover in Cairo when the war on drugs ensnared and imprisoned them. They had been there all these years. Their loved ones did not know where they were or if they were still alive. When I reread portions of my writing and journaling from **ΧΗΜΙ** back to west Africa as I mapped and located the family home of each Nigerian I met in that Egyptian prison, I am reminded of the panic I felt as the unexpressed loss of my ancestral homelands was forced to surface in front of temples and inside that prison, and the anger I felt at the estrangements that Africans enforce against each other through colonial systems of conquest. Internalized colorism in conquered **ΧΗΜΙ** is so vicious. It has become clearer to me in recent years that I research and write about colonial, enslaving, imprisoning violence, I study white supremacy, I study and practice anticolonialism because of grief, because of estrangement, because we must process and mourn in order to continue on our journeys to be free. That is why I am abolitionist. Because I yearn to be free from the weight of all that has been lost. I yearn to be free.

Wild Seed Justice

Wild Seed Justice is a call to sketch new worlds for us to grow into. It is a call to imagine and create sustainable gardens with abundant, changing, growing pathways to freedom so that we can have beauty and justice as the standard, instead of continuing to loop into repressive colonial thought and systems of crime, punishment, deterence, and rehabilitation. Wild Seed Justice is a call to reclaim and rebirth justice beyond the shadows, traps, and white power delusions of colonialism, and to do so we must situate ourselves far beyond the limiting and twisting narratives of criminology the colonizing systems of law and control it rebirths and upholds.

In so many ways, the seeds painted into this book's cover by Imani represent Wild Seed Justice flowing through the knowledges and stories shared throughout this book. Each chapter challenges and undoes the white seams holding carceralist logic in place, working together to pull back criminology's thin veil by exposing its lies and mythologies on humanity and justice. This book is full of seeds and flowers resisting the continuing occupation of justice that occurs within colonialism and criminology. Refusing to accept toxic narratives that we have been force-fed about ourselves and our communities throughout these last few hundred years, each chapter engages with the sketches of the new worlds we are creating together.

Criminology's seeds harvest white supremacy within our imaginations and expectations of justice, and Wild Seed Justice emerges through unexpected moments of freedom and resistance, planted for centuries within collective and individual acts for freedom, against all odds, to remind us of the majesty of creation, the power of our inter-sectional existence, and the significance of our pathways and relational journeys on this earth. Wild Seed is a call to see justice as a practice that extends (not limits or arrests) access to our truest selves and collective freedoms. Abolitionist pathways towards justice must, above all else, pave ways for us to access our fullest potentials so that we can live our lives within worlds that uplift and shine beyond the shadows and seemingly endless miseries and incurred losses of carceralism, white supremacy, heteropatriarchy, and colonialism. Wild Seed Justice is the visual that Imani gave us for this book's cover. It is our ancestors whispering through our actions, and our descendants waiting to be born into freedom. It is Anyanwu seeing Doro for all that he is and beginning the journey of detanglement and liberation from his ways, while working to ensure that the direct descendants of his experiments and his violations are protected and supported in their march towards his demise and our liberation.

As you work your way through this and other abolitionist books and materials imagine and know that each Wild Seed planted outside the box of criminology's delusions and lies is going to grow into the liberating futures we need and deserve. Each Wild Seed chapter in this book and all Wild Seed movements and moments in the world contribute to the messy but necessary process of birthing new expectations and demands for justice. We must abolish criminology's carceralist, fear-fueling cultures of scarcity, burnout, and desperation so that we can begin to imagine, plant, and create a Wild Seed journey into justice, so that we can exist and flourish beyond white power's pathologizing and punitive imaginations and systems of conquest – so that we can achieve and extend Anyanwu's shape-shifted time away from Doro, so that we can be free.

What is Wild Seed Justice? It is the abolition of criminology and all the systems this ideology upholds. It is a sketch of the possibility that we can and the promise that we will flourish outside the borders and beyond the colonizing mythologies of crime and criminology.

Notes

1 www.imaniarts.com/ is Dara Kwayera Imani Bayer's website featuring some of her paintings, wisdoms, understandings, and writing.
2 In this chapter, I capitalize *Wild Seed* to refer to Butler's book title and the ideologies of Wild Seed that emerge, and lowercase "wild seed" to refer to the actual process and existence of non-domesticated seeds. The two (capital Wild Seed and lowercase wild seed) are extensions of each other. My use of differentiated lettering is applied for clarity, not to imply that one is vastly separate from the other.

References

Bayer, D.K.I., 2016a. *Imani Arts: Critical and Creative Reflections by Dara Kwayera Imani Bayer.* www.imaniarts.com/ Retrieved December 21, 2021.

Bayer, D.K.I., 2016b. *What Is Imani Arts?* www.imaniarts.com/about Retrieved December 21, 2021.

Butler, O.E., 1976. *Patternmaster.* New York: Avon Books, Inc.

Butler, O.E., 1977. *Mind of my Mind.* New York: Warner Books, Inc.

Butler, O.E., 1978. *Survivor.* New York: Signet Books, Inc.

Butler, O.E., 1980. *Wild Seed.* New York: Warner Books, Inc.

Butler, O.E., 1984. *Clays Ark.* New York: Warner Books, Inc.

Butler, O.E., 1993. *Parable of the Sower.* New York: Warner Books, Inc.

Butler, O.E., 1998. *Parable of the Talents.* New York: Warner Books, Inc.

Butler, O.E., 2000. "A Few Rules for Predicting the Future." *Essence Magazine*, May 2000, 31, 1; Women's *Magazine* Archive pg. 164–166; continued on 264.

Cohen, S. 1985. *Visions of Social Control.* Oxford, UK: Polity Press.

Gerlak, A.K., Louder, E., Ingram, H., McBride, J., Fox, C.A., Reo, N.J., Fessell, B., Dituri, F., Hasan, S., Evers, J. and Zwarteveen, M., 2022. "An Intersectional Approach to Water Equity in the US." *Water Alternatives*, 15(1), 1–12.

Manthey, G., Esposito, F. and Hernandez, A., 2022. "Despite 'Defunding' Claims, Police Funding Has Increased in Many US Cities", *ABC News.* https://abcnews.go.com/US/defunding-claims-police-funding-increased-us-cities/story?id=91511971 Retrieved March 10, 2023.

Mathiesen, T., 1974. *The Politics of Abolition.* Oslo: Scandanavian University Books by Universitetsforlaget.

The Official Mapping Police Violence Database. https://mappingpoliceviolence.us/ Retrieved March 10, 2023.

Saleh-Hanna, V., 2008. *Colonial Systems of Control: Criminal Justice in Nigeria*. Ottawa: University of Ottawa Press.

Saleh-Hanna, V., 2015. "Black Feminist Hauntology: Rememory the Ghosts of Abolition?", *Champ pénal/Penal Field*, 13. http://journals.openedition.org/champpenal/9168.

Saleh-Hanna, V., 2017a. "An Abolitionist Theory on Crime: Ending the Abusive Relationship with Racist-Imperialist-Patriarchy [R.I.P.]." *The Contemporary Justice Review*, 20(4), 419–441.

Saleh-Hanna, V., 2017b. "Reversing Criminology's White Gaze: As Lombroso's Disembodied Head Peers Through a Glass Jar in a Museum Foreshadowed by Sara Baartman's Ghost." In J.Z. Wilson, S. Hodgkinson, J. Piche and K. Walby (Eds.) *The Palgrave Handbook on Prison Tourism* (pp. 689–711). Hampshire, UK: Palgrave Macmillan.

2

UNWANTED

Epistemic Erasure of Black Radical Possibility in Criminology

Jason M. Williams

Introduction

As a so-called scientific discipline, criminology has been at the forefront of tremendous harm bestowed onto marginalized communities. Since its infancy, criminology has manifested primarily in a white male heteropatriarchal context. Since then, the discipline has also focused mainly on marginalized populations, especially racial-ethnic people. These groups, who have faced immeasurable barriers due to structural racism, inequality, and political abandonment, have long faced the brunt of white criminologists' need to support the statecraft of white supremacy and retribution against marginalized people. White criminologists have long been complicit in labeling Black communities as prone to violence and deserving of punishment and outright abandonment by the state. They have put forth these arguments via incomplete and flawed conclusions that form the basis of a largely obsolete and lazy body of knowledge. Brazenly, these are the writings that inform and control the orthodoxy today. Their lionized writings have stolen and diminished classrooms, theses, and careers for over a century – to the utter detriment of other ways of meaning-making in criminology.

This chapter will detail my trajectory in the discipline as a Black radical criminologist whose epistemic frame is opposite of the expected norm. I will chart my story briefly as a graduate student and my transition into the professoriate. I intend to tell a story of feeling unwanted and excluded from the enterprise. This story is not only mine, but it resonates with many others who have had to fight for legitimacy in a discipline that does not see them. I argue that our exclusion is the manifestation of epistemic battles long fought by ancestors past. However, the war continues today in a so-called more inclusive academy.

DOI: 10.4324/9780367817114-4

Foregrounding Situated Knowledges

As a graduate student, I was well grounded in my positionality as a radical Black criminologist. I frequently spoke up in classes against patently racist and inaccurate commentary from students and professors alike. I was well prepared for such a battle, since my undergraduate experience was fiery, battling the ignorance of classmates' youth and a series of unfit, practitioner-oriented adjuncts. However, during this experience, I never forgot where I came from and how important my roots were in helping me to shape my understanding of the world. While mainstream scholarship is quick to denounce the utility of one's self-awareness, others have long argued that our understanding of the world is inextricably tied to the lens from which we come (Haraway, 1988). Such a departure from mainstream epistemology has long been championed by radical scholars of color (and allies) across the social sciences, especially Black feminist scholars (Almeida, 2015; Bell, 1992; Bhattacharya, 2017; Crenshaw et al., 1995; Delgado, 2005; Gordon, 1990; Harding, 1991; Hill Collins, 2006, 2013, 2019; Hill Collins & Bilge, 2021; Ladson-Billings, 2003; Potter, 2015; Saleh-Hanna, 2015; Stanfield, 1985).

However, foregrounding lived experiences is key when critiquing the administration of justice. I often rely on a triangulation of historical knowledge and contemporary narratives to form the basis of my analyses and conclusions. That way of creating knowledge is on par with tradition in African American culture; indeed, my people are capable of developing science to understand the world. It is important to note that US justice has never been indigenous to those who bear the brunt of its reach. For instance, Berry (1995), in her seminal book *Black Resistance/White Law*, charts the course of history regarding social and racialized control in the US. She accentuates that the law is created for and by whites to control those groups they deem deviant or unfit for full citizenship. She articulates this provocative thesis through painstaking historical analysis beginning with the inception of the US. Berry notes how the law has played a pivotal role in suppressing the humanity of Blacks – and this was masterfully done by controlling their movement:

> [I]n 1806, the Virginia legislature passed an act which required free blacks who were manumitted to leave the state. Many free blacks left the lower South to resettle in the Upper South and Midwest. States in these areas began enacting legislation to prevent the entry of free blacks within their borders. As the number of free blacks in the United States increased from 59,000 in 1790 to 319,000 in 1830, many blacks faced the problem of finding a place to live.
>
> *(p. 16)*

Thus, processes of (in)formal governance and control have consistently charted the course for Blacks in the US. The refusal, of course, to allow Blacks to move freely stemmed from white supremacist ideals that sought to relegate nonwhites to the undercarriage. Much of the terroristic strategy to control nonwhites manifested out of white fear, in the hope that they could stifle revolts and stymie the imaginations of the oppressed. Laws like the slave codes and others worked fantastically to remove even the remote imagined thought of being free. So, while these laws were created to oppress physically, they also did grave psychological harm, halting their victims from accessing their freedom of mind. Blacks could not live free in the physical society and were also not free in their secrecy. The damage of such a system cannot be underestimated and written off as rogue laws of their time, as the extent of their damage is immeasurable, with a legacy that haunts today.

Conroy (2005) provided insight, noting how past legal regimes that controlled the movement of Blacks have reemerged via the judicial affirmation of Black subjective citizenship. He unpacks the meaning of the US's founding documents while also calling out the false promise they provide for Blacks and, therefore, the delusion they represent to all:

> Out of a strong democratic history and sacred founding documents, our nation was created as a refuge from tyranny. The Constitution and subsequent Amendments promised such basic rights as freedom of religion, speech, and expression. The Constitution also guaranteed protections against government oppression and unreasonable search and seizure. These ideals, however, have never been uniformly applied. African Americans have never enjoyed the benefits of full and equal rights, but have instead suffered oppression, racism, and degradation.
>
> *(Conroy, 2005, p. 149)*

It is within this historical and contemporary reality that my epistemic framework emerges. As a descendant of slaves who bears their legacy today, my lens is riddled with their memory and my experiences of being a Black American. I cannot rid myself of such a lens any more than my white colleagues can erase their lens, yet my counterparts easily seek refuge in a space that centers them as the default. It centers whites even as it claims to be objective, never realizing that objectivity is almost always defined by those who control the metrics of knowledge.

My situated knowledeges and way of understanding social control and the administration of justice are not readily accepted by the so-called scientific discipline(s) charged with studying crime and social control. Understanding that the process of meaning-making is influenced by our histories and singular experiences navigating the world, criminology, as a so-called scientific discipline, is compromised, as it is incomplete, fallible, and exists in a Eurocentric default. Moreover, at their root, genuine scientific disciplines are democratic and inclusive of the plurality of perspectives in their field. Under such a scheme, all perspectives would receive equal recognition as contributions to the field. This is not the case for criminology. Criminology has chosen to stand as a weapon of the state, always being willing to uphold the state's rogue strategy of racialized social control and willing to invent new technologies of oppression and death. Criminology has been complicit in human suffering and manufacturing the same crime and deviance it claims to study. Criminology is criminogenic.

Black radical epistemology would understand the state as a singular force of immense oppression and terror in collusion with white supremacy (Lawrence-McIntyre, 1992). History and today reveal how organized anti-Black decapitation has long been a focal point of governance for the US government (Balbus, 1973; Civil Rights Congress, 1952; Higginbotham, 1996). Therefore, one cannot undertake any criminological analysis without considering those core facts of reality. We cannot believe that the basis or the science of criminology is somehow objective and value-free. However, much of criminology is based on the lie of racelessness, the wanton exclusion of history, and the politics that create the law (Quinney, 1970). Like US jurisprudence, criminology does not see the significance of race; it is purposefully too complex. Instead, it concedes to white sentimentalism (Browne-Marshall, 2013, 2021; Crenshaw et al., 1995; Delgado & Stefancic, 2012), rendering its conclusions incomplete. Criminology hides its marriage to white supremacy through so-called objective logic that praises race neutrality and apolitical, value-free assumptions. Clearly, the discipline exists in a delusional reality that only makes sense to itself.

A liberative criminology understands the usefulness of self-awareness and situated knowledges. Under such a paradigm of practicing criminology, the multitude of perspectives existent within the broader universe of the discipline would be recognized as legitimate ways of cultivating knowledge. Standpoint epistemology (Haraway, 1988) is a necessary component in bulldozing the criminogenic, inhumane nature of criminology as it stands today. As such, I choose to execute my standpoints within criminology as a way of not only liberating my people but also as an act of pure resistance against an undemocratic and rogue governing ethos whose desire is to destroy me.

Abolishing the Default

Despite some paradigmatic changes in the discipline, criminology has remained a tool of imperialism (Agozino, 2003; Cunneen & Tauri, 2016). While criminology is a tool for pillaging lands and silencing marginalized people, war is also brewing around the meaning-making process inside the discipline (Saleh-Hanna, 2015, 2017; Williams, 2019; Williams & Battle, 2017). Some scholars have called attention to these power dynamics inherent in the discipline, describing diverging perspectives as deviant (Walters, 2003). Walters (2003) has highlighted the discursive connection between the state and the discipline by unpacking the appropriation of state funds to study crime, for example. Suppose it is the will of the state to maintain differential systems of racialized social control. In that case, it will demand absolute obedience to this order from scholars who beg for its money. Walters (2003) argues that the default methodology for acquiring such funds is almost always quantitative, ignoring other ways of cultivating knowledge.

Critical scholars who focus on rich data seldom have a chance at obtaining state funds because their knowledge is unwanted. This collusion between the state and scholars in the field helps to legitimate the governing ethos that diminishes other ways of knowing. Under such a program of strict methodological control, qualitative research becomes moot, illegitimate, and banished from the halls of criminological science (Young, 2011). It is important to note that the erasure of voice significantly impacts marginalized communities that bear the brunt of intervention from the criminal legal system. This is no coincidence, as an oppressor will never allow the voices of its victims to be heard. Therefore, criminology is complicit in silencing scholars who wish to proceed differently and human beings whose voices and lived experiences could help to improve and inform the discipline and the administration of justice.

I mostly look toward the girth of knowledge in the field of education to decontextualize the epistemic realities in criminology. For instance, other scientific fields have accommodated debates around meaning-making. These fields understand that the social is political; therefore, any discipline that deals with society should not uncritically accept objectivity as a legitimating force of the status quo. There is always more to the story, and context matters greatly within a purposefully complex system of racial inequality. We can rely on Ladson-Billings (2003) to remind us that meaning-making and our understanding of said meaning take place within the sociopolitical context of its time. Thus, liberating epistemologies in criminology must take heed of the revolts that occurred, for instance, in the summer of 2020. How might criminology reconstitute its understanding of policing in the aftermath of George Floyd, Breonna Taylor, Toni McDade, and others? Will the discipline adopt an intersectional strategy, or will it remain obedient to the state?

Haraway (1988) reminds us that it is important to argue that "politics and epistemologies of location, positioning, and situation, where partiality and not universality is the condition of being heard" (p. 589). We must undo the governing ethos that tries to restrict how we practice criminology because the products of what we do "are claims on people's lives" (p. 589) and not some abstract conclusion that rests in some book or journal, never to be actualized by others. Unfortunately, policymakers and police and correctional administrators have used hyper-positivist conclusions from criminology to harm society members (Saleh-Hanna, 2017). It has also had its share of influence in the courts, legitimizing race neutrality in how courts decide on matters concerning race (see Cleve, 2016). Under hyper-positivist control, people of color (especially Blacks) have had to absorb the force of administering justice in ways that claim not to see the humanity of racialized people. The marriage between criminology and the system is painstakingly discovered through these processes. As Haraway (1988) lamented, "admitted or not, politics and ethics ground struggles over knowledge projects" (p. 587). Therefore, abolishing criminology and adopting a more humanistic approach is the only way to ensure genuine justice that would center reparative strategies in the community. Ethnocentric variations within the broader scope of social science have not helped marginalized people, and they do not lead to a more healthy, liberated society (Stanfield, 1985).

One way to change the current in criminology is to adopt concepts rooted in theoretical sensitivity. For instance, Strauss and Corbin (1990) purported that theoretical sensitivity refers to:

> [a] personal quality of the researcher. It indicates an awareness of the subtleties of meaning of data. One can come to the research situation with varying degrees of sensitivity depending upon previous reading and experience with or relevant to the data. It can also be developed further during the research process. Theoretical sensitivity refers to the attribute of having insight, the ability to give meaning to data, the capacity to understand, and capability to separate the pertinent from that which isn't.
>
> *(pp. 41–42)*

Moreover, adopting theoretical sensitivity gives way to accepting critical traditions such as Critical Race Theory (CRT). In my research, I have chosen to use CRT as a theoretical, methodological, and analytical tool (see Williams, 2019). As Solórzano and Yosso (2002) argue, rich traditions like CRT help to provide a counter-story to hyper-positivist orientations that refuse to hear the stories of marginalized people. They also advocate for the adoption of critical race methodologies to combat the erasure of marginalized humanities, as "counter-stories can shatter complacency, challenge the dominate discourse on race, and further the struggle for racial reform" (p. 32).

Within the context of what African Americans have to offer to the discipline, there needs to be some regard for what Gordon (1990) describes as a Black intellectual discourse and cultural knowledge. For instance, she defines Black epistemology as "the study or theory of knowledge generated out of the African-American existential condition, that is, of the knowledge and cultural artifacts produced by African-Americans based on African-American cultural, social, economic, historical, and political experience" (p. 90). In responding to the mainstream, she laments, "[M]ainstream academicians have experienced difficulty with African-American thought – and its potential to influence education – because it is often both holistic and nonsynchronous" (p. 90). Here she condemns white sentimentalism in deference to the right of all peoples to cultivate knowledge from within their traditions. In response to the need to resist, despite immense erasure, Gordon proposes that "we must look for the reason for such marginalization in the emancipatory and empowering nature of serious dialogue and debate within the scholarship produced by people of color" (p. 90).

Conclusion: Toward Future Black Radical Knowledges of Liberation

Therefore, if criminology is to be a genuine science, it must open its doors to the full scope of knowledges available to us so that we may have a more holistic understanding of crime and social control. This is why many Black scholars, in particular, choose to foreground lived experiences and histories in how we compute criminological knowledge. Any science worth its weight would not mandate the obliteration of the self in constructing knowledge. Criminology is afraid of what might be discovered if the inclusion of equally other epistemic frameworks suddenly came into play. Perhaps the other ways of knowing may abolish or cancel its status as a weapon of the state. Nevertheless, we must remember, too, that these processes of marginalization within science are human led. While criminological science holds much weight in society, we must not forget that it takes human intervention to actualize what these knowledges purport. For instance, while the broken windows theory was created within the untouchable and elite confines of academia, it was nonetheless put to practice by police practitioners and further legitimated via criminological studies affirming its position.

The future of Black radical imaginations within criminology rests in our ironclad resistance against the mainstream and our ability to provide counter-narratives, even in the face of not being heard. It becomes a matter of being on the record, having something out there for future generations to embrace. For me, being able to read the works of radical Black scholars provided me a haven within a space that only sought to terrorize me. In much of my work, I often cite the criminally undercited Georges-Abeyie (2001) theory of Petit Apartheid in the criminal justice system. While he is not widely spoken about in criminological theory, he has nonetheless produced quite a canon of knowledge that will speak to future generations who are also looking to claim and establish Black real estate in the criminological enterprise. Thus, our future depends on our ability to imagine a better tomorrow for ourselves and those behind us. Our future also depends on us unyieldingly revealing the role imperialism has played in how we define knowledge (Go, 2016). We have to keep the flame going through each storm the orthodoxy throws at us because our mere presence lets them know that our whole selves are here to stay. Like those before us, the artifacts of our contributions will be a constant reminder that we were here and persevered. #BLM!

References

Agozino, B. (2003). *Counter-Colonial Criminology: A Critique of Imperialist Reason*. Pluto Press.

Almeida, S. (2015). Race-Based Epistemologies: The Role of Race and Dominance in Knowledge Production. *In Wagadu: A Journal of Transnational Women's and Gender Studies, 13*, 28.

Balbus, I. D. (1973). *The Dialectics of Legal Repression: Black Rebels Before the American Criminal Courts*. Russell Sage Foundation.

Bell, D. (1992). *Faces at the Bottom of the Well: The Permanence of Racism*. Basic Books.

Berry, M. F. (1995). *Black Resistance/White Law: A History of Constitutional Racism in America*. Penguin.

Bhattacharya, K. (2017). *Fundamentals of Qualitative Research: A Practical Guide*. Routledge.

Browne-Marshall, G. J. (2013). *Race, Law, and American Society: 1607-Present*. Routledge.

Browne-Marshall, G. J. (2021). *She Took Justice: The Black Woman, Law, and Power – 1619 to 1969*. Routledge.

Civil Rights Congress. (1952). *We Charge Genocide: The Historic Petition to the United Nations for Relief from a Crime of the United States Government Against the Negro People*. Civil Rights Congress.

Cleve, N. G. V. (2016). *Crook County: Racism and Injustice in America's Largest Criminal Court*. Stanford University Press.

Conroy, J. S. (2005). Show Me Your Papers: Race and Street Encounters. *National Black Law Journal, 19*, 149.

Crenshaw, K., Gotanda, N., Peller, G., & Thomas, K. (Eds.). (1995). *Critical Race Theory: The Key Writings That Formed the Movement*. The New Press.

Cunneen, C., & Tauri, J. (2016). *Indigenous Criminology*. Policy Press.

Delgado, R. (Ed.). (2005). *The Derrick Bell Reader*. NYU Press.

Delgado, R., & Stefancic, J. (2012). *Critical Race Theory: An Introduction, Second Edition*. NYU Press.

Georges-Abeyie, D. (2001). Petit Apartheid in Criminal Justice: "The More 'Things' Change, the More 'Things' Remain the Same." In *Petit Apartheid in the U.S. Criminal Justice System: The Dark Figure of Racism* (pp. ix–xiv). Carolina Academic Press.

Go, J. (2016). *Postcolonial Thought and Social Theory*. Oxford University Press.

Gordon, B. M. (1990). The Necessity of African-American Epistemology for Educational Theory and Practice1. *Journal of Education, 172*(3), 88–106. https://doi.org/10.1177/002205749017200307

Haraway, D. (1988). Situated Knowledges: The Science Question in Feminism and the Privilege of Partial Perspective. *Feminist Studies, 14*(3), 575–599. https://doi.org/10.2307/3178066

Harding, S. (1991). *Whose Science? Whose Knowledge? Thinking from Women's Lives*. Cornell University Press.

Higginbotham, A. L. (1996). *Shades of Freedom: Racial Politics and Presumptions of the American Legal Process*. Oxford University Press.

Hill Collins, P. (2006). *Black Sexual Politics African Americans, Gender, and the New Racism*. www.vlebooks.com/vleweb/product/openreader?id=none&isbn=9780203309506

Hill Collins, P. (2013). *On Intellectual Activism*. Temple University Press.

Hill Collins, P. (2019). *Intersectionality as Critical Social Theory*. Duke University Press.

Hill Collins, P., & Bilge, S. (2021). *Intersectionality*. Polity Press.

Ladson-Billings, G. (2003). It's Your World, I'm Just Trying to Explain It: Understanding Our Epistemological and Methodological Challenges. *Qualitative Inquiry, 9*(1), 5–12. https://doi.org/10.1177/1077800402239333

Lawrence-McIntyre, C. C. (1992). *Criminalizing a Race: Free Blacks During Slavery*. Kayode.

Potter, H. (2015). *Intersectionality and Criminology: Disrupting and Revolutionizing Studies of Crime* (1st edition). Routledge.

Quinney, R. (1970). *The Social Reality of Crime*. Transaction Publishers.

Saleh-Hanna, V. (2015). Black Feminist Hauntology. *Champ Pénal/Penal Field, XII*, Article Vol. XII. https://doi.org/10.4000/champpenal.9168

Saleh-Hanna, V. (2017). Reversing Criminology's White Gaze: As Lombroso's Disembodied Head Peers Through a Glass Jar in a Museum Foreshadowed by Sara Baartman's Ghost. In *The Palgrave Handbook of Prison Tourism* (pp. 689–711). Springer.

Solórzano, D. G., & Yosso, T. J. (2002). Critical Race Methodology: Counter-Storytelling as an Analytical Framework for Education Research. *Qualitative Inquiry, 8*(1), 23–44. https://doi.org/10.1177/107780040200800103

Stanfield, J. H. (1985). Chapter 10: The Ethnocentric Basis of Social Science Knowledge Production. *Review of Research in Education*, *12*(1), 387–415. https://doi.org/10.3102/0091732X012001387

Strauss, A., & Corbin, J. M. (1990). *Basics of Qualitative Research: Grounded Theory Procedures and Techniques*. SAGE Publications.

Walters, R. (2003). *Deviant Knowledge: Criminology, Politics, and Policy*. Willan.

Williams, J. M. (2019). Race as a Carceral Terrain: Black Lives Matter Meets Reentry. *The Prison Journal*, *99*(4), 387–395. https://doi.org/10.1177/0032885519852062

Williams, J. M., & Battle, N. T. (2017). African Americans and Punishment for Crime: A Critique of Mainstream and Neoliberal Discourses. *Journal of Offender Rehabilitation*, *56*(8), 552–566. https://doi.org/10.1080/10509674.2017.1363116.

Young, J. (2011). *Criminological Imagination* (1st edition). Polity.

3

THE HISTORY OF CRIMINOLOGY IS A HISTORY OF WHITE SUPREMACY

Viviane Saleh-Hanna

My time as a student in criminology and criminal justice programs at the turn of the 21st century was littered with classroom teachings and readings obsessively docu- menting, reiterating, fetishizing, justifying, and building careers that legitimized or dissected 'the over-representation of minorities' (their language) in prisons and other carceral, family-breaking, community-destroying institutions. Any freedom-minded teachings I received occurred within the small arenas of abolitionism and restorative justice (RJ) briefly in the mid-1990s, before RJ was gobbled up by the state, moving us quickly to turn towards Ruth Morris's (2000) definitions and ideologies of trans- formative justice (TJ) at the turn of the century. TJ is now being gobbled up and co-opted as power structures grapple with demands to defund the police throughout Turtle Island, so we know it is time to move on, once more, to new sketches within unfinished (Mathiesen, 1974) arenas of justice.

Criminology disallows students from considering justice as possible beyond the limitations and oppressions of white supremacy, heteropatriarchy, and colonialism. In those early years of my crim education in Canada, all lessons I learned on anti- colonialism, anti-oppression, and anti-racism happened through my work with imprisoned people serving life sentences in Collins Bay Penitentiary in Kingston, Ontario and later Matsqui Penitentiary in Abbotsford, British Columbia. I also received significant teachings through my work with the Prison Arts Foundation and the hundreds of imprisoned artists and people I met and worked with inside penitentiaries, prisons, and jails across Canada. The years I spent working with peo- ple imprisoned in Nigeria, and briefly in Ghana and Egypt, imparted lessons and teachings that continue to position colonialism and enslavement as synonmous with criminal legal systems and ideologies. Years spent working with prisoners through- out Turtle Island and Africa are foundational to my understandings of criminology's colonizing and enslaving roots. Those years, and the lived realities of millions of

DOI: 10.4324/9780367817114-5

imprisoned people and their loved ones across time and place, witness and contradict criminology's mythologies and assumptions every day.

While many of criminology's classrooms and research projects rely upon the aggressions (they are not 'micro') of colorblind racism (Bonilla-Silva, 2021), my position a young north African woman volunteering inside prisons in the 1990s and 2000s demanded I stand firmly and without hesitation within Blackness. Inside prisons, the race-ethnicity blinders and silences imposed within 'polite' white spaces are not only dysfunctional and harmful to me, they came with immense risks to imprisoned people I was working with. Inside prison there are no pretenses about identity and with so much at stake, I entered into overt north African Blackness through the ways that prison guards responded to me versus white volunteers, through the ways that young white women volunteering alongside me fetishized and criticized any extended time I spent in dialogue with imprisoned Black people, and within the immediate kinships and unspoken understandings that imprisoned Black adults and youths formed with me through unspoken exchanges and glances, or the details they chose to share when they spoke about their experiences and reflections on arrest, courtrooms, and imprisonment. Eventually, my work with imprisoned Africans in Kirikiri Medium and Maximum Security Prisons and Kirikiri Prison for Women in Nigeria brought me larger understandings of why Pan Africanism truly is an antidote to colonialism and white supremacy: seeing Africa and being African through a wholistic lens full of Africa's wide spectrums of Blackness produced a relationality that pushed and broke the borders of the white settler landscapes and the holographic identities I had grown up within. Those precious years in Africa at the turn of the 21st century deepened my understanding of the nuances and indirect rulings of carceralist cultures and economies, and allowed me to see parallels that tie all colonial systems of control (Saleh-Hanna, 2008) within global, heteronormative, white power dynamics (Saleh-Hanna, 2015).

I completed two degrees in criminology and one in criminal justice in three rather large and prestigious university programs, in eastern, western, and midwestern regions, in Canada and the U.S. Regardless of the stereotypes each of these regions and nations hold, criminology and criminal justice remained consistent. Except for my last class during my last degree, none taught about white supremacy and colonialism as the precursors to enslavement and imprisonment. We learned about classism and sexism but never within the contexts of racism, white supremacy, heteropatriarchy, and colonialism. A select few professors assigned Black and Indigenous prison writings, though none assigned Black and Indigenous methods or theory: it was the story and the struggle we learned about in criminology in those days, not the ontology or epistemology of Black and Indigenous thought and ways of knowing (Agozino, 2003; Absolon, 2022; Kitossa, 2012; Tauri and Porou, 2014). According to the criminology I experienced and had to survive, critical thinking and true access to justice existed only within the stale and sterilizing writings of critical criminology's labeling theorists, or Marxist and feminist (aka class-only and white-women-only) criminology. The ontological assessments I received in my undergraduate and master's degrees in Canada were anchored within critical and radical criminology's critiques of positivism and classical criminology, and these continue to shape my understanding of the field today. While that education prepared me for an academic deconstruction of a doctoral criminal justice degree in the U.S., none of the critiques of criminology provided anti-racist or anti-colonial frameworks, limiting their scopes and potentials. The only truly significant teachings I received within criminology in those undergraduate years came in the form of Dr. Bob Gaucher's abolitionist teachings, anchored within the classics of prison and penal abolition ideologies, an unwavering and nuanced deconstruction of institutions and their wide-reaching social control mechanisms, and a clear understanding that social movements centering as much solidarity with those imprisoned and formerly imprisoned as possible are the key to any substantial social change and actual realization of justice (Mathiesen, 1974; Cohen, 1985, Cohen, 1988; Hulsman, 1986; Bianci and van Swaaningen, 1986; Christie, 1993; Culhane, 1985, Morris, 2000).

In 2005, during my last course for my last degree in criminology's wretched and barren trenches, I had my first experience of being in a Black professor's Black-affirming classroom. Dr. Leon Pettiway assigned *The Bluest Eye* by Toni Morrison (1970) and my mind grew exponentially in liberating directions, appropriately as I was ending my time as a student in a field that had invented and continued to enforce growing forms of imprisonment. Gaining much-needed distance from criminology through my dissertation on Black musicianship (Saleh-Hanna, 2007) and then the establishment of my own career with some personal agency (provided through academic freedom, what little bit we have left in the U.S.) opened doors for me to dedicate time towards Black feminist methodologies and understandings. During those short few months in Dr. Pettiway's classroom at the end of my doctoral studies at Indiana University, my heart, mind, and soul sparked new life as I began healing journeys into Black feminism through Toni Morrison's work. After the *Bluest Eye* I read all of her novels, and moved on to read her essays, interviews, and speeches – I read all that I could find by Toni Morrison and Black women who emerged as her intellectual kin. I spent almost ten years reading, writing, and exorcizing criminology's impact through Black Feminist teachings. Not until 2015 could I express my own Black feminist voice and understandings in *Black Feminist Hauntology: Rememory the Ghosts of Abolition?* (Saleh-Hanna, 2015). Essentially, the aftermath of my three degrees in criminology and criminal justice required more than ten years of learning and healing. I used to wonder where I would be had I met Dr. Pettiway sooner or had been introduced to Black feminist teachings in place of all my miserable years in criminology. On other days, I know those years provided access, details, and clear-as-day understanding of criminology's imaginations, narratives, assumptions, histories, politics, thought patterns, mannerisms, cultures, intentions, and tactics. Because the criminal legal system is amongst the most viscious and powerful systems of violence and oppression weaponized against Black and Indigenous people today, knowledge of the details and nuances of criminology's imaginations, intentions, and behaviors are valuable for our struggle to be free.

Teaching the History of Criminology

Abolitionist professors who teach in criminology and criminal justice programs do the important work of exiting the ideological echo chambers where most (on all sides of western political spectrums) tend to remain. As abolitionist professors we enter classrooms that have overtly and openly pushed white power agendas for hundreds of years, and we work to open new pathways of thought, vision, and understanding for our students to consider. We are surrounded by saboteurs and racists in the academy – some masquerading as allies and experts in our struggles for freedom – but we also tend to have strong roots within our chosen communities and solidarity with other abolitionist, anti-colonial, freedom-driven scholars. It is through these contexts that many of us manage to navigate through the colonizing dynamics of western academic settings. Below I share some tools and stories about this process.

One of the first courses I was assigned to teach as an assistant professor in Crime and Justice Studies was a third-year course called Criminological Theories. As soon as possible, I rewrote the course into a second-year class and renamed it A History of Criminology. I reassigned it as a second-year course because criminology's theories are actually quite remedial in thinking and structure (though the use of obscure terms and colonial logic casts them as scientific and technical). I changed 'theories' to 'history of thought' because students seldom think of the study of western theory as a history of white men's musings about the world they seek to conquer and the humans they seek to exploit. After years of sitting in criminology's classrooms, I knew it is neither ethical nor accurate to teach 'theories of crime' without a wholistic context of the white men (and starting in the 1970s, the white women) whose policies, political world views, and allegiance to institutionalized colonialism birthed and shaped criminology's assumptions about humanity, society, and the role of colonial law in our lives.

To properly teach the history of criminology's thoughts and behaviors we must first develop a bird's eye view of the field. This allows students a fair chance to deconstruct the myths and pervasive untruths that colonize justice, destabilize our communities, and stunt our abilities to create and sustain infrastructures and justice-oriented models of collective care and support. To build that larger world view in my classrooms I have relied on two conceptual tools of analysis: first, a deconstruction of criminology's opposites as aligned, and second, a comprehensive mapping of criminology's dominant theories and schools of thought within their political contexts, institutionalizing praxis, and white power allegiances.

Criminology's Opposites Are Actually Aligned

There are many opposites and binaries presented in criminology that are not oppositional in theory nor practice. Often, these 'opposites' are presented as classical criminology versus positivist criminology debates, when in truth, both work hand in hand, employing elasticity along criminology's spectrum of tactics to institutionalize and expand the powers of the criminal legal system. This is best explained through the fake dichotomies narrated about punishment (classical criminology's theories of rationality, hedonism, and deterrence) versus rehabilitation (positivist criminology's theories of treatment, self-improvement, and risk management). This debate is often performed through the following scripts.

First, classical criminologists assume that human nature is hedonistic (wanting to maximize pleasure and minimize pain), therefore the law and law enforcement agents must provide deterrence (the threat of punishment followed by the actual use of state-endorsed violence) to encourage 'rational' thought. In a white power context, being 'a rational human being' is synonymous with being a self-serving, calculating, narcissist who seeks to gain power/pleasure without regard for others. Thus, according to supporters/believers of these theories, the law provides external stimuli needed (i.e., the wrath of the state's punishment mechanisms) to ensure humans make 'good, rational decisions'. Without the law's threat to punish, colonizers believe that people will go about their daily lives doing exactly what colonizers have done: stealing, murdering, raping, abusing, and harming each other repeatedly.

Through classical criminology, the declaration of human nature as hedonistic is presented as 'logical', even though we know that individual human behavior, societal interactions, and all systems of power are much more complex than the calculating mathematics of deterrence. Three hundred years into the criminal legal system's existence (the first prisons used for the purpose of deterrence date back to the 1700s), we have yet to see evidence to support the outlandish colonizing claims that hedonism is universal to all humanity. Stepping beyond the abusive projections of criminology (Saleh-Hanna, 2017) allows us to see how ludicrous criminology's claim on human nature as hedonistic is, as it fails to account for the very complex nuances held within the many behaviors or realities of 'humanity' or 'all people' and instead, more accurately describes the behaviors of colonizers and slavers who maximized their own pleasure and wealth on the backs, lands, and suffering of Black and Indigenous peoples, lands, and nations. Bentham and Beccaria's assumptions about human nature should be applied to themselves and to their colleagues in the western academy, partners in all colonial institutions of land theft and occupation, enslavement, arrest, imprisonment, psychological and physical warfare, and exploitation – and not to the rest of us situated on the other side of white-hetero power structures. It is also important to map the assumption that 'human nature is hedonistic' within old-school, sexist, racist, impoverishing narratives used by colonizers, enslavers, imprisoners, and arrestors. White power and colonizing cultures socialize and groom members of the dominant group to view us as 'savage' (hedonistic), as infantalized and dependent upon carceral control and the heavy, paternalistic, abusive (punitive) hands of the colonial state. The result of these theories is not justice and security but instead further control over the lives of oppressed peoples, and a continued avoidance of consequences and systemic accountability for colonizers, enslavers, imprisoners, and their beneficiaries. To summarize the obvious: there is no proof that all human nature is hedonistic. Hedonism exists within the institutionalized (not human) nature of slavers, colonizers, imprisoners, and their benefactors. And yet, all of classical criminology's theories of deterrence as well as the very existence of the criminal legal system, the penal code, and all criminal legal enforcement agencies rely upon the foundational mythology and colonial lie that claims human nature is hedonistic. Instead of deconstructing the absurdity of this assumption, criminologists shifted into a debate framing hedonism and rational choice as the categorical opposite of positivism's assumptions about human nature as determined and shaped by a plethora of colonizing variables and forces.

Positivist criminologists claim that human nature is not rational and hedonistic but instead is determined or influenced by *something*. This is not a stand-alone claim – it is a literal response to the claims of classical criminologists. By deterministic they mean that human behavior is not shaped by hedonism and rational-decision-making, but instead by genetics, brain size, social organization (or lack thereof), subcultures, neighborhoods, mental health, family structures, immigration status, friends, the weather, erection and ejaculation, the onset of menstruation, and so on. Therefore, what determines our behavior (genetics, lack of control over our emotions, living in a 'bad' neighborhood, growing up around 'bad' cultures, being raised within a 'broken' family, hanging out with the 'wrong' crowd) needs to be rehabilitated, cured, or curtailed in order for the state to manage crime. In the name of rehabilitation, criminology has endorsed and performed lobotomies (surgical severing of the brain in areas criminologists believed were linked to anti-social and criminal behavior), therapy, anger management, parole and probation stipulations that monitor and control social interactions, chemical castration, and other physical or hormonal manipulations and control over human and social bodies, and a plethora of violently intrusive private and state-sponsored programs and research geared towards eliminating the 'criminal element' from society, from culture, from the human body, or from whatever dimension of our existence criminology's positivists imagine next.

In truth and in practice, the majority who are imprisoned or criminalized belong to or are descended from colonized and enslaved peoples and communities. Thus, to suggest that criminologists can locate 'crime' within culture, family, the human psyche, or social bodies without acknowledgment of the fact that crime emerges through the imaginations and narratives of colonizers and slavers is absurd. To perpetuate the idea that criminology and the criminal legal system can 'rehabilitate criminals' – most of whom are impoverished, gendered, sexualized, and racialized through colonial systems of control – is to perpetuate white supremacist belief systems that declare whiteness (and its gendering, impoverishing, racializing, and sexualizing formations) 'superior' while the rest of us continue to be framed as 'deviant'.

To state the obvious, which tends to be hidden in plain sight within criminology's theoretical smoke and mirrors: the only 'determinism' we have in this world is the inevitability of institutional violence. As long as there are colonial institutions of enslavement and imprisonment, they will determine violence and continue to place all oppressed peoples at risk of remaining colonized. The result of positivism's biological, psychological, and sociological frameworks is the same as that of classical criminology's old and new formations: further exploitation and control over the lives and resources of colonized peoples, and a continued avoidance of consequences and systemic accountability away from colonizers and their beneficiaries.

From the perspective of these two schools of thought, we can see that classical and positivist criminology are simply two limbs serving the same colonizing body. One hand feeds and holds the other as needed. Punishment and rehabilitation accomplish the same thing. They both institutionalize and expand colonization by providing an elasticity that extends the life and reach of carceral power. In practice, they gain power when framed as opposites – for classical and positivist criminology are the original 'good cop/bad cop' dance that keeps us tangled within criminology's paradigms and interrogative frameworks (Saleh-Hanna, 2017b). Although the two appear oppositional, punishment and rehabilitation duplicate and nourish each other in theory and action along the same carceralist spectrum of state violence.

Within colonial societies and their cultural landscapes, the language and politics of 'punishment' feed the bloodthirsty, controlling dogmas of conservative-leaning audiences seeking to conserve and extend all that white supremacy has robbed from Black and Indigenous peoples and lands. Simultaneously, the language and politics of 'rehabilitation' feeds the white savior, needy-charity frameworks of liberal-leaning audiences seeking to reform old systems of exploitation so that they can legitimize, conserve, and extend all that white supremacy has robbed from Black and Indigenous peoples and lands. These are two sides of the same coin: both punitive (classical criminology) and rehabilitative (positivist criminology) approaches seek to sustain and grow colonial conquest. They are nothing more and nothing less than the spectrum of white power options needed to feed the various expectations and political leanings of contemporary colonizer audiences and benefactors. They both empower the criminal legal system to enforce and extend colonialism. Their dual (not oppositional) existence along the spectrum of armed criminal legal power and ideology provide the much-needed elasticity of give and take, without which the exploitative and vicious systems of colonial carceral power would snap under the pressure of their own true savagery, hypocrisy, and moral bankruptcy (Saleh-Hanna, 2015).

It is also important to recognize that presenting rehabilitation and punishment as two separate options that law can pursue severely limits most people from recognizing that we are trapped within a system that gives us no true options or pathways into justice. The fake opposites of criminology's aligned methodologies and practices create a dizzying debate that prevents many from stepping back to understand and work to create justice beyond the punitive and torturous imaginations of white power. To achieve justice we must map and pursue anticolonial options and pathways beyond the violent binaries and fake opposites of criminology. Only when we climb over the walls of criminology and its false assumptions about our own humanity and societal needs, can we begin to create a world where justice can escape the clutches of white power, where we become justice because justice has been liberated, decolonized, and indigenized with us out of the grasping deathly grips of prisons, courts, and policing.

A Map of Criminology's History of Thought: White Power Landmarks and Entanglements

The second tool I offer towards deconstructing criminology's mythologies comes in the form of a chronological map of the history of criminology's thought within the context of white supremacist behaviors and policies. The map I have drawn to capture the history of criminology within the U.S. is clear and helps students in the U.S. see how every dominant theory of crime is directly associated with and simultaneously emerging to endorse white power policies and historic events. I suspect that any scholar teaching criminology within a colonized, white, or white-settler landscape can produce the same map of allegiances between dominant theories of crime and specific colonial violence, public discourse, and policy battles for those places and times.

For example, criminology's demonic theorists in the 1500s and 1600s (pre-dating the formal creation of criminology yet forming significant precursors and foundation forming dogmas), conveniently identified the practitioners and holders of Europe's land-based spiritualities and practices as the weakest and therefore most dangerous bodies, minds, and spirits of their times. They theorized that the devil could possess spiritually weak people, targeting people who threatened power structures or whom they aimed to exploit. Once possessed, these 'weaker souls' would be influenced (or 'determined', to use positivist criminology's language) by the devil to commit the vilest forms of violence against individuals and society – and by 'society' they really meant priests, bishops, popes, and the wealthy who aligned with the political goals of the monarchy (Federici, 2004). Because demonic theories of deviance aligned with the goals of the wealthy and powerful, they gained dominance and became institutionalized and enforced through Europe's inquisitions. Demonic theories also played a key role in how white colonizers drafted 'manifest destiny' policies and how they legitimized (for themselves) mass crimes against humanity in the form of colonial land-theft and occupation, genocide, and chattel slavery. Demonic theories of crime started with hundreds of years of inquisitions in western Europe and white settler nations within the continent, and extended to target and exploit knowledges and spiritualities of Black and Indigenous peoples dating from time immemorial. These theories conveniently provided the story of why white people were compelled by their God to commit mass violations against the majority of the world's population: to civilize, to missionize, to Christianize, and so forth (Césaire, 1955). From this context and direct overlap between white theories of danger and colonial systems of exploitation, we can trace the roots of criminology to long before Bentham and Beccaria's classical criminology, Lombros and Durkheim's positivism, and Marx's critical criminology.

Bentham and Beccaria are cited as 'founding fathers' of the field, for they conceived of the theories of deterrence that underlie the modern criminal legal system. Their ideologies and assumptions form the story of why the state must have a right to punish the people. Unfortunately, these theories are seldom taught in criminology within the context of the largest institutions of their times: global chattel slavery and colonial wars to enforce global white supremacy and theft of Black and Indigenous lands, lives, and futures.

In my undergraduate years, during the 1990s in Canada, I remember a course on sentencing with teachings on the history of the penal code. We peripherally visited Bentham and Beccaria's work from the 1700s. I asked my mildly famous British professor, who was a 'sentencing expert' how they were able to write a penal code without including the acts of enslavement as a crime punishable by law. It was a naïve question, but that was where I was in my learning journey. He replied something along the lines of: they were not thinking about slavery as a problem – why would they? It was everywhere and therefore normalized. They were studying crime, and as far as they were concerned that had nothing to do with slavery. And he moved on to the next question.

Years later, when I read the original works of Bentham and Beccaria alongside scholars who engaged directly and critically with these writings, I found that both Bentham and Beccaria explicitly wrote about slavery. Further, Agozino (2003) points out that France's first penal code emerged at the same time as the Haitian revolution. He explains how impossible it would have been for the classical theorists of the penal code to fail to realize the terrors of slavery during those years. From my own studies I have learned that Beccaria literally cited the punitive and terrorizing praxis of chattel slavery's plantations as his inspiration for theories on deterrence:

> The strongest deterrent to crime . . . [would be] the long and painful example of a man deprived of his freedom and become a beast of burden, repaying with his toil the society he has offended. . . . No one today, in contemplating it, would choose total and perpetual loss of his own freedom, no matter how profitable a crime might be. Therefore that intensity of the punishment of lifelong slavery as a substitute for the death penalty possess that which suffices to deter any detrimental soul. I say that it has more. Many look on death with a firm and calm regard – some from fanaticism, some from vanity, which accompanies a man beyond the tomb, some in a desperate attempt to cease to live or to escape misery – but neither fanaticism or vanity dwells among fetters and chains, under the rod, under the yoke or in an iron cage, when the evildoer begins his sufferings instead of terminating them. . . . Were one to say that perpetual slavery is as painful as death and therefore equally cruel I would reply . . . the former would be even worse.
>
> *(Beccaria, translated and quoted in Sellin, 1976: 66)*

Jeremy Bentham (1748–1832), also often cited as a 'founding father' of classical criminology, was an outspoken antislavery (but not anti-carceralist or penal) abolitionist. In *The Works of Jeremy Bentham, Principles of Penal Law* (John Bowering edition, Edinburgh, 1859, 444) he wrote:

> It is not to be disputed that sugar and coffee, and other delicacies, which are the growth of those islands, add considerably to the enjoyments of the people here in Europe; but taking all these circumstances into consideration, if they are only to be obtained by keeping three hundred thousand men in a state which they

cannot be kept but by the terror of such executions: are there any considerations of luxury or enjoyment that can counterbalance such evils?

(translated and cited in Klingberg, 1926: 51)

It is within Bentham's use of 'enjoyments' and 'pleasures' that we can begin to trace the roots of classical criminology's views on human nature as hedonistic. On the evils he mentions at the end of the above quote, Bentham, both a slavery abolitionist and the architect of the prison's first blueprint, wrote:

In the West India colonies, a freeman . . . could enjoy the benefit, such as it was, of committing at pleasure all manner of enormities, short of murder, on the bodies of all persons in a state of slavery. . . . In some places the substitution of a small fine to all other punishment, the licence to add or substitute murder to every other injury is completed.

(translated and cited in Klingberg, 1926: 53)

In this we locate Bentham's musings that human nature is both rational and hedonistic (key components of criminal legal systems) as <u>not</u> inspired by his observations or reflections on the human condition in general but instead as inspired by the behaviors and priorities of slavers and colonizers who 'enjoy the benefit' and 'commit at pleasure' mass crimes against humanity. Even as Bentham notes his own critiques of slavery, he draws a clear line when it comes to adding the act of enslavement to the penal code as a crime punishable by law. Circling back to my naïve question in that undergraduate course on sentencing, having now read Bentham and Beccaria's original writings I can confidently conclude that classical criminology's theories on deterrence and the penal code's threat of punishment were never meant to deter the violence of those who hold power. Their views of 'humanity' were never informed by a reflection on the human condition, nor of the experiences and behaviors of those who experience and incur Europe's crimes against humanity. The fact that Bentham, the antislavery abolitionist, did not write chattel slavery into the penal code as a criminal behavior that necessitated deterrence serves as a clear indicator of the fact that he, like so many white antislavery abolitionists, had never considered Black freedom and protections from violence as something the criminal legal system can or should guard (Saleh-Hanna, 2015, 2017a). Beccaria's very direct reference to plantation violence as his inspiration to suggest imprisonment (or perpetual slavery) as a form of punishment is also key for our understandings of the roots and realities of the criminal legal system's foundations and current behaviors.

My deep dive into classical criminology over the years has made clear that it is not just about the administration of policies and manners of law enforcement and imprisonment as so many liberal and conservative criminologists insist. Within the writings of classical criminology's founding fathers is the elusive yet obvious slavery-to-prison pipeline. Inside the theories on deterrence and assumptions about hedonism, right at the core of all crime and punishment narratives and debates, is the plantation. Bentham and Beccaria's theories and horrors assumed about human nature (as rational and hedonistic) and the role of the law (for deterrence) only work to extend white slaver plantations occupying Indigenous lands, further ingraining and extending slavery's power through a criminal legal system whose thought processes, housed within criminology, are inherently malicious and full of enslaving pathways leading us further into carceral imaginations through damning assumptions about our needs, natures, and potentials.

Turning towards the rise of positivism and the growing popularity of Cesare Lombroso (1835–1909), we can trace criminology's allegiance to white power structures as they begin to reckon with the end of chattel slavery. Without chattel slavery in place to indoctrinate, enforce, and exploit, criminology begins to turn away from classical theories (although they stay alive and well within the now established criminal legal system) and invests heavily in eugenics and the racial 'sciences' to extend and professionalize the rise of white nationalism and white power at the start of the 20th century (Saleh-Hanna, 2017b).

As the carnage of eugenics and the visceral nature of that research reaches its bloodiest heights, biological criminologists start to lose legitimacy as other social scientists in surrounding disciplines start turning their backs on their openly genocidal trajectories. This happened not because sociological theories were less racist or less problematic than biological theories on crime, but because biology had taken the field as far is it could go at that time. Sociological directions became the most appropriate place for white power to go. Sociological positivism extended the violent work of biological criminologists by constructing distance between the criminal legal system and the bloody practices of eugenics. Also expanded was the focus of criminology's carceral power from the human body into an interrogation of entire social bodies along the same racialized evolutionary scale used by biologists.

Durkheim published *The Rules of Sociological Method* in 1895. In it he states that sociological data becomes research when it stops being a 'simple descriptive inventory of political or administrative divisions' and becomes a 'veritable explanatory science' when placed within a racialized, evolutionary framework:

> Such an explanation can naturally be attempted by means of broad comparisons, including the most varied forms of human groupings, from the most rudimentary and most primitive to the most recent and most advanced, for there are none that cannot be instructive. Here, as in the other life sciences, it is often the embryo types that on occasion shed the most light. Thus political geography will not be limited to a consideration of the most civilized states in their perfected form: it will go back to the lowest type of political establishments. By comparing those societies that are best constituted it will succeed in determining the laws of their geographical evolution. . . . [Friedrich Ratzel, creator of the genocidal theory *lebensraum*] refers back to the geography of ancient peoples or the most savage tribes as well as that of the great European States.
>
> *(translated and cited in Durkheim and Giddens, 1986: 53)*

Building upon Durkheim's sociological positivism, the Chicago School of Thought began applying racialized, evolutionary notions of development towards entire neighborhoods (Park and Burgess, 1925). These shifts in focus from the human body to the social body were mirrored in the U.S. as public violence in the form of lynching expanded from targetting individuals to lynching to entire Black neighborhoods. During the 'red summer of 1919', the police in Chicago sided with white mobs to murder Black adults and children, making this mass lynching one of many explosions of white racial violence. Between April 14 and October 1 of that year, white mobs targeted and attacked at least 22 Black, racially segregated cities and towns. In addition, at least 74 Black individuals were publicly lynched during that same time span (Norvell and Tuttle, 1966).

In 1921 white mobs attacked and murdered Black residents in the Greenwood district of Tulsa, Oklahoma, burning down Black Wall Street, the epicenter of flourishing Black economies under Jim Crow segregation, resulting in lasting impacts and continued implications (Messer et al., 2018). Cumulatively, these massacres caused the onset of mass Black migrations from the US south into northern cities, not because the north was safer (mass lynchings happened there too), but because there were more opportunities for nonagricultural work in these regions. As Black communities faced white terror, trauma, literal displacement due to 'race riots' as mass lynchings, folks started to move north in search of work away from the trauma-filled fields of southern plantations (Bonilla-Silva, 2001; Douglas, 2005).

Between 1910 and 1940 almost 2 million Black people migrated from south to north in the U.S. (Bonilla-Silva, 2001). Between 1910 and 1930, Chicago's Black population increased from 44,100 to 233,900 (Douglas, 2005: 132). In response, the racist 'local real estate board took action in 1917 to restrict Black migrants to certain blocks in the city' (Douglas, 2005: 136). In 1925, when Park and Burgess published *The City* (1925), the following was the context in Chicago:

> Those states receiving the largest number of black migrants . . . were, in descending order, Pennsylvania, Illinois, Ohio, New York and Michigan. Most black migrants settled in cities. Indeed by 1920, almost 40 percent of northern blacks resided in just eight cities – New York, Philadelphia, Chicago, Detroit, Pittsburgh, Cleveland, Cincinnati, and Columbus.
>
> *(Douglas, 2005: 132)*

Black migrations into Chicago coincided with Asian and 'ethnic European' immigration (Chinese, Irish, Greek, Jewish, and Polish are named in Douglas's charts) and these absolutely propelled criminology's sociological positivists to write theories that endorsed racial segregation in Chicago's neighborhoods. Emerging from a white power paradigm, criminology's Chicago School of Thought was mobilized to legitimize and institutionalize classism and racism within increasingly diverse northern cities. Park and Burgess (1925) set a tone and tenor that criminology carries on today: they determined (im)migration and mobility to be social ills; criminalized 'single-parent homes'(which always increase in the aftermath of race massacres and other forms of mass violence); fetishized and pathologized Black diaspora cultures with an entire chapter in *The City* on "Magic, Mentality, and City Life" that spewed racism against the persistence of west African spirituality in Black diaspora societies (establishing a foundation for the criminalization of hip hop, hoodies, and countless formations of Black cultures and ways of life); and sexualized young girls with a perverted hyper-focus on any links they could invent between 'promiscuity and juvenile delinquency'. Without mincing words, Chicago School of Thought theorists formed a white supremacist foundation for the 'broken windows' theories (Kelling and Wilson, 1982) herald the current framework for policing in 'urban' (code for Black, working-class, and 'ethnic' immigrant) communities. In Park and Burgess's own words,

> [t]he differentiation into natural economic and cultural groupings gives form and character to the city. For segregation offers the group, and thereby the individuals who compose the group, a place and a role in the total organization of city life. Segregation limits development in certain directions, but releases it in others. These areas tend to accentuate certain traits, to attract and develop their kind of individuals, and so to become further differentiated.
>
> The division of labor in the city likewise illustrates disorganization, reorganization, and increasing differentiation. The immigrant from rural communities in Europe and America seldom brings with him economic skill of any great value in our industrial, commercial, or professional life. Yet interesting occupational selection has taken place by nationality, explainable more by racial temperament or circumstance than by old-world economic background, as Irish policemen, Greek ice-cream parlors, Chinese laundries, [Black] porters, and Belgian janitors, etc.
>
> *(Park and Burgess, 1925: 56–57)*

These musings and racist 'observations' imply that it is the city's 'natural ecological' setting (as originally defined by Durkheim), and not structural racism's white occupation of Indigenous lands and slavery's racist colonial economies (as originally implemented by white supremacists) that produce racially differentiated access to employment and decent housing. Using sociological positivism's assumptions and methodologies, Chicago School of Thought theorists were able to conclude that the only way to prevent a large, diverse city from descending into social disorganization, chaos, and crime is to enforce racial, ethnic, and class segregation. Further, such musings and writings on segregation within the context of mass Black migrations beset by white mob violence in the form of individual and group lynchings are not the 'innocent' or 'ill informed' writings of white men who did not know better. The history of criminology's sociological positivism is not just emblematic of the times – they are the shapers and influencers of the policies that sustained Jim Crow violence and racial segregation. These were white men who witnessed a huge increase in mass, racialized white violence and proceeded to write theories that would legitimize and further fuel white rage against Black and racialized communities. The Chicago School of Thought (and many descendant sociological positivists) are too often framed as 'the opposite' of racist biological (now biosocial) theorists, but in reality, they are not – they are an abstraction, extension, and expansion of positivist criminology's western medical model in biology's arena weaponized against individual human bodies, and in psychology or sociology's other arena abstracted but just as lethal, can now be weaponized against entire social bodies.

It should be noted, before I end this brief map of criminology's history of thought within the U.S., that criminology's first comprehensive book fully dedicated to the criminalization of youth was *Delinquent Boys*, written by Albert Cohen. It was published in 1955, the year after the U.S. Supreme Court, in *Brown v. Board of Education of Topeka*, declared racial segregation in public schools unconstitutional (1954). Albert Cohen's theories, suggesting that race and class mixed schools are dangerous, festering pits for gang creation and violence emerged at the height of anti-apartheid organizing in the U.S., and stood firmly on the side of the angry white mobs gathering in front of schools to assault and terrorize Black children assigned the heavy and still unsuccesful task of desegregating the U.S. public school system. It was during this era that Albert Cohen published the following:

> The diverse ethnic and racial stocks have diverse and incongruent standards and codes, and these standards and codes are in turn inconsistent with those of the schools and other official representation of the larger society. In this welter of conflicting cultures, the young person is confused and bedeviled. The adult world presents him with no clear-cut authoritative models. Subject to a multitude of conflicting patterns, he respects none and assimilates none. He develops no respect for the legal order because it represents a culture which finds no support in his social world. He becomes delinquent.
>
> *(Cohen, 1955: 33–34)*

Cohen's subcultural theory suggests that racial, ethnic, gendered, and class-based 'mixing' in schools is a recipe for gangs because working-class people, and racialized working-class people in particular, will not 'measure up' to white middle-class expectations, standards, intelligence, work ethic, and conduct. This will result in collective feelings of insecurity and inadequacy that will inspire mistreated schoolchildren to form a 'subculture of violence' against the norms and standards of the school environments that have rejected them. Cohen's entire theory is anchored within a critique against desegregation in school settings at the same time that Black social movements in the U.S. mobilized to gain access to decent, well-funded schools for Black children. In response, Cohen published a theory warning that 'mixed school settings' will result in a failure for newcomers to meet the 'middle class measuring rod' (his language), and that this will push young boys further into aggressive masculinity and young girls into promiscuity and other sexual 'deviations'.

Not only is Cohen's premise of subcultural theories flawed and rife with heterosexism, classism, genderism, and racism, the core of Cohen's theory on delinquency and 'the culture of the gang' falsely suggests that gangs form because of a personal sense of insecurity and inadequacy amongst disenfranchised and working-class youths. Cohen pathologizes and scapegoats young people by risk-assessing them towards violence while failing to critique or criminalize the violent, white, affluent school settings that discriminate against and violate students. His theory worked to fuel the fear-mongering white power narrative of 'danger' as a natural by-product of 'culture clashing' that is often framed as inevitable within desegregated social and educational settings. The context and precedent of openly aligning with white power set by the Chicago School of Thought at the height of Black migrations and ethnic white immigrations was carried on by subcultural theorists at the height of the fight to desegregate public schools. Criminology's alignment with white power is ongoing and traceable through the return of neo-classical and rational choice theories to shape the rise of mass incarceration and the war on drugs in the aftermath of Black power, Brown Berret, LGBTQI+, and American Indian Movement organizing in the 1970s–80s, and criminology's current debates on 'expanding, reforming, or further militarizing the police' in the aftermath of BLM uprisings in 2020.

The History of Criminology Is the History of White Supremacy

White power has always relied upon criminology to instigate, legitimize, and enforce its segregationist, pathologizing, and punitive behaviors. When we step back to consider criminology's larger contexts, foundations, and theories in relation to time, place, policy, and politics, we cannot help but trace the unwavering allegiances between criminology's dominant schools of thought and white power. It is important to map these correlations and political influences upon the field so that we can clearly and without hesitation understand how the history of criminology is the history of white supremacy, so that we can once and for all see that criminology and white power are extensions of each other.

References

Absolon, K. 2022. *Kaandossiwin: How We Come to Know*. Halifax, Nova Scotia: Fernwood Publishing.

Agozino, B. 2003. *Counter-Colonial Criminology: A Critique of Imperialist Reason*. London: Pluto Press.

Bianci, H. and van Swaaningen, R. 1986. *Abolitionism: Towards a Non-Repressive Approach to Crime*. Amsterdam: Free University Press.

Bonilla-Silva, E. 2001. *White Supremacy and Racism in the Post–Civil Rights Era*. Boulder, CO: Lynne Rienner Publishers.

Bonilla-Silva, E. 2021. *Racism Without Racists: Color-Blind Racism and the Persistence of Racial Inequality in America* (6th Edition). Lanham, MD: Rowman & Littlefield Publishers, Inc.

Césaire, A. 1955. *Discourse on Colonialism*. New York: Monthly Review Press.

Christie, N. 1993. *Crime Control as Industry: Towards Gulags Western Style*. Oslo, Norway: Scandinavian University Press.

Cohen, A.K. 1955. *Delinquent Boys: The Culture of the Gang*. New York: The Free Press.

Cohen, S. 1985. *Visions of Social Control.* Oxford, UK: Polity Press.

Cohen, S. 1988. *Against Criminology.* New Brunswick, NJ: Transaction Publishers.

Culhane, C. 1985. *Still Barred from Prison: Social Injustice in Canada.* Chicago: Black Rose Books.

Douglas, D.M. 2005. *Jim Crow Moves North: The Battle Over Northern School Segregation, 1865–1954.* New York: Cambridge University Press.

Durkheim, E. and Giddens, A. 1986. *Durkheim on Politics and the State* Edited with an Introduction by Anthony Giddens Translated by W. D. Halls. Redwood City, CA: Stanford University Press.

Federici, S. 2004. *Caliban and the Witch.* Brooklyn, NY: Autonomedia.

Hulsman, L. 1986. Critical Criminology and the Concept of Crime. In *Abolitionism: Towards a Non-Repressive Approach to Crime.* Amsterdam: Free University Press.

Kelling, G.L. and Wilson, J.Q. 1982. Broken Windows. *Atlantic Monthly,* 249(3), pp. 29–38.

Kitossa, T. 2012. Criminology and Colonialism: Counter-Colonial Criminology and the Canadian Context. *Journal of Pan African Studies,* 4(10), pp. 204–226.

Klingberg, F.J. 1926. *The Anti-Slavery Movement in England: A Study in English Humanitarianism.* New Haven: Yale University Press.

Mathiesen, T. 1974. *The Politics of Abolition.* Oslo: Scandinavian University Books by Universitetsforlaget.

Messer, C.M., Shriver, T.E. and Adams, A.E. 2018. The Destruction of Black Wall Street: Tulsa's 1921 Riot and the Eradication of Accumulated Wealth. *American Journal of Economics and Sociology,* 77(3–4), pp. 789–819.

Morris, R. 2000. *Stories of Transformative Justice.* Toronto, ON: Canadian Scholars' Press.

Morrison, T. 1994. *The Bluest Eye.* 1970. New York: Alfred A. Knopf Inc.

Norvell, S.B. and Tuttle Jr, W.M. 1966. Views of a Negro During "The Red Summer" of 1919. *The Journal of Negro History, 51*(3), pp. 209–218.

Parks, R.E. and Burgess, E.W. 1925. *The City: Suggestions for Investigation of Human Behavior in the Urban Environment.* Chicago: University of Chicago Press.

Saleh-Hanna, V. 2007. Lyrical Passages Through Crime: An Afrobeat, Hip Hop, and Reggae Production featuring Black Criminology. *Dissertation towards Doctor of Philosophy in Criminal Justice.* Indiana University, Bloomington.

Saleh-Hanna, V. 2008. *Colonial Systems of Control: Criminal Justice in Nigeria.* Ottawa: University of Ottawa Press.

Saleh-Hanna, V. 2015. Black Feminist Hauntology: Rememory the Ghosts of Abolition? *Champ pénal/Penal Field,* p. 13. http://journals.openedition.org/champpenal/9168.

Saleh-Hanna, V. 2017a. An Abolitionist Theory on Crime: Ending the Abusive Relationship with Racist-Imperialist-Patriarchy [R.I.P.]. *The Contemporary Justice Review, 20*(4), pp. 419–441.

Saleh-Hanna, V. 2017b. Reversing Criminology's White Gaze: As Lombroso's Disembodied Head Peers Through a Glass Jar in a Museum Foreshadowed by Sara Baartman's Ghost. In J.Z. Wilson, S. Hodgkinson, J. Piche and K. Walby (Eds.) *The Palgrave Handbook on Prison Tourism* (pp. 689–711). Hampshire, UK: Palgrave Macmillan.

Sellin, J.T. 1976. *Slavery and the Penal System* (Vol. 27 – Classics of Law and Society Book Series). New York and Amsterdam: Elsevier Scientific Publishing Co.

Tauri, J.M. and Porou, N. 2014. Criminal Justice in Contemporary Settler Colonialism. *African Journal of Criminology and Justice Studies,* 8(1: Special Issue: Indigenous Perspectives and Counter-Colonial Criminology), pp. 20–37.

4

THE HISTORY OF CRIMINAL JUSTICE AS THE ACADEMIC ARM OF STATE VIOLENCE

Brian Pitman, Stephen T. Young, and Ryan Phillips

Introduction

The need to abolish the academic discipline of criminal justice is made evident by its existence as a tool of the racist criminal legal system. Its founders, both in the US and abroad, developed the field from the tenets of scientific racism, which existed to reinforce the status quo of white supremacy, heteropatriarchy, and imperialism (Roberts, 1999; Washington, 2006; Muhammad, 2010). Since the early works of August Vollmer, the academic discipline of criminal justice in the US has sought to sustain its existence by advocating for the expansion of the criminal legal system. Thus, criminal justice exists to rationalise, legitimise, and participate in the violence of the system itself. In this chapter, we discuss the history of the academic discipline of criminal justice in the US, including its roots in scientific racism. We connect this history with August Vollmer's creation of criminal justice in the US and its subsequent expansion via federal funding. We end by connecting criminal justice research to the racist political ideologies of the state.

The History of Criminology

Wetzell (2000, p. 16) defines criminology as "the scientific study of the causes of crime", which is traced to late 18th- and early 19th-century medical explanations of behaviour (Rafter, Posick and Rocque, 2016). Some attribute criminology's beginning to moral insanity theory, the belief that "criminals" are without remorse and morally inferior. Moral insanity theory conceptualised these "defects" as innate and exacerbated by biological factors, including diet and alcohol consumption (Rafter, Posick and Rocque 2016, p. 24). By the late 1800s, white male scholars had constructed "criminals" as undeterrable and driven by a "malignant

DOI: 10.4324/9780367817114-6

heredity" (Matsubara, 1998). These "scientific" explanations were an extension of western medicine's colonising racial sciences and genocidal praxis against Black, Indigenous, and colonised people (Roberts, 1999; Washington, 2006; Muhammad, 2010).

It was in this context that Cesare Lombroso, an Italian physician, psychiatrist, and anthropologist, gained notoriety. Lombroso, known as "the father of criminology", developed the theory of "the born criminal" (Caglioti, 2017). The theory is rooted in the white supremacist and heteropatriachal idea of atavism, which posits that certain groups are "biological throw-backs" who counter the rules and expectations of the "civilised" world (Wolfgang, 1961). Lombroso argued that "criminals" are subhuman with inherited inferior characteristics such as varying head, jaw, and cheekbone sizes, unusually sized ears, "defective" eyes, "homosexuality", and other "peculiarities" (Wolfgang, 1961; Woods, 2015). This placed his work within the confines of scientific racism, which was accepted in fascist regimes like the US and Nazi Germany "to justify their ventures in colonialism and imperialism" (Rafter, Posick and Rocque, 2016, p. 77).

Lombroso grounded his explanations of crime in positivist criminology, defined as "the project of subjecting criminal behavior to scientific study and bringing the findings of this science to bear in the practice of criminal justice" (Simon, 2006, p. 2136). He believed that being overly logical could disrupt the existing social order, thus his use of positivism was "performative art in service of European power" (Morrison, 2004, p. 79). Specifically, Lombroso brought together pseudo-Darwinian biology and older scientific trends to reinforce the power of the existing white supremacist, heteropatriarchal institutions, specifically the penitentiary.

Lombroso's work was foundational for Italian eugenics (Caglioti, 2017) and influenced other European criminologists, including Enrico Ferri, Alfredo Niceforo, Hans Gross, and Raffaele Garofalo, who coined the term "criminology" in his book *Criminologia* (Beth, 1941). Niceforo studied within the Italian positivist tradition, and, along with Ferri (D'Agostino, 2002), was instrumental in the racialisation of southern Italy. He used Lombrosian criminology to argue that crime rates differed between the north and south "because a Mediterranean race from Africa inhabited the South and a Celtic-Aryan prevailed in the North" (Caglioti, 2017, p. 465). Niceforo concluded that southern Italy "was trapped in a 'social atavism', extending Lombroso's concept of degeneration from the individual to an entire population based on statistical thinking" (p. 465).

Niceforo contributed to the rise of statistical methodology as the primary method used in studying crime in Italy (Caglioti, 2017). His research focused on "quantifying the degree of superiority and inferiority of civilizations and social groups" (Caglioti, 2017, p. 470). Niceforo understood that statistics were crucial to keeping the positivist understanding of crime going, as it could establish connections between crime and anthropometric measures. "Thus, statistics were the tool and eugenics the theory used to reject the charges of scientific inaccuracy levelled against the positivist school of criminology" (Caglioti, 2017, pp. 468–469).

The lasting effects of this pro-eugenics history is still apparent in Italy. Immigrants, especially in southern Italy, continue to face racism. Earlier research demonstrates that these white supremacist sentiments resulted in disproportionate complaints and arrests against immigrants, specifically Moroccans and Senegalese, as well as other groups from Africa, Latin America, and eastern Europe (Angel-Ajani, 2002). Over the past few decades these racist and pro-eugenics sentiments have shifted to target Muslim people, as Islamophobic and anti-Muslim rhetoric is persistent in both northern and southern Italy (Fekete, 2004).

Lombroso's Influence in the US

During the Reconstruction era in the US, white male scholars and policymakers utilized Lombrosian criminology to reinforce the white supremacist status quo of colonialism and slavery by categorising Black, Indigenous, and colonised peoples as "dangerous" (Robertson, 1996). After the abolition of slavery, formerly enslaved people were criminalised under Black Codes, which were designed to control and surveil them (Ritchie, 2017). These codes also reinforced "the continued subordination of black labor to white economic power" (Bass, 2001, p. 160). In what was essentially a continuation of slavery, Black people were arrested disproportionately for various quality-of-life offenses and leased out to businesses to do forced labor (Bass, 2001; Blackmon, 2008). By 1890 Black people were 12 percent of the population and 30 percent of the people incarcerated, findings the ruling class used to substantiate racist notions of innate Black criminality (Hinton and Cook, 2021). As Simon notes:

> Lombroso's appeal in the United States was how well this scientific racism fit with the new Jim Crow governance strategy of the post-Reconstruction South and the acceptance of that new arrangement by the centers of elite opinion in the North who had backed the Civil War and Reconstruction.
>
> *(Simon, 2006, p. 2155)*

Lombroso's work also inspired US immigration law in the early 20th century. In 1911 a US congressional investigation by the Dillingham Commission utilized Lombrosian-style criminology and the works of Nicefero in its report to justify selective admission of mostly white northern European immigrants and the criminalization of southern European, Mediterranean, and African immigrants (D'Agostino, 2002). This report was the basis for the 1924 Johnson-Reed Act, which created quotas on the number of immigrants allowed in the US, while excluding immigrants from Asian countries. The act was heavily enforced by police and ultimately led to the creation of the US Border Patrol under the National Origins Act of 1924 (Ngai, 1999).

August Vollmer and the Creation of academic Criminal Justice in the US

August Vollmer was a military veteran from Berkeley, California, who served during the US invasion and counterinsurgency occupation of the Philippines from 1898 to 1899 (Welch Jr., 1974; Oliver, 2017; Go, 2020). After returning to Berkeley, Vollmer was asked to run for town marshal by the editor of the local newspaper, who felt that his experience in the Philippines would serve him well in the position. Berkeley's population was growing fast (Douthit, 1975) and the editor pleaded to Vollmer that he was needed to fight off "dope dens and gambling joints and crooks [who] are coming here too fast" (Parker, 1961, p. 39). This was part of the broader anti-immigrant sentiment in Berkeley and throughout California, particularly as capitalists no longer needed cheap labor and used immigrants as the scapegoat for rapidly rising inequality (Mark, 1975).

Vollmer agreed to run and in 1905 was elected town marshal. He implemented military techniques, including intelligence gathering, hierarchy, and surveillance (Oliver, 2008; Go, 2020). One of his first acts as marshal was the targeted raid of a Chinese opium and gambling den. Vollmer even "noted similarities between the 'yellow hatchet men' guarding the Chinese dens and Filipino insurgents" (as cited in Go, 2020, p. 1217). His first raid led to the arrest of 14 Chinese people, who would eventually be let go because of insufficient evidence (Parker, 1961). Afterwards, Vollmer made it his mission to target similar settings around Berkeley. He also spearheaded the response to the San Francisco earthquake of 1906 that left many refugees homeless and fleeing to Berkeley. Vollmer deputised hundreds of men in response, including veterans of the Civil War and the invasion of the Philippines. He petitioned the governor to institute martial law and organised efforts to surveil and deport earthquake refugees deemed as "criminals" (Schwartz, 2005).

In this position, Vollmer also laid the foundation of the white supremacist US criminal justice academic discipline. In 1907, he began exploring how scientific racism could be applied to policing "by reading works by such people as Gross, Pinkerton, Garofalo, Ferri, and Lombroso" (Oliver, 2008, p. 95). He was initially introduced to *Criminal Psychology* by Hans Gross, the founder of racial profiling, who "promote[d] policies such as the deportation and castration of criminals" (Hertz, 2019, p. 61). Vollmer went on to organise required "crab sessions" for off-duty Berkeley police officers, which he used to impart "upon them some of the knowledge he had been learning about police procedures, evidence, collection, or criminal psychology" (Oliver, 2017, p. 230). He also offered courses on the pseudo-sciences of fingerprinting and anthropometry, among others (Douthit, 1975).

Vollmer and Dr Albert Schneider, professor of medicine at University of California, Berkeley's Medical School, published their three-year summer course curriculum for police training in 1917 (Oliver, 2017). Courses offered included "Criminological Anthropology and Heredity", "Criminology: Theoretical and Applied", and "Police Methods of Procedure" (Vollmer and Schneider, 1917). Students in "Criminological Anthropology and Heredity" studied topics that included eugenics and "race degeneration", both of which were influential in shaping white supremacist and heteropatriarchal opinions and policies regulating and criminalizing Black people, particularly Black women (Roberts, 1999). In "Criminology", students studied atavism, specifically physical "abnormalities", including multiple pregnancies and baldness. Students also studied mental "abnormalities" like socialism, and mental and educational "perversions" that included "Orientalism, hindooism, [and] occultism" (Vollmer and Schneider, 1917, p. 889). The required texts included works by Lombroso, Gross, and Ferri and represented the early entrenchment of white supremacist, heteropatriarchal, and colonising ideologies in academic US criminal justice programs.

The professionalization of policing via college education and the development of criminal justice as an academic discipline was part of the broader police reform movement that was shaped by the US empire's colonialist endeavors overseas, particularly in the Philippines (Go, 2020). Vollmer, along with police reformers more broadly, molded police programming based on "the army's new professionalization schools and training methods" (Go, 2020, p. 1205). The implementation of these military-style programs was largely driven by the white supremacist logics occurring within cities like Berkeley (Go, 2020). Vollmer believed that college credentials provided legitimacy and respect to policing, and in essence white supremacy, and he worked diligently for the next 15 years to fully develop his academic program (Vollmer, 1932). He accomplished this in 1931, integrating his curriculum while emphasizing the mechanics of police work (Koehler, 2015). He was hired by the University of California, Berkeley, with the help of a Rockefeller Foundation grant in 1931, leading the university to officially approve the major in 1933 (Oliver, 2017).

The George-Deen Act and the Expansion of Police Education

Vollmer and his protégés, known as V-Men, were part of the implementation of police programs across the country "modeled after military training" (Go, 2020, p. 1205). At San Jose Teachers College, Vollmer worked with future Supreme Court Chief Justice Earl Warren to develop a police program with V-Man George H. Brereton as director (Oliver, 2017). Another V-Man, O.W. Wilson, started a police program at the University of Wichita (Gammage, 1963). Michigan State University developed its police administration program in 1935, a program notorious for its involvement in foreign police assistance (Triplett and Turner, 2010; Seigel, 2018).

The federal government further incentivised police education expansion by passing the George-Deen Act, which provided funding for vocational education in public occupations (Prout, 1972). Under this legislation, the US Office of Education supported police training by providing funding and teaching assistance. Motivation for this funding was outlined in the federal government's guide to police training:

> [A]n efficient police training program is one of the principal means for increasing and maintaining a high degree of efficiency in law enforcement work. . . . As a result of this training, supplemented by efficient and intelligent supervision, [the police officer] will learn to work cooperatively with others toward the common objectives of law enforcement, the preservation of peace, and the maintenance of law and order.
>
> *(Adams, 1939, p. 3)*

In the academy, the George-Deen Act funded police training through the creation of a variety of criminal justice programs at colleges and universities. The federal government saw the value of funding these academic programs to legitimize its colonialist agenda. In 1935, Purdue University began offering traffic courses and crime prevention and detection training. In 1936, the University of Alabama, Harvard University, and the University of Michigan offered a police administration course. Ohio State University, the University of Minnesota, the University of Maryland at College Park, the University of Chicago, Northeastern University, Rutgers University, and Texas A&M University offered courses in police work (Gammage, 1963; Triplett and Turner, 2010). By 1937, California, Kansas, Oklahoma, Utah, Alabama, Oregon, Kentucky, Illinois, Minnesota, South Dakota, and Texas were offering police training courses funded by the state (Gammage, 1963). The next year, Colorado, Idaho, Pennsylvania, and New Hampshire began providing funding, and Wisconsin, Oklahoma, and Utah hired police officers to travel the states and give training courses (Gammage, 1963). By 1963, there were "[n]inety-five institutions – junior colleges, colleges, and universities in twenty-nine states and the District of Columbia offer[ing] 204 programs leading to academic degrees in law enforcement" (Gammage, 1963, p. 93).

Police education expansion coincided with the escalation of white riots in the North and racist lynchings in the South, both of which involved police violence (Murakawa, 2014). States sought to address this by developing state police departments with the hope that these departments would "rise above the rogue racial violence of local, rural police officers" (Murakawa, 2014, p. 47). Despite these changes, there were 242 "racial battles" in 47 cities in 1943 alone (Murakawa, 2014). Many of these involved direct violence by police and white people against communities of colour. In Detroit in June 1943, one of these "racial battles" ended with 17 Black people killed by police and 1,893 arrested, of which 85 percent were Black (Sugrue, 1996). Political concern following these violent white riots along with grassroots pressure led the federal government to advocate professionalizing the criminal legal system throughout the 1950s. This culminated in the "massive funding for police modernization" (Murakawa, 2014, p. 47) that occurred in the 1960s, which included the expansion of criminal justice programs that served the white supremacist status quo in the US.

Police Education Expansion During the Civil Rights Era

The 1964 presidential election marked a new beginning of federal government involvement in the academic development of criminal justice. Presidential candidates George Wallace and Barry Goldwater used crime to rile up conservatives and counter the growing Civil Rights movement (Savelsberg, 2018). Though they both lost, the political pressure led the federal government to ignore the underlying social issues associated with crime. President Lyndon B. Johnson established the Office of Law Enforcement Assistance in 1965, which distributed $21 million in grants, most of which went to colleges for police education (Morn, 1995). He was in pursuit of the "Great Society", foundational to which was the belief that police and prisons should be federally funded, similar to education (Murakawa, 2014).

In 1966, the Office of Law Enforcement Assistance released a memo titled "Work Plan: Police-Community Relations," defining good police–community relations to anyone applying for funds from the organization (as cited by Murakawa, 2014). These points included improving respect for and public confidence in police, encouraging citizens to report crime, or at the very least abstain from interfering with arrests, and "[t]o *remove incidents which can lead to riots*" (as quoted in Murakawa, 2014, p. 81). Then, in 1968, with increased radical organizing and uprisings, Richard Nixon and George Wallace ran for president on "law and order" platforms. This inspired a right-wing oriented rewriting of the 1968 Crime Control and Safe Streets Act, which transferred control of aid from state and local governments to large federal block grants (Murakawa, 2014; Savelsberg, 2018). The act created the National Institute for Law Enforcement and Criminal Justice (later renamed the National Institute of Justice) which was responsible for providing grants and loans to educational institutions to support research, programming, and training (Savelsberg, 2018). It replaced the Office of Law Enforcement Assistance with the Law Enforcement Assistance Administration (LEAA), which contained the Law Enforcement Education Program (LEEP).

The Law Enforcement Education Program provided government assistance to allow police and other in-service personnel to earn any criminal justice–related degree from an associate's to a PhD or JD if they worked for a certain number of years in a criminal justice agency (Bennett and Marshall, 1979; Allinson, 1980). Over its 12-year existence, the Law Enforcement Education Program distributed $322 million to provide higher-education credentials to people already working in policing (Weirman and Archambeault, 1983). The provision of these funds was directly tied to the creation and legitimacy of criminal justice programs, as the Law Enforcement Education Program "took both a supply and demand approach to education by helping fund police officers to go to college and helping colleges create or expand the criminal justice programs to fit their needs" (Oliver, 2016, p. 463). This program alone helped increase the proportion of police officers with a college education from 20 percent to 46 percent from 1960 to 1975 (Allinson, 1980).

In 1969 there were 485 higher education institutions receiving $6.5 million from the Law Enforcement Education Program. By 1975 this expanded to 1,065 colleges receiving upwards of $40 million, increasing students in police science courses to nearly 180,000 (Morn, 1995). From 1967 to 1977 the program was responsible for the number of criminal justice bachelor's degree programs skyrocketing from 39 to 376 (Walker, 1998). From 1966 to 1973, criminal justice programs at community colleges increased from 152 to 505 (Brown 1974). In 1977, 1,027 criminal justice–related programs existed around the US in colleges and universities (Bennett and Marshall, 1979). By 1995, there were 18 doctoral programs and 157 master's programs (Adler, 1995).

The 1968 Crime Control and Safe Streets Act tied criminal justice to the "professionalization" of policing by incentivising programs to focus their teaching and academic training on pro-policing technologies and reforms through the allocation of grant funding (Agozino, 2003; Schept, Wall and Brisman, 2014; Correia and Wall, 2018; Seigel, 2018). Given that policing and its associated technologies are rooted in maintaining the status quo of colonialism and white supremacy, it was, in essence, a way to professionalize and legitimize those ideologies. One example of this was at John Jay College of Criminal Justice, when a student who was also a Federal Bureau of Investigation agent did a research paper on the bureau's involvement in the Civil Rights movement. After being reported by the agency typing pool, he was suspended and transferred to Butte, Montana (Morn, 1995). Shortly after, the Law Enforcement Education Program authorised criminal justice agencies to modify courses covered by its funds to those that "have direct bearing on the officer's future role as a law enforcement agent or criminal justice representative" (Morn, 1995, p. 120). Criminal justice departments were now dependent upon substitute revenue sources, especially as the universities went through a neoliberal transformation that diminished state and federal funding (Schept, Wall and Brisman, 2014; Savelsberg, 2018). Consequently, criminal justice's purpose "to credential, not to educate" (Farrell and Koch, 1995, p. 54) was reinforced as backlash to the Civil Rights movement.

The expansion of this professional model did encounter backlash within the academy (Platt, 1974). Jeffery (1977) noted that "nothing has been more destructive of the academic base of criminology than LEAA and LEEP funding" (p. 284). Germann (1977) referred to the field as "rigid, anti intellectual [sic] amateurism and mechanical hyper-pragmatism" (p. 5). The Academy of Criminal Justice Sciences' president Gordon Misner was quoted as referring to college presidents as "hustlers" and "pimps" and believed the funding had created one of the greatest scandals in education (Morn, 1995).

Outside criminal justice, funding from the Law Enforcement Assistance Administration and the Law Enforcement Education Program was unsuccessful in accomplishing its stated goals. For example, one stated goal was to reduce crime by 20 percent over five years in cities receiving funding (Murakawa, 2014). This was never achieved and in reality many of these cities saw increases in arrests for robbery and other violent crimes. In fact, those stated goals were never the point. Instead, the point of the 1968 Crime Control and Safe Streets Act was to centralise the criminal legal system, professionalise its employees through education, and further entrench the criminal legal system in general as a tool of colonialism and white supremacy, particularly as a response to the rising radical elements of the Civil Rights movement of the 1960s. As Seigel (2018) notes:

Police education and criminal justice have approximated mass incarceration and academia by involving more university-based people in courts and prisons as "experts", investing universities in the growth of the system as a site for jobs for its graduates, and interweaving prison–industrial and academic–industrial complexes.

(p. 144)

Consequently, criminal justice programs in the academy legitimise the criminal legal system and its colonising function, while training many of the systems' employees for the violent offensive of hyper-policing and hyper-incarcerating Black, Indigenous, and colonised people (Murakawa, 2014; Hinton, 2016).

The Closure of the Berkeley School of Criminology

At the University of California, Berkeley, where criminology and criminal justice in the US began, there was significant pushback to the changes initiated by the Law Enforcement Education Program and the Law Enforcement Assistance Administration. The official "School of Criminology" was established in 1950 with O.W. Wilson as dean. The new school continued the white supremacist and colonialist aspirations:

> dedicated to creating a "Westpoint" [sic] for the domestic "law enforcement army". . . . It was a program of good old-fashioned law and order, albeit of Vollmer's reformist brand and it had little patience even for the niceties of liberal social science.
>
> *(CSJ Editors, 1976, p. 131)*

Initial faculty included various criminal justice practitioners, including Vollmer, a former district attorney, a Federal Bureau of Investigation official, and an assistant chief of security of a California Japanese concentration camp (CSJ Editors, 1976). After Wilson's departure, however, the new dean, Joseph Lohman, shifted the school's curriculum. He entrenched the coursework formally in the social sciences with a sociolegal orientation, moving away from the training style preferred by Vollmer and Wilson (Geis, 1995; Morn, 1995). This shift in curriculum subsequently paved the way for the groundbreaking work that would follow through the 1960s and 1970s. Some of the school's faculty directly engaged with political activism and heavily critiqued the criminal legal system and Berkeley police, which the school was created to serve (Morn, 1995).

Despite the popularity of the school and faculty, the program came under intense political pressure due to ties to antiwar and liberation groups like the Black Panther Party (Geis, 1995; Myers and Goddard, 2018). With very few tenured faculty, the passing of Joseph Lohman in 1968, and the lack of political support from local police who often helped deflect criticism during the Vollmer years, the school was unable to prevent its eventual closure in 1976 (Koehler, 2015). The closure of the Berkeley School of Criminology points to the continued power of Vollmer's legacy by reaffirming his vision for criminal justice as an academic discipline.

Vollmer's legacy, however, did not determine the development of all criminology and criminal justice programs. Some Justice Studies programs developed following the closing of the Berkeley School of Criminology. The first of these programs was housed at Arizona State University, beginning in 1983 with the creation of the School of Justice and Social Inquiry (Velasco, 2008). Other universities followed suit with a broader focus on social justice instead of "training". Programs now exist across the US, including at James Madison University, University of Massachusetts, Dartmouth, Montclair State University, Northern Arizona University, Rutgers University, San Jose State University, Winston-Salem State University, and many others. Despite the emergence of these Justice Studies programs, the level of impact on the broader field is still limited due to the control and dissemination of knowledge based on the Vollmer-inspired curriculum structure of many criminal justice and criminology programs in the US.

Criminological Research

The federal government also became more involved in criminological research beginning in the 1960s. The Kennedy administration signed the Juvenile Delinquency and Youth Offenses Control Act, providing $10 million in grants for research on juvenile delinquency (Hinton, 2016). Prominent criminologists Lloyd Ohlin and Richard Cloward orchestrated antidelinquency initiatives that "targeted the behavior of individual children and teenagers, rather than systems and institutions" (Hinton, 2016, p. 20). These initiatives viewed crime and delinquency as a pathology of the individual and community absent structural forces. The lineage of this argument can be traced to Lombroso's individual, biological argument. Like Lombrosian criminology, this cultural pathological understanding was rooted in white supremacist views of crime. The Ford administration later weaponised this argument by promoting a crime plan, the Juvenile Delinquency and Prevention Act, that criminalized and imprisoned Black youth (Hinton, 2016).

From 1969 to 1976, federal funding for criminological research increased from $13.4 million to $110.2 million (Seigel, 2018). These funds were used to complete research like the 1975 study *The Effectiveness of Correctional Treatment: A Survey of Treatment Evaluation Studies* by Robert Martinson. This work produced the thesis that "nothing works" when it comes to rehabilitating so-called criminals (Hinton, 2016) and was exploited politically even after Martinson's retraction (Seigel, 2018). For example, as a result of this thesis, the federal government's sentencing guidelines changed to forbid "imposing a term of incarceration on the view that it will lead to rehabilitations" (Barkow, 2009, p. 1173). These findings, along with those of other crime researchers, came "as racially marginalized Americans became majorities within the nation's prisons" (Hinton, 2016, p. 244). The "nothing works" and cultural pathology theories shaped crime and incarceration policies for decades to come.

In the 1980s, President Ronald Reagan's advancement of racist crime policies directed criminal justice research to focus on social control. The National Institute of Justice (formerly the National Institute for Law Enforcement and Criminal Justice) used its newfound funding to push specific agendas through the formulation of "predefined specific research questions and specified methods or data sets to be used" (Savelsberg, 2018, para. 27). Other entities, like the US Sentencing Commission and the National Science Foundation, manipulated the various objectives and units of analysis of criminal justice research for political purposes, ensuring that it would continue to focus on punishment and incapacitation (Savelsberg, 2018). A content analysis of flagship criminology and criminal justice journals published from 1951 to 1993 provides additional evidence of this change in ideology (Savelsberg, Cleveland and King, 2004). It was found that

> changes in criminological work are associated with shifts of implicit political ideologies and penal strategies, away from a concern with sociological conditions of crime toward a concern with control, and, within control institutions, away from informal toward formal social control. The new organizational specialization of criminology (strongly) and criminal justice agency funding (somewhat) engender a politically favored focus on control institutions.
>
> *(Savelsberg, Cleveland and King, 2004, p. 1295)*

Criminal justice's focus on social control led to the prominence of Wilson and Kelling's broken windows theory. Broken windows theory drew directly from the racist ideologies of conservative thinkers like Edward Banfield, who believed the physical deterioration of neighborhoods stemmed from a cultural and biological inferiority of poor, Black, Indigenous, people, and people of colour (Thompson, 2015). The theory "surmised that fear of violent crime and societal dysfunction directly correlated with the prevalence of 'broken windows,' or minor criminal offenses left unchallenged in neglected communities" (Hinton and Cook, 2021, p. 276). Police departments across the country used broken windows theory to transition to "order-maintenance and disorder-management" policing (p. 276), which police used to justify targeting colonised communities. The legacy of this shift in policing has been "further expansion in the field of police research and development . . . via interagency partnerships between police practitioners, academic researchers, and police-community partners" (Hinton and Cook, 2021, p. 277), further entrenching academic criminal justice's role in continuing the legacy of colonialism and white supremacy through police education and research.

Conclusion

With its roots in scientific racism, criminology and academic criminal justice has been in service to white supremacy and colonialism. In the US specifically, academic criminal justice programs have largely served as a colonising mechanism to legitimise the criminal legal system's targeting of Black, Indigenous, and colonised communities. Reliance on federal funding for both program expansion and research ensures criminal justice will always prioritise reforming to maintain the existing system. Any time the system experiences a legitimacy crisis targeting its white supremacist and colonialist roots, it employs criminal justice academics to reaffirm its existence, necessity, and legitimacy through federally funded empirical research and training. The result in the US has been the continuous expansion of the carceral state (Schenwar and Law, 2020). This chapter provided an overview of the history of US academic criminal justice programs and research so that we can better understand these roots and future trajectories. Ultimately, two paths are available for the discipline: (1) continue down the same path of supporting the racist criminal legal system; or (2) abolition.

References

Adams, O.D. (1939) *Training for the Police Service*, Washington, DC, US Department of the Interior.

Adler, F. (1995) 'Who Are We? A Self-Analysis of Criminal Justice Specialists.' *ACJS Today*, vol. 14, no. 1. Available at: https://cdn.ymaws.com/www.acjs.org/resource/resmgr/ACJSToday/ACJSTodayMayJune1995.pdf (Accessed 27 November 2020).

Agozino, B. (2003) *Counter-Colonial Criminology: A Critique of Imperialist Reason*, London, Pluto Press.

Allinson, R.S. (1980) 'A Great LEEP Backward?' *Change*, vol. 12, no. 1, pp. 14–16.

Angel-Ajani, A. (2002) 'Diasporic Conditions: Mapping the Discourses of Race and Criminality in Italy', *Transforming Anthropology*, vol. 11, no. 1, pp. 36–46.

Barkow, R.E. (2009) 'The Court of Life and Death: The Two Tracks of Constitutional Sentencing Law and the Case for Uniformity', *Michigan Law Review*, vol. 107, no. 7, pp. 1145–1205.

Bass, S. (2001) 'Policing Space, Policing Race: Social Control Imperatives and Police Discretionary Decisions', *Social Justice*, vol. 28, no. 83, pp. 156–176.

Bennett, R. and Marshall, I.H. (1979) 'Criminal Justice Education in the United States: A Profile', *Journal of Criminal Justice*, vol. 7, pp. 147–172.

Beth, M.W. (1941) 'The Sociological Aspect of Criminology', *Journal of Criminal Law and Criminology*, vol. 32, no. 1, pp. 67–71.

Blackmon, D.A. (2008) *Slavery by Another Name: The Re-Enslavement of Black Americans from the Civil War to World War II*, New York, Doubleday.

Brown, L. (1974) 'The Police and Higher Education: The Challenge of the Times', *Criminology*, vol. 12, pp. 114–124.

Caglioti, A.M. (2017) 'Race, Statistics and Italian Eugenics: Alfredo Niceforo's Trajectory from Lombroso to Fascism (1876–1960)', *European History Quarterly*, vol. 47, no. 3, pp. 461–489.

Correia, D. and Wall, T. (2018) *Police: A Field Guide*, Brooklyn, Verso Books.

CSJ Editors. (1976) 'Editorial: Berkeley's School of Criminology, 1950–1976', *Social Justice*, vol. 40, no. 1–2, pp. 131–136.

D'Agostino, P. (2002) 'Craniums, Criminals, and the "Cursed Race": Italian Anthropology in American Racial Thought, 1861–1924', *Comparative Studies in Society and History*, vol. 44, no. 2, pp. 319–343.

Douthit, N. (1975) 'August Vollmer, Berkeley's First Chief of Police, and the Emergence of Police Professionalism', *California Historical Quarterly*, vol. 54, no. 2, pp. 101–124.

Farrell, B. and Koch, L. (1995) 'Criminal Justice, Sociology, and Academia', *The American Sociologist*, vol. 26, no. 1, pp. 52–61.

Fekete, L. (2004) 'Anti-Muslim Racism and the European Security State', *Race & Class*, vol. 46, no. 2, pp. 3–29.

Gammage, A. (1963) *Police Training in the United States*, Springfield, Charles C. Thomas.

Geis, G. (1995) 'The Limits of Academic Tolerance: The Discontinuance of the School of Criminology at Berkeley', in Blomberg, T. and Cohen, S. (eds.) *Punishment and Social Control: Essays in Honor of Sheldon L. Messinger*, New York, Aldine de Gruyter, pp. 277–304.

Germann, A.C. (1977) 'Criminal Justice Leadership *Bankrupt Forever?*' *Criminology*, vol. 15, no. 1, pp. 3–6.

Go, J. (2020) 'The Imperial Origins of American Policing: Militarization and Imperial Feedback in the Early 20th Century', *American Journal of Sociology*, vol. 125, no. 5, pp. 1193–1254.

Hertz, G. (2019) 'From Epistemology of Suspicion to Racial Profiling: Hans Gross, Mobility, and Crime Around 1900', *Transfers*, vol. 9, no. 1, pp. 59–81.

Hinton, E. (2016) *From the War on Poverty to the War on Crime: The Making of Mass Incarceration in America*, Cambridge, Harvard University Press.

Hinton, E. and Cook, D. (2021) 'The Mass Criminalization of Black Americans: A Historical Overview', *Annual Review of Criminology*, vol. 4, no. 1, pp. 281–286.

Jeffery, C.R. (1977) 'Criminology: Whither or Wither?' *Criminology*, vol. 15, no. 3, pp. 283–286.

Koehler, J. (2015) 'Development and Fracture of a Discipline: Legacies of the School of Criminology at Berkeley', *Criminology*, vol. 53, no. 4, pp. 513–544.

Mark, G.Y. (1975) 'Racial, Economic and Political Factors in the Development of America's First Drug Laws', *Issues in Criminology*, vol. 10, no. 1, pp. 49–72.

Matsubara, Y. (1998) 'The Enactment of Japan's Sterilization Laws in the 1940s: A Prelude to Postwar Eugenic Policy', *Historia Scientiarum: The International Journal of the History of Science Society of Japan*, vol. 8, no. 2, pp. 187–201.

Morn, F. (1995) *Academic Politics and the History of Criminal Justice Education*, Westport, Greenwood Press.

Morrison, W. (2004) 'Lombroso and the Birth of Criminological Positivism: Scientific Mastery or Cultural Artifice?' in Ferrell, J., Hayward, K., Morrison, W. and Presdee, M. (eds.) *Cultural Criminology Unleashed*, London, The GlassHouse Press, pp. 81–94.

Muhammad, K.G. (2010). *The Condemnation of Blackness: Race, Crime, and the Making of Modern Urban America*, Cambridge, Harvard University Press.

Murakawa, N. (2014) *The First Civil Right: How Liberals Built Prison America*, New York, Oxford University Press.

Myers, R.R. and Goddard, T. (2018) 'The Berkeley School of Criminology: The Intellectual Roots and Legacies', in Triplett, R. (ed.) *The Handbook of the History and Philosophy of Criminology*, Hoboken, NJ, Wiley Blackwell. Available at: https://onlinelibrary.wiley.com/doi/book/10.1002/9781119011385 (Accessed 29 December 2020).

Ngai, M.M. (1999) 'The Architecture of Race in American Immigration Law: A Reexamination of the Immigration Act of 1924', *The Journal of American History*, vol. 86, no. 1, pp. 67–92.

Oliver, W. (2008) 'August Vollmer', in Bumgarner, J.B. (ed.) *Icons of Crime Fighting: Relentless Pursuers of Justice*, New York, Greenwood Press, pp. 83–115.

Oliver, W. (2016) 'Celebrating 100 Years of Criminal Justice Education, 1916–2016', *Journal of Criminal Justice Education*, vol. 27, no. 4, pp. 455–472.

Oliver, W.M. (2017) *August Vollmer: The Father of American Policing*, Durham, Carolina Academic Press.

Parker, A.E. (1961) *Crime Fighter: August Vollmer*, New York, The Macmillan Company.

Platt, T. (1974) 'Prospects for a Radical Criminology in the United States', *Crime and Social Justice*, no. 1, pp. 2–10.

The President's Commission on Law Enforcement and Administration of Justice, "Work Plan: Police-Community Relations," January 14, 1966, Folder: Law Enforcement Assistance Act-1, Box 102, Clark Papers, quoted in Naomi Murakawa, *The First Civil Right: How Liberals Built Prison America* (New York, Oxford University Press), 81.

Prout, R.S. (1972) 'An Analysis of Associate Degree Programs in Law Enforcement', *The Journal of Criminal Law, Criminology, and Police Science*, vol. 63, no. 4, pp. 585–592.

Rafter, N., Posick, C. and Rocque, M. (2016) *The Criminal Brain: Understanding Biological Theories of Crime*, New York, New York University Press.

Ritchie, A. (2017) *Invisible No More: Police Violence Against Black Women and Women of Color*, Boston, Beacon Press.

Roberts, D. 1999. *Killing the Black Body: Race, Reproduction, and the Meaning of Liberty*, New York, Vintage Books.

Robertson, C.W. (1996) 'Representing "Miss Lizzie": Cultural Convictions in the Trial of Lizzie Borden', *Yale Journal of Law & the Humanities*, vol. 8, no. 2, pp. 351–416.

Savelsberg, J.J. (2018) 'Criminology in the United States: Contexts, Institutions, and Knowledge in Flux', in Triplett, R. (ed.) *The Handbook of the History and Philosophy of Criminology*. Hoboken, NJ, Wiley Blackwell. Available at: https://onlinelibrary.wiley.com/doi/book/10.1002/9781119011385 (Accessed 29 December 2020).

Savelsberg, J.J., Cleveland, L.L. and King, R. (2004) 'Institutional Environments and Scholarly Work: American Criminology, 1951–1993', *Social Forces*, vol. 82, no. 4, pp. 1275–1302.

Schenwar, M. and Law, V. (2020) *Prison by Any Other Name: The Harmful Consequences of Popular Reforms*, New York, The New Press.

Schept, J., Wall, T. and Brisman, A. (2014) 'Building, Staffing, and Insulating: An Architecture of Criminological Complicity in the School-to-Prison Pipeline', *Social Justice*, vol. 41, no. 4, pp. 96–115.

Schwartz, R. (2005) *Earthquake Exodus, 1906: Berkeley Responds to the San Francisco Refugees*, Berkeley, RSB Books.

Seigel, M. (2018) *Violence Work: State Power and the Limits of Police*, Durham, Duke University Press.

Simon, J. (2006) 'Positively Punitive: How the Inventor of Scientific Criminology Who Died at the Beginning of the Twentieth Century Continues to Haunt American Crime Control at the Beginning of the Twenty-First', *Texas Law Review*, vol. 84, pp. 2135–2172.

Sugrue, T.J. (1996) *The Origins of the Urban Crisis: Race and Inequality in Postwar Detroit*. Princeton, NJ, Princeton University Press.

Thompson, J.P. (2015) 'Broken Policing: The Origins of the "Broken Windows" Policy', *New Labor Forum*, vol. 24, no. 2, pp. 42–47.

Triplett, R.A. and Turner, E.M. (2010) 'Where Is Criminology? The Institutional Placement of Criminology Within Sociology and Criminal Justice', *Criminal Justice Review*, vol. 35, no. 1, pp. 5–31.

Velasco, E. (2008) 'School of Justice and Social Inquiry Commemorates 25 Years', *ASU Now: Access, Excellence, Impact*, 29 February. Available at: https://asunow.asu.edu/content/school-justice-and-social-inquiry-commemorates-25-years (Accessed 25 November 2020).

Vollmer, A. (1932) 'Abstract of the Wickersham Police Report', *Journal of Criminal Law and Criminology*, vol. 22, no. 5, pp. 716–723.

Vollmer, A. and Schneider, A. (1917) 'The School for Police as Planned at Berkeley', *Journal of American Institute of Criminal Law and Criminology*, vol. 7, no. 6, pp. 877–898.

Walker, S. (1998) *Popular Justice: A History of American Criminal Justice*, New York, Oxford University Press.

Washington, H.A. (2006) *Medical Apartheid: The Dark History of Medical Experimentation on Black Americans from Colonial Times to the Present*, New York, The Doubleday Broadway Publishing Group.

Weirman, C. and Archambeault, W.G. (1983) 'Assessing the Effects of LEAA Demise on Criminal Justice Higher Education', *Journal of Criminal Justice*, vol. 11, no. 6, pp. 549–561.

Welch Jr., R.E. (1974) 'American Atrocities in the Philippines: The Indictment and the Response', *Pacific Historical Review*, vol. 43, no. 2, pp. 233–253.

Wetzell, R.F. (2000) *Inventing the Criminal: A History of German Criminology, 1880–1945*, Chapel Hill, University of North Carolina Press.

Wolfgang, M.E. (1961) 'Pioneers in Criminology: Cesare Lombroso (1825–1909)', *Journal of Criminal Law and Criminology*, vol. 52, no. 4, pp. 361–391.

Woods, J.B. (2015) 'The Birth of Modern Criminology and Gendered Constructions of Homosexual Criminal Identity', *Journal of Homosexuality*, vol. 62, no. 5, pp. 131–166.

Criminology's Systemic Violence Against Humanity

5

THE WHITE RACIALIZED CENTER OF CRIMINOLOGY

Holly Sims-Bruno

Introduction

Most criminologists assume that people who come into contact with the criminal justice system are somehow *different* from those who do not. For that reason, criminological theories were created to identify what makes the criminal different from the *normal*, law-abiding citizen.

However, few criminologists have addressed how the physical and cultural traits of the white middle class became synonymous with being law-abiding and decent in the study of criminal behavior (Agozino, 2003; Saleh-Hanna, 2017).

This chapter interrogates some of the more popular theories of positivist criminology to "tease out the subtle or unconscious practices of racial discrimination" that are generally accepted as normal within the discipline (Green, Sonn, and Matsebula, 2007, p. 390). This analysis serves as a reminder to criminologists that our theories were not created in a vacuum. The scholars who constructed these theories were not immune from what Joe Feagin (2010) refers to as the white racial frame (i.e., an overarching worldview that most whites – and those who try to conform to white middle-class norms – use to view society). As an ideological framework, the white racial frame aides the process of racialization via racial stereotypes and biased narratives that convey the belief that whites, particularly members of the middle class, are superior, virtuous, and normal, while people of color and whites of lower socioeconomic status are deficient, dangerous, and inferior (Feagin, 2010). Given the pervasive nature of this framework, one should not be surprised that the scientific gaze of European and white American criminologists focused almost exclusively on impoverished whites and people of color who were supposedly unable to adhere to middle-class standards of decency (i.e., the patriarchal family arrangement, educational achievement, steady employment, and the accumulation of wealth).

DOI: 10.4324/9780367817114-8

From Adolphe Quetelet's statistical principle of normal distribution, to Walter Miller's notion of a "lower-class" subculture, this chapter outlines how and why positivist criminology perpetuated a rigid binary between normality and deviance that remained centered on white middle-class norms. Therefore, this analysis highlights how criminology developed and was inescapably influenced by the white racial frame. It concludes by proposing how criminologists might counter the frame's influence by disrupting the cycle of linking criminality to physical and cultural characteristics that deviate from those associated with the white middle class.

Positivist Criminology

In the early 1840s, Adolphe Quetelet, the French statistician and founder of positive criminology, measured the bodily dimensions of over 100,000 French and Scottish men to calculate the average body type of a normal law-abiding citizen. He believed that all the measurements fell into a natural and determined order which gave rise to the statistical principle of normal distribution. While he observed that some physical variations from the mean were considered natural, extraordinary variations from the mean were considered "monstrous" (Beirne and Messerschmidt, 1991, p. 391). Quetelet believed that all men had the capacity to commit crime but concluded that the criminal tendencies of law-abiding men were rarely if ever translated into criminal actions because they were "morally temperate and mentally healthy" (Beirne and Messerschmidt, 1991, p. 392). Quetelet contrasted these men with individuals of lower socioeconomic status and people of color whom he believed were morally inferior to men like himself. He concluded that biological defects and severe aberrations from his manufactured norm were responsible for moral deficiencies and criminality (Beirne and Messerschmidt, 1991). Therefore, being of Aryan or Caucasian descent implied that a person was of decent moral character, while having physical traits similar to Africans and other people of color suggested that an individual was morally deficient.

The White Racial Frame

Feagin (2010) traced the scientific tradition of describing physical and cultural differences with the intent to divide human beings into inferior and superior groups back to Plato, the father of western philosophy. Plato did not believe that having a human body automatically qualified someone as *human*. According to Marimba Ani (1994), Plato perceived the human identity as a cultural marker of superiority that took an extensive amount of work to achieve – and not everyone could. He believed that some human bodies were inherently defective by birth, biology, or culture.

To illustrate his theory of a natural social hierarchy, Plato identified "the Great Chain of Being" and placed western man at the very top of the order (Feagin, 2010). The higher up the Great Chain ladder, the more valued a human group became, while the groups placed lower on the Great Chain were less valued, less human, and believed to have more in common with nonhuman animals, to whom western man was superior (Ani, 1994; Feagin, 2010). Plato also placed men like himself at the top of the chain to symbolize their close proximity to God. This placement conveyed his belief that western man facilitates God's plan by controlling inferior, less rational people (Ani, 1994).

The intellectual tradition of a superior-inferior logic facilitated the belief that human decency is a constant, unchangeable, trait of western man. Therefore, Plato's Great Chain of Being allowed for western man to become the center to which everything and everyone else was compared.

Like Plato, English colonists were convinced that European patriarchs were the standard for normalcy and that deviation from the body and lifestyle of European man was enough to prove anyone and anything deficient. In fact, Feagin (2010) marks the earliest evidence of a white racial frame with the tendency of English colonists to link the physical and biological traits (i.e., skin color, facial features) of Indigenous and African people to negative moral and cultural stereotypes (i.e., savagery). They used terms like "savage" and "barbaric" to describe African and Indigenous populations not only to imply that African and Native Americans were uncivilized but to convey the notion that people of color were dangerous and *criminal*.

Despite the differences that existed among various African and Native American populations, the English lumped them all together into two large groups. Borrowing from the words used by Spanish colonists in the Caribbean and South and Central America, the English categorized people of color in North America as either Indian or Black (Malcomson, 2000; Feagin, 2010). Both groups were considered less than human and more like the animals to whom European men were superior (Malcomson, 2000). The anti-Black and anti-Indigenous subframe of the white racial frame was spread across North America via European scientists, scholars, ministers, missionaries, and other colonists who interpreted human difference so that the bodies of Indigenous peoples, Africans, and other people of color were always associated with deficiency and danger, and the bodies of European men were always associated with decent and moral character (Maclomson, 2000; Feagin, 2010, Roberts, 2011).

By the 1730s, the dramatic increase in the use of science rather than religion to understand human issues did not disrupt the European colonial tradition of linking physical and cultural characteristics to moral integrity (Feagin, 2010). In fact, scientific thinking throughout the 18th century in Europe and America often involved identifying deviations from the bodies of white men (Ani, 1994). Influential Enlightenment era scientists, like Swedish botanist and taxonomist Carol Linnaeus, and well-known philosophers like Immanuel Kant, were convinced that skin color could be linked to particular cultural traits. Europeans were categorized as "white," Africans were "black," and Natives were "red," but white people were always considered *normal* and decent (Feagin, 2010; Roberts, 2011). Therefore, when Adolphe Quetelet attempted to determine the physical characteristics of criminals, he attempted to prove that their bodies had more in common with the bodily dimensions of Africans, the mentally ill, and other individuals of lower socioeconomic status. Operating from the white racial frame, Quetelet ensured the bodies of middle- and upper-class men of Caucasian descent remained linked to normal and decent character.

Piers Beirne (1987) criticized Quetelet's analysis of crime for perpetuating a rigid binary between *normal* and *deviation*. He argued that it was the creation of this binary that provided the epistemological core for the dominance of biological and economic explanations of crime in criminology. However, Quetelet's analysis also ensured that white middle- and upper-class men were always considered normal and law-abiding, while criminals were always thought of as being different. Therefore, the operation of a white racial frame in positivist criminology ensured the criminal was always inferior, whether biologically and/or culturally, when contrasted with European members of the white middle and upper-class.

Biological Theories of Crime

The Italian physician Cesare Lombroso was another leading figure in the development of criminology. Lombroso was heavily influenced by the evolutionary theories of Charles Darwin and believed that criminals were atavistic throwbacks to less civilized periods in human history. As a consequence, he presumed that the answers to the problem of crime and criminal behavior were located in the bodies of criminals and the mentally ill, who differed from the average law-abiding citizen (Beirne and Messerschmidt, 1991).

After examining the skull of a prominent European criminal in 1871, Lombroso concluded that it had more in common with the skulls of non-Western people than that of the average European man (Bradley, 2010). Then, after examining the heads of deceased white male juvenile delinquents, he claimed that they were significantly different from that of the average law-abiding man and more similar to Africans and the "insane" (Beirne and Messerschmidt, 1991, p. 303).

His comparison of white criminals to Africans and the mentally ill reflected Lombroso's belief in the natural superiority of white men and provides evidence that like Quetelet, he too was operating from a white racial frame. Lombroso concluded that Africans committed crimes because they were naturally inclined to criminal behavior. On the other hand, he concluded that white criminality was only the result of some trait that made white criminals different from other law-abiding whites. In fact, Lombroso believed that white men were normal, naturally honest, and therefore unable to commit crime. He believed that social circumstances activated latent criminal tendencies that were already present in the biology of "abnormal or degenerate" individuals (Ellwood, 1912, p. 718). Although Lombroso failed to locate one distinct characteristic common to all criminals, he identified a range of attributes related to what he identified as the "born criminal." These attributes included but were not limited to individuals with smaller skulls and darker hair, skin, and eyes (Bradley, 2010). His infamous linkage of criminals to Africans and whites with "activated latent criminal tendencies" already present in their biology reinforced the notion of white supremacy.

During the late 19th and early 20th century, theories of social Darwinism significantly influenced the minds of white American businessmen, clergymen, and scholars who believed that extreme wealth was a consequence of moral superiority and that poverty was a consequence of moral depravity. Therefore, it was common for people like John D. Rockefeller to argue that extreme social inequity was the will of God and for prominent white American scholars, like William Graham Summer, to argue that wealthy industrialists and financiers were the true creators of wealth and human virtue (Goldman, 1956, Feagin, 1964). Because it was common for members of the upper classes to believe they were the esteemed product of natural selection, many also believed members of the upper class were obligated to regulate and control the dangerous classes of people who were not white and those whose lifestyles were not quite white enough.

Eugenics

American scholars in the early 20th century combined evolution and natural selection with a biomedical emphasis on blood and genetics to "prove" that whites were more intelligent than Africans and other individuals convicted of crime (Feagin, 2010). The majority of those in the scientific community believed that blood and genes carried mental properties. They were convinced that the bloodlines and the genetics of whites carried more intelligence, greater moral refinement, and a more vigorous spirit of enterprise (Dyer, 1997, Malcomson, 2000). They linked the physical attributes of Africans and other people of color to crime and deviance. For example, American sociologist Charles Ellwood (1912, p. 719) believed it was a "great mistake" to think that biological conditions of the individual organism were not "determinative of individual habits." He concluded that human habits were rooted in instinct and that instinct was essentially a biological matter that varied with racial and individual heredity. Later, in 1939, Harvard anthropologist E. A. Hooton claimed that criminals were organically inferior and reiterated Lombroso's conclusion that the only way to eliminate crime was to remove or segregate physically, mentally, and morally unfit individuals from society (Cullen and Agnew, 2011).

The study of poverty, with the intent to identify racial differences between impoverished and middle-class whites, led many 20th-century American scientists to embrace eugenics. Sir Francis Galton, the founder of the eugenics movement and Charles Darwin's half-cousin, saw class as an integral component of race (Roberts, 2011). In 1883, Galton coined the word *eugenics* from the Greek root word *eugenes*, which meant "good birth," to describe the science of improving humanity by giving the "more suitable races or strains of blood a better chance of prevailing over the less suitable" (Roberts, 2011, p. 36). Galton argued that no one who bred domestic animals would disagree that "the breeding of weak individuals was highly injurious to the race of man" and that hardly anyone was "so ignorant to allow his worst animals to breed" (Roberts, 2011, p. 36). Therefore, rather than relying on natural selection to force inferior groups into extinction, he emphasized that state intervention, via forced sterilizations, would increase the likelihood that only more suitable people procreated (Feagin, 1964; Roberts, 2011). Galton argued that what nature did "blindly, slowly, and ruthlessly," man could do more "quickly and kindly" (Roberts, 2011, p. 36).

Galton further exemplified his own adherence to a white racial frame with his extreme criticism of Africans, who he described as impulsive, unintelligent, and without dignity (Roberts, 2011). Galton's eugenics theory flourished in America during the early 1900s, when poverty and racial oppression were believed inevitable and many white Americans were convinced that the moral character of impoverished whites and people of color needed to be controlled or corrected to protect the integrity of American society (Feagin, 1964). However, the persistence of poverty in urban and rural America did not agree with the assessment held by many middle- and upper-class whites who believed that people of color and whites of lower socioeconomic status were biologically inferior and destined for extinction. Because many middle- and upper-class whites were fearful of the alleged defectiveness of people of color and the impoverished, they believed it was necessary to increase white procreation (Roberts, 2011).

During the age of eugenics, many whites were concerned with the preservation of "racial purity" and strongly opposed mixing with other racial groups. In fact, President Woodrow Wilson advocated the superiority of European civilization over all others and promoted the racial segregation of African Americans during his terms, from 1913 to 1921. Racial separatism and forced sterilization programs became increasingly important as many whites believed such intervention was necessary to protect the longevity of the white race and the greater good of society (Roberts, 2011). This belief was supported by American eugenicist Madison Grant, whose work was widely circulated among white scientists throughout the1920s. He described impoverished whites, people of color, Jews, and criminals as inferiors whose elimination was necessary to preserve white racial purity and social well-being. Grant and other eugenic scientists interpreted inequality as a natural phenomenon dictated by nature (Feagin, 1964; Roberts, 2011). Therefore, they were convinced that any attempt to alter inequality with egalitarian social programs would have dire consequences to the natural order of moral society. However, some middle- and upper-class whites believed that whites of lower socioeconomic status could redeem themselves by conforming to the lifestyle of the white middle class (Wray, 2006). In fact, most whites, regardless of class, believed that if whites worked hard enough, were disciplined, and were the best at what they did, natural law would reward them with success in the form of wealth, property, prestige, and power (Feagin, 1964). Many members of the middle class believed that poverty was a natural consequence of immorality or character flaws that included dishonesty, an unwillingness to work, sexual deviancy, and wastefulness (Barrett and Roediger, 1997). As a result, individuals unable to adhere to white middle-class norms (i.e., the patriarchal family arrangement, educational achievement, steady employment, and the accumulation of wealth) were continuously framed as deviant, indecent, and less than human.

After the defeat of Nazi Germany in World War II, eugenics was discredited as bad science that was used to justify racial hatred. Anti-Semitism and anti–Eastern European racism lost respectability in the US after American eugenic scientists were linked to the Nazi movement (Roberts, 2011). The scientific administrators of eugenic laboratories resigned, and the word "Aryan" was no longer used to describe the white race, given its connotation of Nazi extremism. However, it was not until the 1940s that white Americans began to identify exclusively as Caucasian (Dyer, 1997). The U.S. census stopped differentiating between white people born within, and white people born outside of the United States. European-Jewish and other Euro-ethnic economic mobility were seen as an American triumph over racism. When the United States emerged from World War II with the strongest economy in the world, the boundaries of the white identity shifted to allow Jews and Eastern Europeans to enter the exclusive racial group (Roberts, 2011). However, the upward class mobility of a select group of Europeans did little to unsettle the ideological dominance of the white racial frame and its emphasis on white supremacy.

Cultural Theories of Crime

Throughout the early 20th century, Chicago experienced extreme urbanization, growth, and racial tension as the city quickly transformed from a small trading post to a city with more than 3 million residents. By 1930, the city was home to various European immigrant groups and African Americans seeking distance from rural poverty and the Jim Crow South. In Chicago and across America, urban ethnic centers were increasingly viewed by the white middle and upper classes as both dirty and dangerous (Brodkin, 1997).

Social Disorganization

When Clifford Shaw and Henry McKay (1942) examined the juvenile delinquency rates of Chicago, they concluded that high rates of delinquency and recidivism were strongly correlated with social disorganization (i.e., community problems facilitated by high rates of school truancy, young adult offenders, infant mortality, tuberculosis, and mental disorders). In addition, Shaw and McKay believed that the inner city suffered higher levels of crime because community norms and behavioral standards were set by the various cultural beliefs of migrant groups and unassimilated immigrant groups, and often reflected the moral values of predatory youth gangs and organized street crime. They were convinced that deviant values were in direct opposition to conventional values that were symbolized by the "family, church, and other institutions common to . . . general society" (Shaw and McKay, 1942, p. 171).

While Shaw and McKay did not believe that residents of high crime communities were biologically or psychologically abnormal, they failed to challenge Quetelet and Lombroso's rigid dichotomy that set the *conventional* in opposition to the criminal deviant. They identified two opposing moral values within the city: one that emphasized monetary success derived through criminal enterprise and another that accentuated Christianity, the patriarchal family arrangement, and the more distant possibility of success through legitimate means. They concluded that cities had higher rates of delinquency because conventional morals were challenged by the overwhelming presence of unassimilated European immigrants and African American migrants from the South who accumulated wealth via criminal activity.

The views of Shaw and McKay (1942) differed from those of E. Franklin Frazier, a Black sociologist who also studied urban crime in Chicago around the same time period. Frazier (1939, 1949) refuted the notion that higher crime rates in African American communities stemmed from the inability of Africans to assimilate to *conventional* America because he believed Black culture *was* American culture. However, Shaw and McKay's observation of declining delinquency rates in the rural white-majority towns of Illinois aligned well with their internalized white racial frame. They believed that white suburban and rural communities had lower crime rates because their white inhabitants were *normal* and therefore law-abiding (Beirne and Messerschmidt, 1991, p. 366).

Ultimately, Shaw and McKay constructed deviance simply as they imagined the inverse to normalcy and then linked criminal activity to those perceived as different from members of the white middle class. Their work continued to emphasize and extend the white racial frame as they failed to challenge the notion that deviation from white middle-class culture is associated with criminality.

Social Strain

Sociologist Robert K. Merton was also interested in the high crime rates of urban city centers. In 1938 he published *Social Structure and Anomie*. In the article, he claimed criminal behavior was a symptom of social disorganization that consisted of: (1) a lack of fit between culturally prescribed aspirations and (2) socially structured avenues for achieving them. He focused on the inaccessibility of the American dream, which by the early 1900s firmly centered on the patriarchal family arrangement and the accumulation of wealth and private property. He believed the lack of legitimate means to ensure all people could achieve the American dream forced some individuals to seek alternative measures (i.e., criminal activity) to achieve success. The "lack of fit" Merton referred to in his interpretation of a disorganized society increased what he called societal "strain." Strain was the consequence of a society that was poorly integrated because the promise of wealth and prosperity to all who worked hard was unobtainable for most people (Clinard, 1964). At the same time, however, Merton was highly critical of the way American society saw impoverishment as evidence of personal failure rather than social inequality. He believed the negative framing of impoverishment only intensified the strain felt by individuals of lower socioeconomic status, which explained higher crime rates in the highly populated and ethnically diverse American cities (Beirne and Messer-schmidt, 1991).

Merton's introduction of strain theory in 1938 remains one of the most influential sociological explanations of crime ever presented. However, his theory assumed that all people consistently adhered to or aspired to achieve the white middle-class lifestyle (Beirne and Messerschmidt, 1991). This belief was more than likely a reflection of Merton's own desire to conform to white norms despite his upbringing in an impoverished Jewish community in Philadelphia. The fact that Merton changed his name from Meyer Schkolnick to Robert K. Merton indicates that he was distinctly aware of the anti-Semitic nature of white Americans during his time and therefore did what he believed necessary to acquire opportunities outside of his community. He remained preoccupied with upward mobility and was convinced that monetary success required a certain innovative adaptation (Young, 2010a).

While Merton claimed that the American dream of monetary success predisposed everyone to crime, his strain theory failed to challenge the perception that communities with lower crime rates adhered to the "conventional" norms of the white middle class. His theory continued to cast people of color and impoverished whites as different and more prone to engage in criminal behavior, providing further evidence of his inability to transcend the influence of the ever-pervasive white racial frame.

Differential Association

Following the tradition of Shaw, McKay and Merton, Edwin Sutherland (1947) insisted in his book *Principles of Criminology* that neighborhoods with high rates crime rates were not disorganized. Instead, he concluded that such neighborhoods were organized around a different set of moral values and concerns. He believed that criminal behavior was learned within intimate personal groups through an interactive process of communication. Therefore, a person only became criminal when "definitions favorable to violation of the law" exceeded definitions "unfavorable to violation of the law" and when contacts with criminal patterns outweighed contacts with anticriminal patterns (Beirne and Messerschmidt, 1991, p. 425).

Sutherland's theory of differential association was often criticized for lacking clarity and precision (Gibbins, 1979, p. 56). However, it is important to note that Sutherland failed to challenge the assumption that criminals must think differently or adhere to moral values that are somehow different from the average, white, law-abiding citizen who lives in a community with low official crime rates. Even though Sutherland did not believe crime was largely associated with poverty, he still refused to acknowledge the possibility that people who enter into the criminal justice system might have a lot in common with people who do not. For Sutherland, white middle-class culture remained the standard for what was considered normal and decent, while criminals remained unique to the presumed virtuous nature of white normative behavior.

Criminal Subculture

Albert Cohen was a student of Robert K. Merton at Harvard University in 1938. Cohen graduated from Harvard in 1939 with prestigious recommendations for graduate school and an academic record that should have increased his chances for acceptance. However, like Merton, Cohen was Jewish and therefore denied admittance to several graduate programs. Universities had traditionally functioned within American society as white Protestant finishing schools, so it was not uncommon for universities to have quotas that limited non-Protestant entry or denied non-Protestant admittance altogether (Brodkin, 1997). Cohen eventually gained admission to Indiana University, where he worked with Edwin Sutherland as a graduate assistant. While at Indiana, he challenged Sutherland's theory by questioning the origin of the criminal culture spread by differential association (Young, 2010b). Sutherland originally dismissed Cohen's question as unimportant, but William Foote Whyte's *Street Corner Society* (an urban ethnography conducted in an Italian slum during the late 1930s in Boston) inspired Cohen to continue to investigate delinquent subcultures.

Whyte (1943) made a distinction in his work between "corner-boys" and "college-boys." Corner-boys were preoccupied with the present, spent most of their free time hanging around bars and street corners within their own neighborhood, and were described as being "fiercely loyal to their Italian working-class culture and to each other" (Whyte, 1943, p. 111). The college-boys, on the other hand, were more interested in getting good grades in school, individualistic, and felt they had to sever ties with their working-class friends if they wanted to move up the socioeconomic ladder (Whyte, 1943). Cohen was inspired by Whyte's work and wanted to understand why corner-boys preferred the corner or why some young African American men in the inner city preferred the streets.

In *Delinquent Boys*, Cohen (1955) claimed that a contradiction of culture caused delinquents to engage in crime. He did not believe that delinquents turned to crime only to achieve culturally approved goals; rather, he insisted some juvenile gangs committed crime simply for fun. Furthermore, he did not believe that Sutherland's theory of differential association explained why some juveniles joined gangs and others did not. Cohen thought Sutherland took the existence of gangs for granted when he failed to ask where the delinquent culture of the gang came from in the first place. Therefore, Cohen explained delinquency with what he interpreted as a culture clash that existed between "lower-class" and middle-class kids. He thought children of lower socioeconomic status were ill prepared to measure up to the middle-class standards grounded in the modern education system.

The middle-class standards described by Cohen (1955) included: (1) personal ambition, (2) individual responsibility, (3) academic and athletic superiority, (4) courtesy and respect for private property, and (5) the constructive use of leisure time. Cohen believed middle-class children were more likely to obtain these skills from their parents than children of working-class families. He claimed that because young boys and men from families of lower socioeconomic status were more likely to fail in school, they experienced what he described as status frustration, which promoted feelings of self-hatred. Therefore, Cohen (1955) concluded that failure at school forced working-class men to the lower rungs of the social ladder, which made them more likely to adhere to a delinquent subculture rather than the *conventional* culture of the white middle-class. He believed that delinquent subcultures operated as an adjustment mechanism that enabled adolescents to find alternative ways to achieve their own interpretation of success. For example, Cohen (1955) explained that working-class men were more likely to perceive academic success as unobtainable, so they redefined it as bookish knowledge for "sissies" and regarded street knowledge as a superior form of education.

In 1958, Walter Miller's article "Lower Class Culture as a Generating Milieu of Gang Delinquency" criticized Cohen, who claimed that gang members were typically failures of conventional society. Miller (1958) insisted that delinquents simply had a set of "focal concerns" that were different from those of middle-class individuals. For example, he claimed that "lower-class boys" were preoccupied with concerns of "trouble" and "toughness," while middle-class boys prioritized educational achievement (Miller, 1958, p. 7). However, he also insisted that delinquent boys typically came from only a small percentage of lower-class families who fell into a "hardcore" lower-class group (Miller, 1958, p. 6). One of the distinctive characteristics of the hardcore lower class was the female-headed household, which Miller (1958) linked to delinquent behavior.

Like the social theorists before them, Cohen (1955) and Miller (1958) were operating from a white racial frame that hindered their ability to interpret criminality as anything other than a deviation from white middle-class norms. It was this perspective on deviance that Black civil rights scholars were especially critical of (Holloway and Keppel, 2007). Why were certain people and practices privileged as "normative" while others were categorized as deviant? Joyce Ladner (1971) described the premise of deviant behavior as the invention of a group that uses its own standards as the ideal by which to judge others. Hylan Lewis (2002) concluded that as long as social scientists continued to identify people who live in certain areas by some particular trait, they would continue to learn nothing other than what they already believed to be true.

Conclusion

Positivist criminology was not created by white European and American scholars to reduce or alleviate harm. The overwhelming influence of the white racial frame ensured that criminology remained preoccupied with protecting the boundaries of whiteness. Therefore, a discipline that seeks to identify, control, correct, contain, or eliminate the deviant criminal must be abolished. To counter the influence of the white racial frame, we must redirect our gaze to the devastating consequences of white supremacy, colonialism, heteropatriarchy, and racial capitalism. Abolitionist critiques of chattel slavery mark some of the earliest discussions of crime, law, and justice in American society, yet the theoretical dominance of positivist criminology ensures abolitionist and civil rights scholarship remain at the fringes of the discipline.

New abolitionists (i.e. Black feminists, intersectional, queer, Indigenous, critical race, and anticolonial activists and scholars) seek to disrupt the common understandings of crime, law, punishment, safety, and justice that perpetuates our reliance on criminalization and the criminal justice system (Brown and Schept, 2017). This chapter contributes to the efforts of new abolitionists by attempting to disrupt criminology's 'common' sense about crime and the criminal identity. Until criminologists come to terms with the white racialized center of the discipline, they will continue to achieve little more than contribute to the expansion of police power and the carceral state. Their repetitive attempts to identify how individuals who live in communities where people are disproportionately policed and incarcerated are *different* will continue to teach us nothing other than what most criminologists have always believed – that people in communities with higher arrest rates are deficient and dangerous, and that contrary to evidence and reason, people who live in communities with lower arrest rates are superior and not dangerous.

References

Agozino, B. (2003) *Counter-Colonial Criminology: A Critique of Imperialist Reason,* London & Sterling Virginia, Pluto, Press.

Ani, M. (1994) *Yurugu: An Afrikan-Centered Critique of European Cultural Thought and Behavior,* Washington, DC, Nkonimfo Publications.

Barrett, J., Roediger, D. (1997) 'How White People Became White', in *Critical White Studies: Looking Behind the Mirror,* Philadelphia, PA, Temple University Press.

Beirne, P. (1987) 'Adolphe Quetelet and the Origins of Positivist Criminology', *American Journal of Sociology,* Vol. 92, No. 5, pp. 1140–1169.

Beirne, P., Messerschmidt, J. (1991) *Criminology,* Harcourt, Brace Jovanovich College Publishers.

Bradley, K. (2010) 'Cesare Lombroso', in Hayward, K., Maruna, S., Mooney, J., *Fifty Key Thinkers in Criminology,* New York, Routledge, pp. 25–30.

Brodkin, K. (1997) 'How Did Jews Become White Folk?' in *Critical White Studies: Looking Behind the Mirror,* Philadelphia, PA, Temple University Press.

Brown, M., Schept, J. (2017) 'New Abolition, Criminology, and a Critical Carceral Studies', *Punishment & Society,* Vol. 19, No. 4, pp. 440–462.

Clinard, M. (1964) 'The Theoretical Implications of Anomie and Deviant Behavior', in Clinard, M., *Anomie and Deviant Behavior,* New York, The Free Press of Glencoe, pp. 1–56.

Cohen, A. (1955) *Delinquent Boys: The Culture of the Gang,* New York, The Free Press.

Cullen, F., Agnew, R. (2011) *Criminological Theory: Past to Present,* New York, Oxford University Press.

Dyer, R. (1997) *White,* London and New York, Routledge Press.

Ellwood, C. (1912) 'Lombroso's Theory of Crime', *Journal of the American Institute of Criminal Law and Criminology,* Vol. 2, No. 5, pp. 716–723.

Feagin, J. (1964) *The Subordination of the Poor,* Englewood Cliffs, NJ, Prentice-Hall Inc.

Feagin, J. (2010) *The White Racial Frame,* New York, Routledge.

Frazier, E.F. (1939) *Negro Family in the United States*, Chicago, IL, The University of Chicago Press.

Frazier, E.F. (1949) *The Negro in the United States*, Chicago, IL, The University of Chicago Press.

Gibbins, D. (1979) *The Criminological Enterprise: Theories and Perspectives*, Englewood, NJ, Prentice-Hall Inc.

Goldman, E. (1956) *Rendezvous with Destiny: A History of Modern American Reform*, New York, Vintage Books.

Green, M., Sonn, C., Matsebula, J. (2007) 'Reviewing Whiteness: Theory, Research, and Possibilities', *Journal of Psychology*, Vol. 37, No. 3, p. 389.

Holloway, J., Keppel, B. (2007) *Black Scholars on the Line: Race, Social Science, and American Thought in the Twentieth Century*. Notre Dame, IN, University of Notre Dame Press.

Ladner, J. (1971) *Tomorrow's Tomorrow: The Black Woman*, New York, Doubleday and Company.

Lewis, H. (2002) 'Pursuing Fieldwork in African-American Communities', in Bowser, B., Kushnick, L., *Against the Odds: Scholars Who Challenged Racism in the Twentieth Century*, Amherst, MA, University of Massachusetts Press.

Malcomson, S. (2000) *One Drop of Blood: The American Misadventure of Race*, New York: Farrar, Straus and Giroux.

Miller, W. (1958) 'Lower Class Culture as a Generating Milieu of Gang Delinquency', *Journal of Social Sciences*, Vol. 14, No. 3, pp. 5–19.

Roberts, D. (2011) *Fatal Invention: How Science, Politics, and Big Business Re-create Race in the Twenty First Century*, New York, The New York Press.

Saleh-Hanna, V. (2017) 'Reversing Criminology's White Gaze: As Lombroso's Disembodied Head Peers Through a Glass Jar in a Museum Foreshadowed by Sara Baartman's Ghost', in Wilson, J., Hddgkinson, S., Piche, J., Walby, K., *The Palgrave Handbook of Prison Tourism*, London, Palgrave Macmillan, pp. 689–711.

Shaw, C., McKay, H.D. (1942) *Juvenile Delinquency in Urban Areas*, Chicago, IL, University of Chicago Press.

Sutherland, E. (1947) *Principles of Criminology*, Chicago, IL, JB Lippincott Co.

Whyte, W. (1943) *Street Corner Society*, Chicago, IL, University of Chicago Press.

Wray, M. (2006) *Not Quite White: White Trash and the Boundaries of Whiteness*, Durham, NC, Duke University Press.

Young, J. (2010a) 'Richard Merton', in Hayward, K., Maruna, S., Mooney, J., *Fifty Key Thinkers in Criminology*, New York, New York, Routledge, pp. 88–99.

Young, J. (2010b) 'Albert Cohen', in Hayward, K., Maruna, S., Mooney, J., *Fifty Key Thinkers in Criminology*, New York, New York, Routledge, pp. 105–115.

6

EVOLVING STANDARDS

Derrick Washington

Evolving Standards (Part I)

In *Trop v. Dulles* 356 U.S. 86 (1958), the Supreme Court ruled that the Eighth Amendment prohibition on cruel and unusual punishment "must draw its meaning from the evolving standards of decency that mark the progress of a maturing society." Evolving Standards (ES) starts with abolishing systemic practices of punishment for 'social deviants' and entirely eliminating all concepts of 'crime.' Unfortunately, American society often associates justice with punishment, hindering the growth of an evolutionary practice for addressing social deviancy. Evolving Standards eradicates the idea of social deviancy as 'crime,' does away with the labeling of deviants as criminal[s] and instead takes on a health and human services approach to social deviancy.

Crime essentially is an action that violates laws, regulations, and/or policies that govern societies. In America's representative government, societal relationships between laws, conceptual crimes, and society's responses to deviations from such, ultimately determine a person's quality of life and can define roughly who is likely to become part of the permanent deviant class, or what society labels as 'criminals.' Criminality becomes obsolete in an ES-based society. ES shifts how both governments and societies interpret and respond to deviations, allowing our society to learn why people deviate from the social order of law and aim for solutions as opposed to punishment.

The current system of American justice is all punishment and not in accordance with a better tomorrow, as evidenced by the following email, written in the wake of Covid-19 within a Massachusetts maximum security prison at Souza Baranowski Correctional Center (SBCC). It articulates the need for an Evolving Standards society and for eventual elimination of both crime and punishment.

★★★

DOI: 10.4324/9780367817114-9

Sent 10:04 am, Sunday, May 31, 2020

National riots, mass demonstrations and unending calls for justice beat throughout city streets and prison cellblocks like drums. The snow white prison administration at SBCC make it a point to keep us shielded from hearing the resounding
drum beats from our people calling for accountability concerning the killings of
Ahmaud Arbery, George Floyd, and Breonna Taylor. Administration took our televisions from us months ago. Their reasoning for confiscating our televisions then
was to punish us for a staff/prisoner incident and block us from seeing the coverage
concerning people rising up against how they were/are terrorizing the incarcerated
population at SBCC in retaliation for what had occurred. Now, it's just convenient
for them to keep the light out from us receiving any information.

Because the majority of us in here are unaware of the evolving atrocities occurring in society concerning Ahmaud Arbery, George Floyd and Breonna Taylor,
it was initially difficult to connect why hateful prison officials have ramped up
their bigoted behavior against us. They came through the L1 cellblock yesterday
targeting Black persons, making us strip naked, and going through cells tossing
everything about. That was unusual for a Saturday, as that's one day out of the
week that our PTSD from staff abuse is leveled. However, we are also beating our
drums as well!

As I write this email the music from guys kicking cell gates and shouting for justice can be heard from the solitary unit two levels above the L1 cellblock. We're tired
of not being seen and treated like dirt to be stepped on at any time. I once asked
one of the few Latina minority women who work at SBCC, "How are you able
to stomach the racism and abuse that goes on in here and not speak out against it?"
I think by me simply asking that question her mind instantly shifted to job security
as she quickly retorted, "What are you talking about? I haven't seen that." I'm thinking damn, you have to be brainwashed to work in a place where people are openly
tortured and you can't see it.

We don't have camera phones, social media outlets or formal news coverage
exposing the everyday abuse, racism and hatred from prison guards against the
incarcerated population in here. I wouldn't be surprised if this email isn't released
as they haven't been allowing emails to transfer to and from in the past three days.
Prison is a place where racism can entirely remove its masks and racist guards can be
themselves. When they're angered from listening to our drums beating within society, they can come to work and physically beat us, as we don't have any accessible
surveillance or "credible" witnesses to refute whatever fictitious story they concoct
to justify them splitting someone's head open and knocking them unconscious (as
what happened to me). Regardless of that, we'll continue to beat our drums in
tandem with those outside of these walls calling for equitable treatment, confronting racist authorities, and replacing punishment with love as justice throughout the
legal system.

Black lives matter consists of ending the killing of Black and Brown people imme-
diately. We die a little bit each day when we're not treated with dignity, are not seen
as credible, and thrown into torture chambers to be watched by racist authorities. We
must continue to confront an American spirit of racism which has carried on since
the ending of chattel slavery but has appeared in many different shapes since. We
must confront it until it's entirely exposed and can no longer hide under a badge &
uniform, robe of a judge, suit of a prosecutor, or facemasks of a medical practitioner.

Know that we've found a way to cultivate light within the dark and we see. They
can continue to abuse and antagonize us in here as much as they'd like because it
won't stop us from being heard. The tide of passion for justice is building and can't
be tamed. I'm on the side of love as Justice, as I've grown tired of experiencing hate
filled laws, practices and policies that constitute the current make of justice. We will
continue to rise.

Much love to the families and loved ones of Ahmaud Arbery; George Floyd,
Breonna Taylor and the many victims of hate, racism and injustice.

#FreeThemAll #CloseTheMax

Your Brother, Student & Champion,
Much Love,
Derrick Washington

(FOR THE PEOPLE (SHARE))

Emancipation Initiative (EI)
emancipation@gmail.com
@MassPowerVote
Facebook: @emancipation.initiative
Families for Justice As Healing (FJAH)
Harvard Prison Divestment Campaign (HPDC)
Young Abolitionist (YA)
Formerly Incarcerated and Incarcerated Men (FIIRM)
Party for Socialism and Liberation (PSL)
Corrlinks.com (to set up email, type in slave #W89316)

★★★

The above address is an email I wrote "For The People" that friends post on our
Facebook page and website for Emancipation Initiative, an organization for incarcerated persons in Massachusetts advocating to restore universal prisoner suffrage
and end Life Without Parole (LWOP) sentences. It illustrates how dehumanization
dominates the natural order of Massachusetts prisons in which the harm translates
to and from our communities. Punishment beyond correction is a common way
society addresses deviancy throughout the American punishment system. Evolving
Standards explores how laws can be tailored to reverse a cyclical pattern of class discrimination, unequal opportunity, and a constant reproduction of the status quo, as

law currently serves as an agent of oppression by which communities are deprived of political power as illustrated:

> The less political power a community possesses, the fewer resources a community has to defend itself; the lower the level of community awareness and mobilization against potential ecological threats, the more likely they are to experience arduous environmental and human health problems at the hands of business and government.
>
> *(Faber & Krieg 2005, p. 1)*

The lifeblood of American democracy is representation. Growing up on Cleveland's west side, the only representation we had was each other. Selling illegal drugs was an accessible way for me and many of my peers to escape hardships from 'bare life' and live a life where we could afford to buy basic necessities and enjoy ourselves (Agamben 2005, pp. 1–4). Our association with laws was law enforcement oppressing us and preventing us from putting a stop to hunger pangs by trying to make a dollar the best way we knew how to. Bare life exists on society's margins, homeless shelters, 'inner cities,' and public housing projects, relegating us as naked physical beings without political, legal, or social status within our government, so structured on representation (Ogletree & Sarat 2012, p. 100). Faced with bare life conditions, I found growing up a constant fight for survival.

Evolving Standards combats government exclusion and overhauls failed practices of extending equity among disadvantaged populations. Bare life conditions allow for an old implicit form of what was called 'salutary neglect' to crop up, not only in my community, but in many other disadvantaged communities throughout America.

Salutary neglect is the government practice which leaves common people lawlessly taking their destinies into their own hands in a struggle for upward economic mobility. It's an unwritten policy which dates back to colonial times when colonists bucked British laws that governed trade regulations, as heavy taxation from the British Parliament via the Navigation Act of 1651 caused colonists to foment a sort of underworld economy (Brooks 2016). Analogous to our urban economic plight today, salutary neglect reappears when government failure gives cause for social deviancy to occur and then those who deviate become unfairly labeled as criminals. In the following, I briefly share some experiences I encountered growing up that have shaped my commitment to Evolving Standards. I share such experiences in the hopes of providing insight into how social factors perpetuated a school-to-prison pipeline for me and many others who come from similar backgrounds.

Evolving Standards (Part II)

When Saint John Street awakened, streetlamps would bring life throughout the night sky, illuminating the pearl-black tarred pavements as if they were glowing. Marijuana smoke drifted from sparkling smiles and danced alongside spurts of jeered laughter. The life and attraction of our neighborhood would peak around dice games where scores of men stood in huddled circles, crouched over crumpled bills.

Onlookers made side bets and gossiped about neighborhood politics, making each isolated event timeless in its own light. Every moment proved full of excitement as constant activity reproduced itself. It was another gleeful night on Saint John Street.

The love we shared among each other was strong and our communal spirit was like no other. Sitting atop big shiny rims, our cars stood like mini-castles drenched in candy-colored paint (allowing a constant appearance of wetness) as ground-shaking rhythms belted from door speakers, electrifying the night. Custom built rocket 350 engines roared alongside hypnotizing bass booming from elaborate sound systems wired throughout the American muscle cars we favored. Our cars sat clean, parked beside worn street curbs, creating a concert-like atmosphere. The amount of love and passion translated through a show of sophisticated vehicles was nothing short of impressive. But even more impressive was the unspoken sense of togetherness we shared which proved medicinal for our collective spirit as most of our parents were on drugs, in prison or just simply absent. All we had was each other. Despite our inability to recognize our poverty, environmental neglect, and/or the social pains we all confronted, we moved about wearing million-dollar smiles as if we had not a care in the world. Looking back, we were as graceful and rhythmic as the marijuana smoke we blew into the clouds that swiftly disappeared into the night sky. Unfortunately, many of our lives would also disappear into the night sky or, somewhere in distant cages far, far away from Saint John Street in years to come. I've never accepted many of the negative labels some assumed of us later in life because an image of joy, innocence and humanity within us always preceded any misconstrued image of a deviant response to the social conditions we endured. Unbeknownst to me at the time, we were already assumed, marked and branded simply by the conditions we were born into.

I was born in Cleveland, Ohio, which is where the greater part of my youth was lived. Up until about the age of seven, my life was pretty normal, although my parents were separated (I'm unable to recall a time when my biological parents were ever together despite them being once married). My mother's next relationship was with an abusive guy who she eventually married and had children with. Her husband's impulsive attitude in combination with his rejection of my older brother and me made growing up not easy. His increasing abuse, along with the deteriorating condition of my community throughout the 1990s, flipped my world upside down. It wasn't long before drugs began to flood my community, hitting Saint John Street (my street) and eventually finding their way into my household. The instability of my household caused me to be moved up and down the East Coast and I ricocheted between staying with my mother in Cleveland or my father who was always moving from state to state.

I was now 17 and had triangled between Cleveland, Ohio, Monck's Corner, South Carolina and Springfield, Massachusetts. The moves had been spontaneous, following spurts of conflict within my household. Now returning to Cleveland, after my father's place was no longer an available place for me to live, and learning that my mother's home had been raided by law enforcement (arresting her for allegedly aiding and abetting her husband, who'd been charged with armed robbery), I knew

I was returning to a world I had grown all too familiar with. The west side of Cleveland was not like I remembered it. It now mirrored the torn areas of other states I'd been living in as hardship from poverty had become a constant thread in all the states I had triangled throughout. I initially just needed money to survive.

As a young teenager, I did everything I could think of to make an honest dollar. I cut grass in the summer, raked leaves in the fall, and shoveled snow in the winter. I used to walk for blocks up 117th and Lorain Street into white neighborhoods, under blazing summer heat, lugging a lawn mower. In the freezing cold winter, I wielded a shovel over my shoulder seeking driveways to clear. And, in the fall, I sought yards to rake and leaves to bag. I had a set rate of $5 per yard. Some days I'd come back home with a whole $20 to $25, drained of all my energy. It was an all-year-around gig between going to school and playing with friends. After the work became unsustainable because of the intense labor, I began to look for formal work. Upon searching, I managed to get hired at Cleveland Metro Parks Zoo with a food service company called Ogden Entertainment. I remember waking at 4:00 in the morning to catch the Cleveland RTA bus to make it to work. There'd be countless times I'd miss the bus and find myself power walking, if not light jogging, all the way from Saint John Street to work. After some time, I realized the expenses of taking care of myself, supporting my siblings and affording peace of mind, whether it was going to the movies, buying food or purchasing clothing items that'd cheer us up, was impossible to do. I did not have enough money or time to do anything. Survive or suffer literally had been my reality until I decided to no longer suffer. I began selling weed.

Around this time, most of my friends had already began selling weed, cocaine or crack cocaine (cocaine cooked into its hardened form). In Cleveland, I learned an ounce of marijuana (28 grams) sold for $120. Where I was living in Springfield, Massachusetts, I could buy an ounce of weed for $60 or, if I wanted to purchase more, say a quarter pound (4 ounces), I could get it for $200. The profit would be great; my only problem was getting back and forth from state to state and risking the interstate trafficking charge, although getting caught was never a thought nor was it in my plans.

Violating a law never crossed my mind because it didn't exceed the urgency of having money to live. I actually had no knowledge of laws or how much time I could face by violating a law. In fact, I hated the law because it was the law that seemed to hate Black people. In my mind, it was the law that raised stress levels so high that many Black people turned to using and/or selling drugs. Even more pressing, it was the law that took my mother away from us when all she did was fall in love with the wrong guy. Whatever it was that I had nobody to blame directly for, I knew subconsciously the law and law enforcers likely had something to do with it. My relationship with the law was at the point where law became so oppressive it was no longer credible in my thought process and the only thing that governed my actions was my own law of survival.

If you were from my neighborhood and sold drugs other than weed, you did so elsewhere. Growing up, there was this Hollywood narrative that suggested all 'drug dealers' fell into a single category of heartless, ruthless 'criminals.' However, those adjectives never fit the description of people I knew who I called friends. We were just doing what we knew best to survive. As most of our parents had already either been kidnapped by law enforcement or themselves lulled into the user cycle to escape from daily reality, my generation had been faced with a dynamic of children being left to raise children. The rule proved to be either survive or suffer, in which children were compelled to go out into the late night hours and attempt to profit from selling a drug that was so powerful users would sell their soul if they could – just to get high. Or, there was a choice to starve and likely be shuffled through foster care or government shelters and suffer. It only made sense in most of our minds to survive.

Over time, I had found my rhythm as a survivor. Having made a larger connection while searching for a pound of weed to buy in Springfield, Massachusetts, I stumbled upon a cocaine connect. The demand for crack had been at every turn for me but I had previously been reluctant to sell crack. At the time, people were paying $1,000 for 28 grams (considered equal to an ounce) and my connection would only charge me $22 per gram for coke that appeared so pure it could be cut (diluted) with baking soda and recompressed, turning 28 grams into 56 grams. My only problem was I didn't know how to convert cocaine into crack. I had a friend in Springfield who could teach me, so I made it a point to stay and learn the process as I felt the skill had come as a windfall and would be my ticket out of struggle.

Months Later . . .

Somewhat skilled now, I was mindful to make sure the water temperatures matched between the water inside the pot and the stove I was placing the pot onto. Unequal temperatures could cause the bottom of the glass jar to collapse. I couldn't afford for that to happen again, it unfortunately happened a few times earlier when learning. I had to hurry and finish this batch, my phone had been ringing nonstop with people waiting for me to make drop-offs. I cooked 20 grams at a time because I didn't want to risk putting in too much coke and accidentally messing up – it was a precautionary step. I filled the small pot with cold water and placed it on the counter. Atop the counter, I unwrapped the plastic from the compressed pack of glimmering white powder, grabbing a silver tablespoon to break off a slab and place it on the awaiting digital scale. I weighed it until it read 20.0 grams exactly. Dipping my spoon into the Arm & Hammer box, I retrieved just enough baking soda to cover the bottom of the jar.

It was decompressed into powder form now. I carefully dumped the cocaine into the Smucker's jar and placed the jar inside the pot with cold water. As the water heated, I used my spoon to slowly stir the mix, closely watching as the baking soda combined with cocaine while I simultaneously dipped small teaspoons of hot water alongside the inner walls of the jar. Now as I was rapidly stirring, the coke began to rock up as the water heated and I continued to whip it faster and faster. I discovered the longer I left the now-hardened rock in the jar to consolidate the more excess baking soda would boil off, making the converted crack more concentrated. If I had taken the solid rock out the jar at first sight of consolidation, the excess baking soda would have increased my quantity of crack – I'd have more, but it'd be less potent. It was all street economics. A lot of young men like myself were selling crack to survive/thrive so, knowing how to cook crack, I had to go for quality over quantity to ensure I was the go-to guy when people wanted to get high. I was now eighteen years of age, and with both parents absent from my life, and nowhere to live, it was me against the world.

Meanwhile, Saint John Street had significantly deteriorated by this time. Houses had become dilapidated while wild possums and other rodents found shelter on littered curbs and other neglected spaces. It was saddening how environmental injustice had afflicted my neighborhood in the worst way. Not really much to be proud of, but once I became active in dealing crack, I held true to not selling it in my own neighborhood. Coming back to a torn-down unfamiliar place where my siblings and I, along with neighborhood friends, used to have the grandest times playing street football, doing random kid stuff and attending backyard cookouts where our parents would dance, drink liquor and listen to Motown hits all night was a traumatic change of scenery. It hurt to see my community in such a way.

Throughout the flash of time in my teenage years, I fortunately had a really nice girlfriend who really pushed me. She enrolled me into high school and encouraged me to finish and get my high school diploma. I succeeded. In the process, I managed to save up some money to help my siblings who were still young, and forwarded money to my mother who was serving time at Marysville State Prison. However, a long way away from those sparkling luminous nights on Saint John Street, I found myself in a distant world. It was 7 February of 2005 and I happened to be awaiting trial for murder and armed robbery charges along with two other alleged codefendants, fighting for my life. Sixteen years later, I'm still fighting – only now as a convicted offender within a maximum-security prison cell, inside a cage that's so easy to make it into but so hard to make it out of.

Evolving Standards (Part III)

An inner-city concept of salutary neglect was how I interfaced with the world around me. Structural racism and systemized oppression had been subtly interconnected with our everyday lives. The connection was not obvious to me initially; however, what my mind could process at a young age was "f★★★ the police," as their actions felt like the closest embodiment to racism I could identify. There were many dehumanizing events I experienced growing up, from how schoolteachers and principals excessively disciplined minority children for minor infractions, to overzealous prosecutors cornering friends from my neighborhood with excessive plea agreements to serve time within the punishment system. I knew most of our actions were influenced by our environments and I was sure (subconsciously) that authorities had everything to do with creating our difficult circumstances. It seemed like catching a case and having a criminal record was inevitable.

Criminalizing and systematically punishing Black and Brown bodies is American culture. While I've been incarcerated, the entire administration of every facility I've been held in has been made up of white staff. Same goes for every judge, prosecutor, police officer, and court-appointed attorney I've interacted with throughout my time trapped within the 'criminal' punishment system. My dissatisfaction is not so much with the lack of diversity of racial minorities who work in prisons and are compelled to carry out racist policies from their racist employers, but more so with how the degradation of Black life occurs across all social structures. Urbicide, which has been defined as "the murder of the city" and the "deliberate denial or killing of the city" (Berman 1987), occurs not only in urban communities but is furthered in American prisons. Prisons perpetuate the deliberate denial of growth and development by prioritizing punishment over all else, ultimately at the expense of urban communities.

Law and order is both racist and stratified. Following a violent incident involving incarcerated persons and staff at SBCC's maximum security prison in Massachusetts, where I'm currently incarcerated, administration began terrorizing the entire SBCC population from 10 January of 2020 up until the date of this writing (31 December of 2020). Shortly after the physical abuse calmed, I was interviewed by WBUR about the evolving crisis unfolding at SBCC (Becker 2020). I myself was violently assaulted by officers – tased, beaten, and knocked unconscious until I awoke in an outside hospital feeling my face being stitched together. When the interview aired some days later I listened to myself. I heard the Department of Corrections spokesperson Flanagan's response to the atrocious treatment I communicated. He stated: "They're *criminals*, who are in there for a reason, prison isn't supposed to be comfortable . . ." All I could do was shake my head in disgust.

'Criminal' is a code word for minorities as the majority of peoples branded as such are minority. Actions described as criminal often occur because people generally just want to live with dignity, not in constant struggle. However, because authorities fear and are insecure about the conditions they created, they criminalize entire communities to protect their own while they watch how our conditions persuade us to blindly harm each other in desperate fights for survival. I often question, how am I the minority of society but the majority of prison houses? Which is why when Black people come to these torture chambers called prisons and white officers beat us, call us niggers and have privileged white guys like Flanagan justifying it by calling us "criminals" to minimize the horror of it, it only solidifies the notion of "criminal" being a racist code word for Black and/or minority people.

Addressing race and attacking the idea of crime – or how American culture interprets race and its relation to social deviancy – is key to confronting America's amorphous spirit of racism. Racism camouflages itself in many different forms today. The most evident forms of racism and racial disparities flourish through the legal punishment system, education, gentrification, environmental justice, health care, unemployment, and disenfranchisement. Shifting an American culture of punishment must occur simultaneously with ending any policy, practice, or law that disproportionately impacts disadvantaged populations.

How We Influence Evolving Standards

Love. Living life without love, or without people who love you unconditionally, is a hard way of living. I know because I see it all around me and have experienced not feeling love at times, and being aware of how miserable life felt in those moments. Unconditional love is a powerful force. It means no matter what conditions one may be under or however miserable and disgraceful one may feel, the love will remain. This sort of love is usually only found in biological families, close friendships, or lifetime partnerships. However, it must become associated with justice in order for change to happen and come directly from government. Love is tenacious in the face of being wronged, it's concerned and pragmatic in the crux of uncontrollable addiction, and it cannot conceive an idea of something being irreconcilable. Unconditional love survives despite whatever conditions arise. A society that governs its people without love will always experience some form of pain or division because laws will inevitably favor the loved population and discriminate against all others. Unconditional love through practice is the answer: abolish criminology and bring forth a push towards evolving standards.

American democracy is structured on representative government. Laws are tailored to reflect the enfranchised population's image of society. Being incarcerated at age 19 within a county jail (November 2004) prevented me from participating in my first presidential election. I was released 22 December of 2004 and was rearrested on 7 of February 2005, charged with joint venture homicide along with two codefendants. Sixteen years later, I'm still fighting for absolute vindication in a punishment system that knows no other language than punishment. Never having an opportunity to vote in my entire life cast me as a label within a monstrous system which does not represent or reflect my imagination. Some of the state-decreed labels that surround me include "drug dealer," "robber," "murderer," "thief," "addict," and many more exclusive labels which don't include "human." However, the universal brand for deviation, inclusive of all labels, is "criminal." It's time we end branding and begin treatment.

Love as justice is treatment. It's seen in most European societies, isolated regions, and even some small, tight-knit towns in America where county sheriffs reprimand social deviancy with wise lessons, words of love, and no arrest or punishment. Justice as love looks like community building, analogous to the concept of environmental poverty law in which practitioners see environmental issues as opportunities to build broad social movements that will ultimately address other issues. Its goal is not solely to win the battle at hand but to empower the client community (Cole 1992). Love infused throughout the political process as well as the American legal system for justice is a preliminary step to evolving standards.

Conclusion

My experiences throughout life have shown me it takes people to bring out the best in people. In prison, administration operates with an infinite ruler of punishment for every action, despite incarcerated persons already living under punishing conditions. Endless punishment corrects nothing. Prisons only cause harm and must be abolished. For people trapped within this graveyard of exclusion (prison), gang affiliation proliferates simply because they identify gangs as being the closest thing to family. Prisons and punishment do not work.

Under Evolving Standards, resources used to punish children involved in the Department of Youth Services system would instead be used for early education, mental health services, prospects for higher education, and housing (for those who may not have family or residence). Meanwhile, incarcerated adults, in a world influenced by Evolving Standards, would no longer be incarcerated and instead be sheltered, educated, compensated for learning a marketable skill, and given an opportunity to critically engage, confront, and reflect on whatever social deviation they're charged with violating without being incarcerated. Such practices will promote dual restoration, breaking the social cycle of hurt people hurting other people. Evolving Standards focuses on fixing dignity-deprived social conditions that bring out the worst in people.

As a society, we are better than the status quo. Evolving Standards reflects the love we have for ourselves and our family to the human family through passionate policies, practices, and laws.

Works Cited

Agamben, G. (2005) *State of Exception* (trans. K. Attell). Chicago: The University of Chicago Press.

Albert L. Trop v. John Foster Dulles, Secretary of State, et al. 356 U.S. 86 (1958), Supreme Court of the United States.

Becker, D. (2020) "As Prisoners Allege Abuse, Mass. Lawmakers Make Unannounced Visit to Souza-Baranowski Prison." *WBUR*, 3 February. Available at www.wbur.org/news/2020/02/03/max-security-prison-souza-calls-for-investigation (accessed 15 April 2021).

Berman, M. (1987) "Among the Ruins." *The New Internationalists*, 178: 8–9. Also Available at https://newint.org/features/1987/12/05/among/ (accessed 15 April 2021).

Brooks, R. (2016) "What Was the British Policy of Salutary Neglect?" *History of Massachusetts Blog*. Available at https://historyofmassachusetts.org/what-was-the-british-policy-of-salutary-neglect/ (accessed 15 April 2021).

Cole, L. W. (1992) "Empowerment as the Key to Environmental Protection: The Need for Environmental Poverty Law." *Ecology Law Quarterly*, 19(4): 619–684.

Faber, D. R. and Krieg, E. J. (2005) "Unequal Exposure to Ecological Hazards, Environmental Injustices in the Commonwealth of Massachusetts." A Report by the Philanthropy and Environmental Justice Research Project, Northeastern University. Available at https://web.northeastern.edu/ejresearchnetwork/wp-content/uploads/2014/10/Final-Unequal-Exposure-Report-2005-10-12-05.pdf (accessed 15 April 2021).

Ogletree, C. J. and Sarat, A. (2012) *Life Without Parole: America's New Death Penalty?* New York: New York University Press.

7

TRANS BLACK WOMEN DESERVE BETTER

Expanding Queer Criminology to Unpack Trans Misogynoir in the Field of Criminology

Toniqua Mikell

First Things First: Protect Black Trans Women

The criminalization of Blackness and queerness, coupled with the misogynoir[1] entrenched in the fabric of a white hetero-patriarchal society, positions Black trans women[2] in the center of a very dangerous matrix of domination amid interlocking systems of oppression (Collins, 2004; Collins & Bilge, 2016). In November 2020, the Human Rights Campaign (HRC) reported that 37 transgender and gender-nonconforming people had been murdered in what is considered the deadliest year on record to date. Of those 37 victims, 25 are Black and/or Latinx trans women. Relatedly, at the time of this writing in March 2021, the HRC identified 2021 as the most legislatively dangerous year for trans people, with 82 anti-transgender bills introduced throughout the US. For context, 2020 saw 79 anti-trans bills filed over the entire year. Even with these alarming statistics, the queering of criminology studies and practices has alienated people most at risk for criminalization and victimization, specifically Black transgender women (Irvine, 2014). Throughout this chapter, I maintain that current approaches to feminist criminology do a disservice to the activism assumed inherent to feminism by not further incorporating a study of power and institutional structures that allow for systemic genocide against trans Black women – who continue to be central for queer liberation – at the hands of individual citizens, social and carceral institutions, public policy, and research (Russell & Carlton, 2013).

In a world where I acknowledge trans women as women, I also honor Black trans women as Black women. This reality implies, then, that Black trans women and femmes[3] have a "distinct set of experiences that offers a different view of material reality than that available to other groups" (Collins, 1989, p. 747). Furthermore, in the spirit of "it's handled" – as expressed by Black women everywhere – queer

DOI: 10.4324/9780367817114-10

women of Color, especially queer and trans Black women, have been the leaders of movements for the liberation of Black people and LGBTQIA+ people. From the blues women of the Harlem Renaissance (Chen, 2016), to gay liberation leader Marsha P. Johnson, to BlackLivesMatter frontrunners Alicia Garza, Opal Tometi, and Patrisse Cullors, queer Black women have always organized and pushed justice forward (Kiesling, 2017). In the face of Black queer resistance and resilience remains the fact that three out of four deadly anti-LGBTQIA+ hate crimes are committed against trans women and girls of Color (National Center for Transgender Equality, 2015); and this violence remains unacknowledged by the dominant society. Trans activist groups and organizations have proven, empirically, that there is a genocide happening against their communities' members. Criminology has been an unapologetic accessory to these murders by maintaining a direct relationship with policing and carceral violence, and by refusing to take up arms in the way that we study genocide perpetrated against transgender Black women.

Using an intersectional abolitionist lens, I challenge existing queer and feminist criminology paradigms arguing that white cisgender gay men have monopolized the public and academic understanding of queer experiences leading to research and policy that further marginalizes our queer communities' most valuable yet vulnerable people. I advocate for a queer criminology that rejects the idea of essentialism within LGBTQIA+ communities and accounts for the history, positionality, and social navigation of Black queer folks. I conclude with a discussion on the importance of abolitionist approaches and *truly* intersectional queer criminology to understanding carceral state violence against Black trans women.

From Criminalizing Queerness to Queering Criminology

Binary gender identities did not exist, as we currently understand them, in the Americas until European colonization (Beemyn, 2014). Modern views on patriarchal power structures, heterosexuality, monogamy, and dichotomized gender identity are white, Euro-Christian concepts dating back to colonizers equating Native people with biblical presentations of perversion and sinful sexuality. Labels of *perversion, criminal,* and *sinfulness* were the dominant view of LGBTQIA+ folks until the 1970s, though one could argue that, to varying degrees, these labels persist today. Indigenous peoples of the modern-day United States, Latin America, and the Caribbean did not have the rigid dichotomy of maleness and femaleness, man or woman that are generally assumed in today's dominant society. In fact, dichotomous gender assignments were used as a tool to categorize the utility of enslaved Africans and Indigenous populations in the Americas (Camp, 2018; Mogul, Ritchie, & Whitlock, 2011). Prior to their forced enslavement, Africans were also not as rigid in their gender identifications or labels of sexual orientation (Berry & Harris, 2018). As British colonizers forced their ideology and fascist values onto peoples around the world, many of those values reflected anti-homosexual sentiments fueled by religion and camouflaged as holiness (Buist & Lenning, 2015). The assignment of gender roles to sex-based characteristics are ingrained in WASP-based patriarchal ideas about men and women and the assignment of power. Those who exist outside those normative gender and sexuality conventions are subject to criminalization and state control (Stanley & Smith, 2015).

The historical understanding of LGBTQIA+ narratives within criminology has generally been situated between two prevailing approaches – the deviance-centered element and the invisibility element. The former is a lens focused on queer identities and lifestyles as deviant; the latter is a disappearance of any sort of LGBTQIA+ discussion from the field altogether (Woods, 2014). Queer criminology developed in response to these extremes, from the call for more critical approaches to studying and understanding crime committed by people who are not heterosexual or gender-conforming, beyond the assumption of sexual deviance (Ball, Buist, & Woods, 2014; Buist & Lenning, 2015; Panfil & Miller, 2014). It was not until the 1980s that scholars began to engage with social identities and power structures as factors significant to understanding queer people's criminalized behavior and victimization. Of the studies that address the social navigation of queer individuals, we (LGBTQIA+ people, myself included) have been presented as a monolithic "other" juxtaposed alongside assumed cisgender and heteronormative standards (Woods, 2014).[4] In the Ivory Tower, subdisciplines within gender and sexuality studies most certainly cover the victimization of LGBTQIA+ individuals, presumably including the disproportionate victimization of Black trans women following heightened awareness of the phenomenon. However, "the field of transgender studies, like other fields, seems to use this Black subject as a springboard to move toward other things, presumably white things" (Ellison, Green, Richardson, & Snorton, 2017). In other words, attention to queer BIPOC experiences is but a means to an ultimately white-positive end that centers the priorities of the power majority and keeps queer people of Color (QPOC) in the margins.

Similar to the way criminology has initiated moves away from an *add race* (or *sex*) *and mix* approach (Burgess-Proctor, 2006; Messerschmidt, 1997; Unnever & Gabbidon, 2011), so too does the field need to move beyond an *add gay and mix* methodology (Haritaworn, 2007; Panfil & Miller, 2015). This culture of checking a box for the sake of quantitative data analysis has resulted in the erasure of a substantial portion of queer individuals. Research done through a white cis–hetero lens that cherry-picks the inclusion or exclusion of others cannot and does not capture the realities of people who are not white, not cis-gender male, not heterosexual, nor any combination of the three. The reality of Black LGBTQIA+ narratives' absence from queer criminology is endemic not only of society generally but grossly endemic of the discipline as a whole. It is Black feminist theorizing (Collins, 2002; Davis, 1983; Gay, 2014; hooks, 1981; Lorde, 1984) that has provided the very basis upon which we have built intersectional frameworks. It is the work of Black feminists that has pushed to the forefront the matrix of domination that must be acknowledged if we are to dismantle white, cisgender, hetero-patriarchal supremacy.

Color-Evasiveness in QueerCrim: Rejecting Essentialism in LGBTQIA+ Communities

Gay liberation, as most commonly understood, began following the Stonewall riots of 1969.[5] The initial movement, rooted in retaliation against racist, sexist, and elitist policing, was led by Black trans and queer women, and has since been co-opted by white lesbian, gay, and bisexual people who have all but done a complete one-eighty of the movement's expressed goals (Bassichis, Lee, & Spade, 2011). The modern "gay agenda," with its focus on equality over equity, is largely decided on and executed by white, upper-class, gay men with the financial means and social privilege to do so. In turn, battles being fought supposedly on behalf of queer communities tend not to include QPOC, trans folks, or working-class and poor queer people – to the particular detriment of Black trans women, who are most likely to exist at the intersection of all three. The mainstream gay agenda fights for the white privilege of "equality" in acceptance, marriage, and nuclear familyhood while simultaneously perpetuating and benefiting from the same carceral systems that victimize and marginalize oppressed peoples (Saffin, 2015). Even the most radical LGBTQIA+ organizations have drawn from the social movements long employed by Black people and the working class – especially Black, working-class women – yet continue to deny voices of poor QPOC (Bassichis, Lee, & Spade, 2011). Racism against Black people within the LGBTQIA+ community is equally, if not more violent than racism inherent in other pockets of American society and global anti-Blackness (Saffin, 2015).

As I write this essay, I am reminded of the time when adding Black and Brown stripes to the rainbow pride flag was such a visceral offense to white gay people during Pride Month in 2017. Symbolic representation of Black and Brown people was so egregious to gay white people who now felt that they were being excluded from an otherwise unifying symbol. This claim is not unlike more recent arguments implying that expanded protections for marginalized populations have somehow reduced white rights overall (Isom, Mikell, & Boehme, 2021). And, because gayness is perceived as more acceptable as long as it is cloaked in a race-neutral (read: white) body, demarginalizing QPOC allegedly jeopardizes otherwise successful campaigns for gay liberation. By keeping Black and Brown queer folks in the periphery, white gay men and white lesbians communicate notions to the heterosexual power majority that they are "regular" people who just happen to be gay. This effectively disconnects lesbian and gay liberation from Black liberation.

Queer policies actively avoid being tied to Blackness and poor/working-class people, despite queer progress being made on the backs of low-income Black queer and trans activists. Separating increasingly criminalized Black people from decreasingly stigmatized queer lifestyles has resulted in the erasure of Black queer people, especially those who are transgender or gender-nonconforming, from LGBTQIA+ narratives. This sort of colorblind (or color-evasive) intersectionality, as described by Carbado (2019), requires that LGBTQIA+ civil rights faces be "gay like a white heterosexual man" – in other words, they must access liberation by looking white and acting straight (p. 213). To illustrate the monopoly of white issues in LGBT-QIA+ activism, consider the following: the first openly gay soldier to successfully challenge the US military's Don't Ask, Don't Tell policy was a Black man named Perry Watkins. Yet the face of the 1993 campaign against the policy was a white navy man named Keith Meinhold (Carbado, 2019). The first couple to appeal for same-sex marriage, in 1993, was an interracial lesbian couple. However, the face of marriage equality in 2015, James Obergefell, is a white man – this despite the diversity of the claimants in the *Obergefell v. Hodges* (2015) landmark case. White LGBTQIA+ advocacy groups have not only erased strides initiated by QPOC, but have also remained largely silent on the racism and violence experienced by Black and Brown people, in general. For example, the 2009 Matthew Shepard and James Byrd Jr. Hate Crimes Prevention Act (the Matthew Shepard Act) – named after and in response to two hate crimes that took place in 1998, the first a gay white man tortured in Wyoming and the second a Black man lynched by white supremacists in Texas – received general support from the public due, at least in part, to the icon of the act being a seemingly "normal" young white man who *just happens* to be gay. Though this chapter does not attempt to encourage "oppression Olympics," it should not be lost on us that the naming of the act, in full and in short, carries primarily Matthew Shepard's name and underscores the value of whiteness in relation to awareness and action. A tragically sad reality is that Black people are routinely terrorized and victimized by regular citizens, suffer substantially from state-sanctioned violence, and are never protected with the same gusto or outrage as our white counterparts. Instead, people who are racialized as Black are criminalized and portrayed as magnets for violence despite any information to the contrary.

Some advocacy groups, though, reject hate crime laws meant to protect queer people because they actually make LGBTQIA+ communities and people much more visible and subject to surveillance (Panfil, 2018), suggesting instead a dismantling of hate crime legislation that calls for enhanced sentences for targeted violence towards certain groups of people (Lambel, 2015). However, BIPOC have always known that increased legal presence does not protect us. The historical and contemporary lynching of Black folks is a constant reminder that the law is not for our protection, but for our control and death. Therefore, enhancing punishment does not undo nor does it address the various -*isms* weaved into the fabric of society. Echoing Stanley and Smith (2015), "[P]rison abolition must be one of the centers of trans and queer liberations struggles" (p. 12). To that end, it cannot be overstated that any number of years in prison increased via hate crime sentencing enhancement laws does nothing to dismantle the white supremacy, heterocentrism, or misogynoir that led to the violence. Instead, it does the opposite – strengthening the power of the state to punish, thereby, expanding the reach of the carceral state.

The Necessity of Abolitionist QueerCrim

The violence of the criminal legal system at each stage is a reformation of a process rooted in chattel slavery and slave catching, with the punitive reach of the state driven and sustained by carceral systems that extend far beyond the physical prison space (Stanley & Smith, 2015). As this system, like so many before it, seeks to reinforce racial, gender, and sexual control, the prison industrial complex "harms trans and gender-non-conforming and queer people" and "produces the gender binary and heteronormativity" (Stanley & Smith, 2015, p. 12). The inherent violence of implicitly or explicitly carceral spaces means that the pathway to abolition must decenter white experiences as universal and "displace heterosexuality and gender normativity as measures of worth" (Stanley & Smith, 2015, p. 14). As trans Black women are subjects targeted for genocide, an abolitionist queer criminology is imperative. We must move beyond viewing *hate* as the driving motivator behind anti-trans or anti-Black hate crimes. We must recognize that transphobia, racism, sexism, and heterocentrism is endemic to U.S. social structures. Individual acts of hatred and malice are but illustrations and examples of larger structural messages that paint not-white/cis/hetero/male bodies as violable, expendable, exploitable, and exterminable. Abolitionist trans and queer approaches are in the best interest of the LGBTQIA+ community at large, and are particularly salient for the justice that Black trans women are often denied (Lambel, 2015).

LGBTQIA+ individuals, especially those who are transgender, are often exposed to carceral spaces from an early age. Parents' disproval or suppression of a child's sexuality or gender can foster negative familial relationships, home instability, neglect, and abuse (Fedders, 2013; Stanley & Smith, 2015). Negativity experienced within the homes of queer or gender-nonconforming youths lends itself to the likelihood of the child either running away or being kicked out of their home, which leads to disproportionately higher risks of homelessness for LGBTQIA+ young people (Knauer, 2013). For many LGBTQIA+ youth, unstable housing and/or homelessness persists into adulthood, accompanied by cycles of poverty, unemployment, and informal-economy involvement. Because the carceral state criminalizes being poor, the criminalization of survival is borne heavily on Black and Brown people and LGBTQIA+ folks, who are more likely to hold lower socioeconomic statuses. Those at the intersections of these identities are especially vulnerable. Homelessness exposes LGBTQIA+ individuals to increased harassment and sexual and physical victimization, including at the hands of police officers. Crimes of survival – prostitution, selling drugs, or theft – increase the risk of carceral state involvement by making LGBTQIA+ people more visible to police and more likely to come into contact with law enforcement. After initial contact with police, queer youth are more likely to be held in pretrial detention, perceived as flight risks due to records of running away to escape harassment and abuse, as well as the assumption that they are sexual predators from whom the community needs protection (Holsinger & Hodge, 2016; Majd, Marksamer, & Reyes, 2009).

Research has shown that police intentionally target LGBTQIA+ youth based on their perceived sexuality or expressed gender identity (Majd, Marksamer, & Reyes, 2009). Queer folks' bodies, mannerisms, and language are implicitly and explicitly sexualized, racialized, gendered, and scrutinized. Generally, police read and interpret the bodies of LGBTQIA+ individuals as not-heteronormative and interact with them based on those interpretations (Dwyer, 2009, 2011). In particular, trans women are especially vulnerable to have their identities overpoliced based on ill-informed reading of their bodies. Police interpretations of gender performance are particularly salient for Black trans folks, who are almost twice as likely to be assumed sex workers as the general transgender population, with trans women of Color being significantly more likely to be suspected and arrested for sex work (James et al., 2016).

Studies have also shown that QPOC are disproportionately targeted for "crimes against nature" offenses (Buist & Lenning, 2015). Queer people of Color, particularly Black and Brown adolescents, are more likely to be arrested for, charged with, and convicted of sex crimes classified as *morals regulations, quality of life* offenses, and *crimes against nature* (Fedders, 2013), which effectively criminalizes being a lesbian, gay, bisexual, trans, or queer person. QPOC, especially Black and multiracial women and poor folks, are disproportionately charged and convicted of such crimes and forced to register as sex offenders – a label that has tremendous sociolegal implications and collateral consequences. Constant entanglement with the criminal legal system reinforces the cycle of homelessness and criminalized modes of survival that are already heavily policed. This process is both a contribution to and outcome of the prison industrial complex and increases the power that the police state maintains over BIPOC, poor people, and trans/gender-nonconforming individuals – the very people whose backs continue to be the bridge to social justice (Stanley & Smith, 2015). The National Center for Transgender Equality reports that almost one-fourth of trans and gender-nonconforming folks have been harassed by police and nearly 40 percent of Black people within this category experience police harassment. Yet, the violent policing of QPOC is an issue that is either blocked from gay advocacy campaigns as a Black problem or hidden within an assumption that "sensitivity training" is sufficient in addressing police harassment of all LGBTQIA+ people (Bassichis, Lee, & Spade, 2011). Even reporting victimization to police seems to result in negative outcomes and police interactions that are discriminatory, homophobic, or transphobic when addressing LGBTQIA+ concerns (Dwyer, 2011; James et al., 2016; Wolff & Cokely, 2007). The 2015 US Transgender Survey reported that 57 percent of transgender people are afraid to go to the police even when they need to. This number increases to more than two-thirds for Black transgender individuals (James et al., 2016); unsurprising, considering the historical and contemporary abuses of power imposed on Black communities by law enforcement. Those who navigate the world in a middle-class nonracialized, cisgender-conforming body do not bear the weight of social controls in place for those who need the most protection from state-sanctioned violence.

Of all justice-involved queer individuals, one could argue that trans folks suffer substantially more due to indifference of court actors. In addition to blatant bias and prejudice towards LGBTQIA+ individuals, many children's prison workers claim to not understand what it means to be transgender, nor do they honor how it is different from being lesbian, gay, or bisexual (Majd, Marksamer, & Reyes, 2009). As a result of their ambivalence, lawyers, judges, and prison workers are unprepared, or perhaps unwilling, to meet the needs of trans youth or provide supportive services (Marksamer, 2008). LGBTQIA+ individuals, both children and adults, in prisons are subjected to verbal, sexual, and physical victimization from other incarcerated persons and prison workers, they receive differential treatment from staff, and they are denied various support services (Estrada & Marksamer, 2006). Across adult and child prison systems, incarcerated queer people report higher rates of abuse based on their sexuality or gender while under punitive supervision (James et al., 2016). Appropriate trainings and antidiscrimination policies to protect LGBTQIA+ individuals in prisons and jails are largely absent, and these institutions are ill equipped to provide proper care and services, which leads to extensive emotional, physical, and sexual abuse of incarcerated queer people (Holsinger & Hodge, 2016; Majd, Marksamer, & Reyes, 2009). Abused prisoners are often moved to isolated protective custody (read: solitary confinement) with little attention being paid to the actual abusers or the dangers of long-term isolation.

Prisons are particularly dangerous for trans youths and adults. Jails and prisons are sex-segregated and transgender individuals are often placed based on their sex assigned at birth, not their actual gender. The National Center for Transgender Equality's US Transgender Survey finds that incarcerated transgender individuals report high rates of physical and sexual abuse from other prisoners and prison guards (James et al., 2016). These numbers are especially staggering for Black transgender prisoners – 40 percent report physical assault from guards or other prisoners and 20 percent have experienced sexual assault from prison guards (James et al., 2016). The brutality of prison is criminogenic and does not rehabilitate the so-called offender or the community to which they may belong. Confinement neither prevents people from further offending nor does it protect those placed under the "care" of the state.

For queer BIPOC, the prison is a dangerous space that perpetuates violence, upholds heteronormative assumptions about sexuality and gender, maintains LGBT-QIA+ entrenchment with the carceral state, and reinforces white supremacy. Like many low-income Black and Brown folks who enter prison, the factors that contribute to queer people's involvement in crime are still present upon release back into society. Trans Black women return to a society with institutional structures that favor those who are wealthy, white, and male through state-sanctioned and state-supported violence that keeps trans folks, Black people, and women in the margins.

Conclusions

Feminist and queer criminology scholars must expand their intersectional scopes considering that race and gender expression – especially within an assumption of white male heteronormativity – are immediate markers of how white peo-ple identify someone as an "other," more specifically an "other" to be oppressed and criminalized (Isom Scott, 2018; Mogul, Ritchie, & Whitlock, 2011). Color-blind essentialist approaches towards a queering of criminology in which offend-ing and victimization are unilaterally structured "gay issues" do not address systemic power structures – which are gendered, racialized, and sexualized – that criminalize nonbinary, gender-nonconforming, and transgender people and ultimately advance white hetero-patriarchal supremacy. For transgender persons, the matrix of domina-tion serves as an elephant of interwoven otherness in a room of cis-hetero white privilege. To that end, queer criminology's advancement must be decolonized and include Black feminism, particularly Black feminist criminology, at its core. Queer criminology scholars have highlighted the importance of intersectional frameworks with the acknowledgment of race, class, sexuality, and gender intersections in an effort to interrogate the assumption of whiteness in lesbian, gay, and queer research and decolonize the discipline as a whole (Ball, 2016, 2019; Ball, Buist, & Woods, 2014). Though, it is important to acknowledge that calling for more work in an area does not necessarily always translate to the work being done.

Like most things in a Western setting, Black women and femmes have led the way with little acknowledgment, reward, or protection. Queer Black scholars and widely cited Black feminists are the lead voices in what we now study as queer criminology. Yet, current queer criminology works do little to draw from the likes of Black queer studies and Black feminist thought. Academe has leached off the backs of Black women – our labor and intellect –in virtually every field to build up disciplines that ultimately disrespect us, ignore us, and take credit for our efforts. Black feminist theory is central to the study and evolution of criminology, queer theory, Black queer theory, and transgender studies. In a society that crimi-nalizes every aspect of Black trans women's lives, bodies, and being – especially race, class, gender, and sexuality – criminology must be disrupted and rebuilt in a way that recognizes these interwoven sources of oppression. It is impera-tive that queer and feminist criminology pay attention to the ways that all Black women – queer, cisgender, trans, femme – are harmed, oppressed, and killed by the carceral state.

Notes

1 "Misogynoir" (a portmanteau of *misogyny* and *noir*) is anti-Black, racist hatred of women experienced, uniquely, by Black women (Bailey, 2010).
2 In some writings, the alternative spelling of *womxn* is used to reiterate women as individu-als independent of men (as the traditional spelling implies dependence) and to represent an intersectional feminism that was being ignored within white feminist circles using the spelling *womyn*. However, this spelling is avoided in this work because I elect to lift up trans women as women and honor their specific experiences as women in varying loca-tions along the gender and sexuality spectrums. While the spelling of woman/women is an unfortunate side effect of patriarchal control over language, it is important to the overall aims of my work not to perpetuate the othering or exclusion of trans women through alternative spellings.

3 "Femme" has traditionally referred to feminine-presenting lesbians, in contrast to masculine-presenting (butch) women. However, the language has evolved wherein femme can refer to any range of femininities that are resistant to patriarchal definitions of femininity (Hoskin, 2017).
4 See Woods (2014) for a complete lineage of criminology's engagement with the study of LGBTQIA+ people across theories and time.
5 Stonewall was not the literal beginning of the contemporary gay liberation movement but one of several movements at the time in protest of police brutality experienced by queer folks of Color.

References

Bailey, M., 2010. "They aren't talking about me", *Crunk Feminist Collective*, 14.
Ball, M.J., 2016. "Towards a decolonisation of queer criminology", *British Society of Criminology, London,* 16, pp. 6–19.
Ball, M.J., 2019. "Unsettling queer criminology: Notes towards decolonization", *Critical Criminology*, 27(1), pp. 145–161.
Ball, M.J., Buist, C.L. and Woods, J.B., 2014. "Introduction to the special issue on queer/ing criminology: New directions and frameworks", *Critical Criminology*, 22, pp. 1–4.
Bassichis, M., Lee, A. and Spade, D., 2011. "Building an abolitionist trans and queer movement with everything we've got", in Stanley, E.A. and Smith, N. (eds.) *Captive Genders Trans Embodiment and the Prison Industrial Complex*. AK Press, pp. 15–40.
Beemyn, G., 2014. "Transgender history in the United States", in Erickson-Schroth, L. (ed.) *Trans Bodies, Trans Selves: A Resource for the Transgender Community*. Oxford University Press.
Berry, D.R. and Harris, L.M. eds., 2018. *Sexuality and Slavery: Reclaiming Intimate Histories in the Americas*. University of Georgia Press.
Buist, C. and Lenning, E., 2015. *Queer Criminology*. Routledge.
Burgess-Proctor, A., 2006. "Intersections of race, class, gender, and crime future directions for feminist criminology", *Feminist Criminology*, 1(1), pp. 27–47.
Camp, S.M.H., 2018. "Early European views of African bodies: Beauty", in Berry, D.R. and Harris, L.M. (eds.) *Sexuality and Slavery: Reclaiming Intimate Histories in the Americas*. University of Georgia Press, pp. 9–32.
Carbado, D., 2019. "Colorblind intersectionality", in Crenshaw, K., Harris, L., HoSang, D. and Lipsitz, G. (eds.) *Seeing Race Again Countering Colorblindness Across the Disciplines*. University of California Press, pp. 200–223.
Chen, E., 2016. "Black face, queer space: The influence of black lesbian & transgender blues women of the Harlem renaissance on emerging queer communities", *Historical Perspectives: Santa Clara University Undergraduate Journal of History*, Series II, 21(1), p. 8.
Collins, P.H., 1989. "The social construction of black feminist thought", *Signs: Journal of Women in Culture and Society*, 14(4), pp. 745–773.
Collins, P.H., 2002. *Black Feminist Thought: Knowledge, Consciousness, and the Politics of Empowerment*. Routledge.
Collins, P.H., 2004. *Black Sexual Politics: African Americans, Gender, and the New Racism*. Routledge.
Collins, P.H. and Bilge, S., 2016. *Intersectionality*. Polity.
Davis, A., 1983. *Women, Race & Class*. Vintage Publisher.
Dwyer, A., 2009. "Identifiable, queer and risky: The role of the body in policing experiences for LGBT young people", in *Proceedings of the 2009 Australian and New Zealand Critical Criminology Conference*. Monash University Criminology, School of Political and Social Inquiry, pp. 69–77.

Dwyer, A., 2011. "It's not like we're going to jump them': How transgressing heteronormativity shapes police interactions with LGBT young people", *Youth Justice*, 11(3), pp. 203–220.

Ellison, T., Green, K.M., Richardson, M. and Snorton, C.R., 2017. "We got issues toward a black trans*/studies", *TSQ: Transgender Studies Quarterly*, 4(2), pp. 162–169.

Estrada, R. and Marksamer, J., 2006. "Lesbian, gay, bisexual, and transgender young people in state custody: Making the child welfare and juvenile justice systems safe for all youth through litigation, advocacy, and education", *Temple Law Review*, 79, p. 415.

Fedders, B., 2013. "LGBT youth in the child welfare and juvenile justice systems: Charting a way forward", *Temple Political & Civil Rights Law Review*, 23, p. 431.

Gay, R., 2014. *Bad Feminist: Essays*. Harper Perennial.

Haritaworn, J., 2007. "Shifting positionalities: Empirical reflections on queer/trans of colour methodology", *Sociological Research Online*, 13(1).

Holsinger, K. and Hodge, J.P., 2016. "The experiences of lesbian, gay, bisexual, and transgender girls in juvenile justice systems", *Feminist criminology*, 11(1), pp. 23–47.

hooks, b., 1981. *Ain't I A Woman: Black Women and Feminism*. South End Press.

Hoskin, R. A., 2017. "Femme theory: Refocusing the intersectional lens", *Atlantis: Critical Studies in Gender, Culture & Social Justice*, 38(1), 95–109.

Irvine, A., 2014. "You can't run from the police: Developing a feminist criminology that incorporates black transgender women", *Southwestern Law Review*, 44, p. 553.

Isom, D.A., Mikell, T.C. and Boehme, H.M., 2021. "White America, threat to the status quo, and affiliation with the alt-right: A qualitative approach", *Sociological Spectrum*, pp. 1–16.

James, S., Herman, J., Rankin, S., Keisling, M., Mottet, L. and Anafi, M., 2016. *The Report of the 2015 U.S. Transgender Survey*. National Center for Transgender Equality.

Kiesling, E., 2017. "The missing colors of the rainbow: Black queer resistance", *European Journal of American Studies*, 11(11–3).

Knauer, N.J., 2013. "LGBT youth: Reconciling pride, family, and community", *Temple Political & Civil Rights Law Review*, 23, p. 297.

Lambel, S. 2015. "Transforming carceral logics: 10 Reasons to dismantle the prison industrial complex using a queer/trans analysis", in Stanley, E.A. and Smith, N. (eds.) *Captive Genders Trans Embodiment and the Prison Industrial Complex*. AK Press, pp. 269–300.

Lorde, A., 1984. "The master's tools will never dismantle the master's house", *Sister Outsider: Essays and Speeches*, 1, pp. 10–14.

Majd, K., Marksamer, J. and Reyes, C., 2009. "Hidden injustice: Lesbian, gay, bisexual and transgender youth in juvenile courts". *Equity Project*, [Online]. Available at https://www.ojp.gov/ncjrs/virtual-library/abstracts/hidden-injustice-lesbian-gay-bisexual-and-transgender-youth

Marksamer, J., 2008. "And by the way, do you know he thinks he's a girl? The failures of law, policy and legal representation for transgender youth in juvenile delinquency courts", *Sexuality Research & Social Policy*, 5(1), p. 72.

Messerschmidt, J., 1997. *Crime as Structured Action: Gender, Race, Class, and Crime in the Making*. Sage.

Mogul, J.L., Ritchie, A.J. and Whitlock, K., 2011. *Queer (in) Justice: The Criminalization of LGBT People in the United States* (Vol. 5). Beacon Press.

National Center for Transgender Equality, 2015. *A Blueprint for Equality: A Federal Agenda for Transgender People*, [Online]. Available at https://transequality.org/sites/default/files/docs/resources/NCTE_Blueprint_June2015.pdf

Obergefell v Hodges, 576 U.S., 2015, [Online]. Available at. https://supreme.justia.com/cases/federal/us/576/14-556/

Panfil, V.R., 2018. "Young and unafraid: Queer criminology's unbounded potential", *Palgrave Communications*, 4(110).

Panfil, V.R. and Miller, J., 2014. "Beyond the straight and narrow: The import of queer criminology for criminology and criminal justice", *The Criminologist*, 39(4), pp. 1–9.

Panfil, V.R. and Miller, J., 2015. "Feminist and queer perspectives on qualitative methods", in *The Routledge Handbook of Qualitative Criminology*. Routledge.

Russell, E. and Carlton, B., 2013. "Pathways, race and gender responsive reform: Through an abolitionist lens", *Theoretical Criminology*, 17(4), pp. 474–492.

Saffin, L., 2015. "Identities under siege: Violence against transpersons of color", in Stanley, E.A. and Smith, N. (eds.) *Captive Genders Trans Embodiment and the Prison Industrial Complex*. AK Press, pp. 161–182.

Scott, D.I., 2018. "Latina fortitude in the face of disadvantage: Exploring the conditioning effects of ethnic identity and gendered ethnic identity on Latina offending", *Critical Criminology*, 26(1), pp. 49–73.

Stanley, E.A. and Smith, N. eds., 2015. *Captive Genders. Trans Embodiment and the Prison Industrial Complex*. AK Press.

Unnever, J.D. and Gabbidon, S.L., 2011. *A Theory of African American Offending: Race, Racism, and Crime*. Taylor & Francis.

Wolff, K.B. and Cokely, C.L., 2007. "To protect and to serve? An exploration of police conduct in relation to the gay, lesbian, bisexual, and transgender community", *Sexuality and Culture*, 11(2), pp. 1–23.

Woods, J.B., 2014. "Queering criminology: Overview of the state of the field", in *Handbook of LGBT Communities, Crime, and Justice*. Springer, pp. 15–41.

8

BARRIO CRIMINOLOGY

Chicanx and Latinx Prison Abolition

Xuan Santos, Oscar F. Soto, Martin J. Leyva, and Christopher Bickel

> *"Oye Loco, El mundo es un Barrio, Homie!"*
> ("Hey Crazy, The world is a neighborhood, Homie!")
> – DJ Muggs and Sick Jacken

Martin Leyva thought stepping off the bus and walking onto the college campus was difficult. That had me feeling overwhelmed, and it had been the first time I felt a flight response. Not even in prison or the barrio did I feel a flight or freeze response, it was all about the fight. However, on the first day of school, as a Chicano, with my baggy Dickies, black baggy t-shirt, Chucks (Converse), and a baseball cap, I felt frozen. People noticed me; I stood out. The jura (police) stopped me on campus to ask me where I was going, and they didn't believe me that I was a student. With visible tattoos throughout my body, arms, hands, neck, face, and head, the jura pointed me out. My dress code and tattoos are a barrio marker; they are my armor. Furthermore, on the college campus, I felt like a target for cops and teachers alike. I felt uneasy in the prison system, [but] I knew how to navigate it. The university reminded me that I'm a cultural outsider. I did not know how to navigate that academic social world.

The Roses That Grow From the Barrio

In the United States, the reproduction and maintenance of a white, homogeneous, nationalistic identity pushes marginalized groups into second-class citizenship, which often, if not entirely, devalues their existence as a people. This subordination erases their voices from the literature, academia, and conventional criminological thought. The barrio, a geopolitical space often composed of predominantly

DOI: 10.4324/9780367817114-11

Spanish-speaking poor working-class people, often is depicted as violent, menacing, and a burden to society, which, in essence, justifies the state's punitive, heavy-handed policing, super-surveillance and mass imprisonment. Chicanx[1] and Latinx people[2] who predominantly reside in the barrios, continue to experience systematic oppression, while barrio activists seek to abolish institutional racism and punitive social control. The continued funneling of Chicanx and Latinx people, the second-largest population in the United States, into social control institutions like prisons, schools, segregated barrios, and immigrant detention centers, makes this a concerning topic. Under this capitalist system, captivity limits people's life chances (Bickel, 2010) by creating a buffer between "civil society" and the "Brown cage."[3] This chapter explores how Latinx and Chicanx barrios promote opposition to the discourse that privileges white society. We argue that barrio spaces nurture critical thought and revolutionary politics geared toward promoting systemic change. As formerly incarcerated and system-impacted scholars, we seek to abolish all prisons, the police, and capitalism, an often-unpopular standpoint in academia, media, and conventional criminology.

Often funneled and segregated into ethnic enclaves known as *barrios*, Chicanx and Latinx people come from working-class poor, immigrant, and predominantly Spanish-speaking backgrounds. Barrios provide Chicanx and Latinx people with a sense of community, collective pride, and relatively affordable housing. They act as important transition neighborhoods for new immigrants (Castañeda, 2019). With its dilapidated and low-income housing and weakened infrastructure caused by historical segregation, neglect, and disenfranchisement, the barrio comes to symbolize a geopolitical space with massive government disinvestment.[4] The media focuses on the inhumane living arrangements of "these people," often masking the barrio's ever-abundant cultural wealth. We find value in all cultural traditions and barrio residents. For example, *paleterxs*,[5] *eloterxs*,[6] and *murales*[7] all constitute important identity and cultural markers of the unique barrio geopolitical space, challenging the urban and rural imaginary. Barrios represent, according to Gina A. Pérez (2017),

> a geopolitical space born out of histories of segregation, uneven development, conflict, and marginalization. Still, they are also the precious spaces that affirm cultural identities, nurture popular cultural production, and provide sanctuary for people with long histories of displacement, land loss, repression, and collective struggle.

In essence, the Chicanx and Latinx barrios emerged from places vacated by predominantly white and upwardly mobile residents (Moore, 1991). Barrioization ignited "white flight," meaning that when large numbers of Mexican, Chicanx, and Latinx people moved into white communities, such as Los Angeles in the mid-1900s, whites relocated to the suburbs to feel a sense of safety (PBS, 2017; Hernandez, 2017; Sanchez, 1995). Today, barrio gentrification marks the return of white people, resulting in the increased assault against barrio residents living in a super-criminalized, 24/7 surveilled, and punitive space where residents confront draconian measures to protect white people, like preemptive strikes against immigrants, gang-involved persons, and the entire Chicanx and Latinx community.

Both Robinson (2018) and Gilmore (2007) show the link between capitalism, incarceration, and surplus humanity. They show how the global political economy played a major role in the prison boom since the 1960s, super-policing, and coercive control via mass incarceration. Robinson (2018) refers to mass incarceration as the global police state. These coercive and punitive control tactics exclusively target specific communities (Wacquant, 2009, 2002, 2001). Robinson suggests that the barrio's 24/7 surveillance, saturated policing, and high incarceration rate, coupled with vast numbers of unemployed and underemployed (or "surplus humanity") push Chicanx and Latinx people into the informal economy – economic activities that are not regulated or protected by the state – such as selling drugs and street vending. This informal economic activity becomes super-policed and super-criminalized. To add insult to injury, barrios confront intergenerational trauma and oppression caused by anti-Chicanx and anti-Latinx legislation, gang injunctions, police repression, immigration raids and checkpoints, poverty, and criminalization. Yet the barrio represents hopeful spaces where we fight against global capitalism and systemic oppression, even as *barrios* emerge as factories manufacturing excess surplus humanity, contentious spaces impacted by the prison industrial complex, gang injunctions, and super-policing. Barrio liberation produces an intellectual tradition that challenges systemic oppression, such as abolishing global capitalism from below.

Barrios become spaces of struggle with abundant cultural and intellectual wealth. Some members of the Chicanx and Latinx community challenge police repression, poverty, and marginalization. Barrios are more than just; Spanish-speaking neighborhoods; they are places composed of vibrant and multicultural communities. Barrios comprise different subcultures that embody and embrace different cultural traditions and group identities, including, but not limited to, immigrants, refugees, and poor Black and Brown people. All these different identities present a challenge to the state's institutional racism and heteronormativity. Thus, to control these identities and barrios, the state pushes for super-criminalization, and super-surveillance through gang injunctions, harassment, and super-policing. Our argument here is that in order to abolish criminal injustice, we must include the voices of those directly impacted by the criminal (in)justice system.

Within prison walls and our barrios, uncredentialed persons and elders with lived experience provide a liberation pedagogy that rests outside of academia. Leyva described the gulag's influential leaders as "cellblock intellectuals," critical self-taught prison scholars with institutional power to redefine education. Caged persons "get schooled" in both the penitentiary and the streets. Cellblock intellectuals offer alternative education to individuals who do not attend formal prison education courses by referencing their joint and barrio knowledge. Men and women become "knowledge givers" and recipients who exchange critical cellblock and critical barrio perspectives, which challenge the systemic status quo. "Critical cellblock intellectualism is the process by which incarcerated people read books they can get their hands on, and engage in deep, intellectual conversations outside of traditional classrooms" (Leyva, 2018). These intellectual practices incorporate barrio oral histories transmitted to youngsters to liberate the barrio and abolish the prison industrial complex.

How can we create an inclusive abolitionist space when barrio constituents remain invisible in the struggle? Academia, prisons, and the community itself continue to dehumanize, exclude, and marginalize members who have radical, revolutionary, and abolitionist ideological thought. Conventional criminology and literature fail to include radical members of the Latinx and Chicanx communities, especially activists directly coming from poor barrios and directly impacted by the criminal (in)justice system. Those chosen to represent Latinx and Chicanx communities come from affluent communities and have never stepped foot inside prisons, jails, or even barrios. The Latinx aristocracy often advocates for reform, rather than abolition. These "honorary white" and white-passing academics of color have become the "voice of reason," representing our communities and having no investment in abolition, political change, or systemic change. These "poster children," tokenized for being Latinx and Chicanx, have become part of the status quo and research our communities as part of their higher education. We do not seek to reinvent the inclusion struggle wheel. Other people attempt to make this field more inclusive, like the Latina/o/x Criminology group Latcrim (2020), mostly comprising Latinx students (undergraduate and graduate) and faculty in the US.

Similarly, barrio criminologists seek to broaden the criminology scope by shedding light on a subset of working-class, formerly and currently incarcerated persons: the system-impacted people and nonacademic voices who rest on the social margins within the Chicanx and Latinx community. We seek to introduce a barrio criminology school of thought that offers a nuanced and radical critique of capitalism, broadening our vision of revolutionary education, and to promote intergenerational advocacy for society's underdogs. Barrio criminology seeks to challenge the barrio palimpsest by describing how barrios generate a praxis for social change.

El Mundo es un Barrio

Before and after my incarceration, I never understood the value of the barrio and its resistance against state repression. I grew up in Valley Center, located on the outskirts of north San Diego County, a small town with a thriving Chicanx and Latinx community, but fraught with racial and class inequality. Institutional racism, police repression, and a flourishing school-to-prison pipeline subjugate poor Brown persons in Valley Center. In this town, super-policing, surveillance, and criminalization become normalized by the youth, that often get funneled into the continuation school system. This arrangement often becomes a badge of honor by those affected by this apartheid educational system. To give context on criminalization in the barrio, I drove a lowered silver 2003 Honda Civic with black 17-inch rims and a sound system that shook the whole car once I maximized the volume. The car was unique and recognizable by everyone, including the sheriff's deputies in the area. I would continuously be pulled over, searched, and given petty citations. Once pulled over, and unaware of my civil rights, I allowed them to search my car. I was arrested, served my time, and was released back into the barrio. After my incarceration, the same cycle of policing, surveillance, and criminalization continued, even though I had paid my debt to society.

The story of policing, mass incarceration, and social control in the barrios is central to global capitalism. As insiders who have experienced incarceration, policing, and reintegration, we have striven in our trajectory as scholar-activists and community organizers to understand the link between global capitalism, hyper-incarceration, policing, and the barrio. In this chapter, we use Robinson's (2004, 2008, 2014) interpretation of globalization as an epochal shift in the world capitalism system dating back to the economic crisis of the 1970s, followed by its restructuring that took place in the following decades.

Robinson (2004), in *A Theory of Global Capitalism: Production, Class, and State in a Transnational World*, argues that global capitalism is in a qualitatively new epoch in the world capitalist system. The new epoch involves the surge of transnational capital and the linkage of every nation into a global maquiladora integrated by the production and finance system, under the social control of a new transnational capitalist class (TCC). The TCC is a group in control of new global markets and circuits of accumulation, shifting from the national markets and circuits of accumulation. The restructuring of world capitalism in the 1970s and since then has involved the global spread of transnational capital through a neoliberal counterrevolution against working-class communities all around the globe (Robinson, 2004; Harvey, 2005). The TCC pushed free trade agreements, such as the North American Free Trade Agreement (NAFTA) and Central American Free Trade Agreement (CAFTA), and neoliberal policy, including privatization and deregulations, that affected millions of people worldwide, generated the vast pools of poverty, unemployment and under-employment, and relegated people into the barrios.

Statistics show that the level of global social polarization and inequality is now at unprecedented levels. Globally, according to the International Labour Organization (ILO), more than 1.5 billion workers or about 50 percent of the global workforce are "vulnerable" workers. This category includes informal, flexible, part-time, contract, migrant, and itinerant workers (ILO, 2018). The ILO (1998) reported that in the late 20th century, one-third of the global labor force or approximately 1 billion workers remained unemployed or underemployed. The murder rate of poor Black, Brown, and white people killed by police is horrendous, but an even higher rate comes from unsafe conditions created by global capitalism. In 2016, more than 5,000 workers died as a result of working conditions (American Federation of Labor & Congress of Industrial Organizations, 2018), and worldwide more than 2.3 million workers die every year as a result of occupational accidents or work-related diseases (World Economic Forum, 2017). Predictably, the Black and Brown racialized groups are overrepresented in these statistics, not because of racial discrimination, per se, but because racialized labor is concentrated in the most hazardous occupations (Loomis and Richardson, 1998). Not only do poor Brown and Black groups worldwide get pushed into dangerous working conditions but, in essence, they are pushed and into poor communities known as barrios. From the favelas in Brazil to the slums on the rims of big cities in Venezuela and the Dominican Republic, barrios are composed of poor people displaced by global capitalism.

Thus, the link between this restructuring of global capitalism starting in the 1970s, the generation of large pools of surplus humanity, and the barrio can be drawn out through Gramsci's concept of hegemony and his insistence on the unity of *coercion* and *consent* in global capitalism. The criminalization, policing, and surveillance of poor Black and Brown communities have involved a vast expansion of the state's repressive apparatuses coupled with the production of a consensus around "law and order" and punishment. *Hegemony*, therefore, entails two forms of power or oppression: *coercive* and *consensual*. According to Gramsci (1971), consent rests at the level of civil society; common sense, as people denote it. Alternately, coercion is on the level of the state, or what Gramsci invokes as the *political society*. The restructuring of the late 20th century came about in response to the massive uprisings against the hegemonic classes in the 1960s and 1970s. Globally, massive anticolonial, anti-imperialist, and anticapitalist movements, including in the United States, where the civil rights movements advanced into radical anticapitalist and antiracist movements. The state's response was an escalation of repressive controls over these communities, including super-policing, massive deportations, hyper-incarceration, the militarization of police and border patrol, and super-surveillance.

Barrio Liberation

Raúl Homero Villa's (2000) study on the cultural politics of space for Chicanx communities in Los Angeles is particularly relevant to the analysis of barrios as contentious spaces and cultural struggle. Villa details how the law and public policy promote "dominating spatial practices" that socially construct the meaning of urban landscapes, and public discourses historically relegate poor working-class people into a specific space, namely the barrio. Poor Chicanx communities have been pushed mainly to the impoverished slums of cities in California but can also be found in dilapidated rural neighborhoods. The social, political, and economic conditions of the barrios are different from upper- and middle-echelon communities, thus relegating barrios to what Michel Laguerre (1999) terms a "minoritized" status. In essence, barrios are spaces of marginality, criminality, poverty, and are mainly, but not exclusively, composed of Black and Brown people. The marginality leads to the normalcy of this designation, and to the practices of super-surveillance and super-criminalization by agents who protect the private property of the superrich. Muniz, for example, highlights that punitive practices like gang injunctions are often not placed in areas with the most crime, but rather can be found in areas where wealthy white communities are in close proximity to working-class communities of color

(Muniz, 2015). Many of our criminal justice policies are designed to contain Chicanx and Latinx communities.

Nevertheless, Villa (2000) notes that the barrio's historical reality is not only repressed and subjugated but a "geographical identity" where cultural material wealth, constant struggle, and resistance to assimilation continue. As Villa (2000) points out, the barrio emerges from the larger city, which defines it as a second city of the more significant metropolis. He notes,

> If not always with the producer's awareness of their collective effect, these practices cumulatively produce and reproduce a mexopolis within the metropolis. . . . This Raza second city – contrary to the rigid laws of physics but consonant with the fluid arts of urbanity – exists in the same space of the putative Anglo-American first city (the visible signs of its decrease exist everywhere), yet in a significant place from its dominant cultural milieu.
>
> *(Villa, 2000, pp. 234–235)*

Thus, barrio communities become sites of struggle against the dominant status quo, like the civil gang injunctions in the region.

In north San Diego County, for example, there are currently twelve gang injunctions dispersed throughout the region.[8] Seven gang injunctions expand in Escondido, Vista, San Marcos, and Oceanside, all targeting Chicanx and Latinx people. A gang injunction is a form of social control that allows the police the discretion to stop, frisk, and detain a person deemed suspicious of being a gang member (Santos and Bickel, 2017; Muñiz, 2015). Thus, gang injunctions constitute a form of selective policing towards working-class poor Latinx and Chicanx communities. Gang injunctions, according to Frank Barajas (2007), restrict guaranteed freedoms of association and expression without affording their targets due process rights under criminal law (p. 394).

The punitive policies that undergird mass incarceration not only bleed into the streets through gag injunctions but also infect our schools. The expansion of the school-to-prison pipeline nationwide preemptively strikes against people of color as well. Kim et al. (2010) argue that children of color are consistently overrepresented at every point of the school-to-prison-pipeline, from the enrollment stage into underfunded public schools to suspensions, expulsions, and referrals to community resource officers, which may lead to their entanglement with the juvenile (in)justice system. State-sanctioned social control takes the form of detainment, super-criminalization, and super-surveillance of poor Black and Brown communities. Gang injunctions and the school-to-prison-pipeline represent two examples of state-sanctioned violence, super-criminalization, and super-surveillance strategies applied in barrios across the nation.

To combat social exclusion and isolation, barrios must create contentious spaces against state-sanctioned violence, militarized police, and policies that exacerbate intergenerational criminalization of poor communities. The barrios emerge as places with an expendable Chicanx and Latinx population that gets funneled into the prison system. The prison system connects state repression, state violence, and corporate gain, becoming the prison industrial complex. The term "prison industrial complex" refers to the interrelated mechanism of social control between corporations, policymakers, and capital that continue to funnel and control vast racialized poor communities into the prison system (Davis, 1995, 1998, 2003). The majority, at least in California, disproportionately come from barrios. Thus, barrios become revolutionary spaces that seek social and systemic change as they continuously are affected by the criminal (in)justice system – a system linked to corporations, massive repression, and caging of poor communities (Armstrong and Seidman, 2020). We have taken over public spaces that limit Chicanx and Latinx inclusion. Spaces like garages, public areas, and parks serve as locations to dialogue and practice revolutionary social change with abolition in mind. Higher education represents another frontier that must address prison abolition.

Chale con Ustedes *(Enough With You All): Academia and Prison Abolition Work*

Often ignored by academic circles, student support services for formerly incarcerated and system-impacted students in university and community college programs often become co-opted by liberal politics, where incarcerated individuals are viewed as "broken" people who need a formal education to become rehabilitated. Although we know that this type of complacency preserves the prevailing industrial complex, very few alternatives exist for people coming home from prison. Some prison education programs and student support services feed people a rational choice[9] and assimilationist[10] pedagogy (both nonthreatening ideologies to the penal system or capitalism) to students during and after confinement. Students are often expected to accept personal responsibility for their "mistakes," while there is little critique of the exclusionary nature of larger social institutions that perpetuate a womb-to-prison pipeline in the barrio. For example, prison administrators and correctional staff do not encourage teachers to introduce critical thought to inmates. Also, the correctional facility usually intervenes to deter the public and educators, particularly faculty of color, from bringing or mailing to inmates any critical education agenda or materials that raise a prison abolition agenda, challenge the status quo, or empower students.

As formerly incarcerated educators, we have consistently faced obstacles when trying to offer a more critical education. I, Oscar Soto, a Chicano coauthor, taught sociology at a federal correctional facility in California. The guards often chastised me in front of students for screening films such as *Freedom Writers* and *13th*. Guards often challenged me under pretenses that these films will retrigger students and insight them into a riot. In doing so, guards overlooked the countless other reasons folks might rebel in a prison: the cramped living quarters, the brutality from guards, and the consistent lack of educational programs. In my case, the students often stood up for me, and they reminded concerned correctional officers that other teachers (usually white teachers) showed them similar movies without consequence. While I sought to create a diverse, intellectually stimulating atmosphere in this gulag, I was heavily surveilled in the classroom, robbing me of the academic freedom to teach without reprisal, like my white counterparts. Still, my barrio appearance[11] results in super-criminality and super-surveillance, preventing me from enjoying the academic freedom to teach without reprisal, like my white counterparts.

Not only are teachers of color differently scrutinized, but critical books also become demonized in the system. I, Xuan Santos, an associate professor at California State University, San Marcos, shipped a series of academic and peer-reviewed articles to a former University of California student from Northern California who is currently serving time in a Central Valley prison. A few weeks later, the prison returned the package, notifying me that these articles represented prison contraband. The return came as no surprise, since some prisons in the U.S. ban books deemed a security threat without explanation, usually making history and civil rights books and articles contraband. Black authors such as Michelle Alexander, James Baldwin, George Jackson, and Malcolm X pose a threat to the existing penal order (Equal Justice Initiative, 2020). Possessing these items may result in a write-up for an inmate's file, which includes sanctions such as the termination of visitation, phone calls, jobs, conjugal visits, and all things that the prison can use as leverage against inmates. A book symbolically becomes a threat, since the system views educated inmates with disdain. This social control system prefers to divide and conquer inmates to deter solidarity *pinta*[12] movements.

Men and women who experienced educational and social distance in their early schooling but now deliver valuable informal pedagogy inside prison walls represent a class of "cellblock intellectuals." These organic intellectuals run the risk of cell raids and write-ups; noncredentialed and stigmatized intellectuals, they become repositories of knowledge as they secretively trade and pass along banned books among inmates. These sanctions include write-ups that can account for the loss of good/work time, visits, commissary, and other institutional privileges. Guards often know cellblock intellectuals who have earned a different level of respect. Senior guards never target them since they know their rights and histories and are well versed in defending their informal educational roles in prison. Elders risk it all in order to keep their books in their cells. Cellblock intellectuals find strategic ways of regularly receiving banned books and new books. The guards receive good payouts from inmates and their families for making these books available. The conflation of inmate resistance and intellectual tradition within the barrio and prisons must be recognized. These subcultural traditions inform us how we, as a society, should run educational programs as part of a more significant abolitionist movement.

The prison system funnels thousands of inmates through its facilities. The Prison Policy Initiative (2020) highlights that "the American criminal justice system holds almost 2.3 million people in 1,833 state prisons, 110 federal prisons, 1,772 juvenile correctional facilities, 3,134 local jails, 218 immigration detention facilities, and 80 Indian Country jails as well as in military prisons, civil commitment centers, state psychiatric hospitals, and prisons in the U.S. territories." In 2019, the California prison system institutionalized 125,472 inmates spread out across 35 prisons (CDCR, 2020). Within the prison system, several community colleges offer a statewide prison structure with in-person, full-credit, degree-building college courses, as well as student support services, to 34 out of 35 detention facilities (California Community Colleges, 2020). In just three years, California has gone from offering face-to-face college in one prison to full-credit, degree-building college courses in 34 of 35 prisons at all security levels. Almost 4,500 students are enrolled in these face-to-face college pathways each semester, and they consistently outperform students at non-penal college campuses (Corrections to College CA, 2020). Carceral education programs mirror privileged spaces that grant a small number of men and women the opportunity to become gainfully educated – the prison administration and corrections staff select program participants, who collectively represent an inmate aristocracy. Opportunity structures to determine which privileged inmates go to college are arbitrary. For example, a correctional officer may deter an incarcerated Latinx prospect from participating in a college program if the officer determines that he or she does not merit it, as observed by Martin Leyva, a formerly incarcerated Chicano scholar-activist. Administrators, counselors, or correctional officers might harbor prejudicial attitudes towards individuals or people. They may also stereotype them without being aware. This "implicit bias" may prevent a person from enrolling in college and even paroling successfully. This selection criterion creates consequences that dictate who reenters society with some college credit, or with associate's, bachelor's, and master's degrees.

On the outside, the privileges that non-system-impacted citizens enjoy means formerly incarcerated and system-impacted persons must cope with systemic inequalities. They confront, as Alexander (2012) notes, "a web of laws, regulations, and informal rules, all of which are powerfully reinforced by social stigma. They are confined to the margins of mainstream society and denied access to the mainstream economy. They are legally denied the ability to obtain employment, housing, and public benefit" (p. 4). In California, the emergence of higher education's prison-to-school-pipeline allows paroled and probationary college students to join post-incarceration programs at similar rates. Some statewide academic programs offer special admissions, student support services, retention, graduation, and advanced degree opportunities. Some students acknowledge how the incarceration stigma may limit their opportunities and often keep their incarceration track record secret. (We find that both people of color and whites join these post-incarceration programs. Still, over time some white students move away from these support groups and remain autonomous throughout their academic trajectories, as noted by Martin Leyva.) These everyday structural arrangements persist as they seek connections with these refuge spaces while maintaining support groups. Most of these programs lack critical thought and often accept the gulag's status quo, which does not promote prison abolition agendas but instead legitimizes these social control institutions. When radical students speak out against this ideological apparatus, some post-incarceration programs push them out for their contentious politics.

Formerly incarcerated and system-impacted Chicanx and Latinx persons also experience the barrioization[13] of higher education through microaggressions[14] (Forrest-Bank and Jenson, 2015; Sue, 2010; Solorzano et al., 2000), macroaggressions[15] (Osanloo et al., 2016), and institutional racism (Bonilla-Silva, 2018; Tucker, 2017; Thomas, 2013; Raza, 2011). Still, higher education can represent a refuge for formerly incarcerated and system-impacted students. Although some support networks exist, the university remains an alienating space as some disciplines and schools of thought become unidimensional. Some Chicanx and Latinx students do not see their lived experiences and struggles in conventional criminology literature or curriculum, which promotes the barrioization of this space. I, Xuan Santos, often experience the barrioization on campus as I organize events related to Chicanx and Latinx criminalization and the prison industrial complex. Campus safety heavily surveils these events and the neighboring law enforcement agencies receive alerts about a threatening presence on campus. An administrative staff member informed me that Campus Safety called her and asked, "Oh, is this a Xuan Santos event?" The police often stereotype Santos as a "gang member" professor, who may potentially invite threatening persons from the Chicanx and Latinx community to campus, including gang-involved persons, which demonstrates how the entire community remains criminalized as a whole. This event featured Father Gregory Boyle, the executive director of Homeboy Industries in Los Angeles, the largest gang prevention and intervention center in the U.S. Although we organize events to inform our students about prison abolition and justice work, we must acknowledge that even though people tell me, "You have made it out of Boyle Heights [my barrio of origin]," punitive social control strategies erase my credentials and delegate me to the status of an academic sCHOLAr[16] (gangster). As a convict criminologist I seek inclusion in the larger organization, but I don't see myself in their organization.

The "New School of Convict Criminology" represents a school of thought that captures criminology from formerly incarcerated persons' and allies' perspectives (Richards, 2013; Terry, 2003; Richards and Ross, 2001). However, the dominant voices in convict criminology remain profoundly white, and people of color often remain underrepresented in the canon, leaving Latinx people as a "little c"[17] subculture in convict criminology even though they represent a large portion of the prison population in the United States. Mainstream convict criminology represents perspectives from a white privileged academic class of scholars, representing a school of thought that reproduces, represents, and maintains an apartheid knowledge system that essentializes all captive knowledge. Convict criminology remains a white, Eurocentric, masculinist, and heteronormative school of thought, which we argue parallels the critiques by feminists of color about academia (Collins, 2009; Anzaldúa, 2012; NietoGomez, 1997; hooks, 1994; Combahee River Collective, 1979; Davis, 1972). The California carceral system cages 79% of people of color compared to their white counterparts at 21%. On the inside, Latinx people represent 44%, Black 28%, and whites 21% in prison; this disproportionality also exists in California jails, with Latinx at 41%, Black 20%, and whites 29% (Vera Institute, 2019).[18] These numbers highlight that in California, people of color remain disproportionately overrepresented in these total institutions,[19] but in the Ivory Tower, the dominant convict criminology voice remains that of the white male ruling class.

Most criminology literature focuses on the Black/white binary, often excluding a Latinx perspective and all other marginalized people (Martinez, 2016; Ramirez, 2002).[20] As more Latinx convict criminologists enter the higher education, we seek to advance a prison abolitionist agenda that promotes our inclusion so that we can build a strong coalition of difference. We aim to shed light on the exclusionary academic status quo, which remains real. Only certain people become the voice in convict criminology, and the experiences of specific groups get notoriety. We seek liberation within a liberation. We recognize that a person's past does not define them, and we aim to destigmatize persons who actively navigate the prison-to-college pipeline.

Conclusion

The demonization and lack of Chicanx and Latinx voices contribute to the continuity and maintenance of oppressive mechanisms that keep the barrio on the margins. Radical and revolutionary people from the barrios often experience marginalization, through coercive militarization, through institutions including education inside and outside the prison walls, job market discrimination, and social death (through poverty, homelessness, and pushed to the margins of the informal economy). The lack of representation, critical analysis, and praxis in the Ivory Tower and elsewhere have led to the continuation of repression, marginalization, and exclusion of poor Latinx and Chicanx populations. We are not asking for representation and inclusion in the system, per se, but rather a total upheaval and a new system as the current system continues to wreak havoc on poor communities, specifically Black and Brown communities in the United States.

Reform Versus Abolition

We are unapologetic abolitionists. Antiracist protests continue to engulf one of the most powerful nation-states in the world. As continued social inequality and criminalization impact our Chicanx and Latinx barrios, we will fight for liberation as we participate in the systemic abolition of prisons, eradication of the police, and promote both anti-imperialist and anti-colonial agendas in our struggle. However, a critique of capitalism, specifically global capitalism, remains evident in our continued abolition struggle. The 2020 wave of mass protests in the United States and around the world should not be reducible to Black and Brown folks being murdered, or racism, but historically tied to the consequences of the global pandemic, "surplus" humanity, class struggles, vast underemployment across the globe, and global capitalism. The same organizations and political agents of the corporate world that in recent decades have praised capitalist globalization and its by-products, hyper-policing, hyper-incarceration, and racist systems, have now come to embrace antiracist protests. This embrace seeks only mild reform to weaken and destabilize demands for revolutionary social change.

Fred Hampton, the charismatic Black Panther Party leader from Chicago who was executed by the FBI and Chicago police in 1969, stated, "We never negated the fact that there was racism in America, but we said that the byproduct, what comes off capitalism, happens to be racism." Hampton argues "that capitalism comes first, and next is racism. That when they brought slaves over here, it was to make money. The idea came that we want to make money, then the slaves came to make that money. That means, through historical fact, that racism had to come from capitalism. It had to be capitalism first, and racism was a byproduct of that" (Ledwith, 2020). In the big picture, the solutions are not to reform law enforcement, the prison system or the criminal (in)justice system, since reforming these will only enforce a system that under capitalism is intended to protect the private property of the rich and powerful from the majority poor and dispossessed through criminalization, stigmatization, and marginalization (Correia and Wall, 2018).

The embrace also shifts attention from a radical critique of global capitalism, including hyper-incarceration, prison and police abolition, reform, and defunding police. Small mechanisms of the injustices of the neoliberal global capitalist generate these conditions (Robinson and Soto, 2019). The newfound corporate interest in antiracist rhetoric and massive funding for "racial justice" is symbolic of corporations' newfound interest in co-opting the Black Lives Matter movement. Amazon, Bank of America, Facebook, Google, Home Depot, Nike, Verizon, and the Walt Disney Company[21] are already welcoming the language of *systemic racism*. Racial justice is now the mantra used by political and economic ruling elites. CEOs of these major corporations whose donations have embraced policing, hyper-incarceration, social inequality, and racial injustices are attempting to commodify the Black Lives Matter movement. History has shown mild reform by corporate elites leads to continued and intensified repression, social control, and oppression. Thus, we must fight instead for the total abolition of the system. In order to achieve full emancipation for all, we must abolish capitalism.

An abolitionist approach involves imagining a constellation of alternative strategies and institutions, with the ultimate goal of abolishing the prison system, policing, and hierarchical systems of inequality perpetuated by the systemic global capitalist regime. This entails developing an alternative framework for social justice and systemic change and the dissolution of the fetishization of material wealth. It is critical to center de-incarceration in strategies to develop alternative systems to imprisonment. Such an approach would include demilitarizing schools and revitalizing public educational systems, revamping the health care system, creating meaningful and rewarding employment, and – why not? – a system without prisons. It becomes clear that abolishing the penal system of super-incarceration ultimately involves a broader struggle against global capitalism. The struggle against global capitalism was the original premise of radical criminology and other approaches to justice that emerged from the mass struggles of the 1960s and 1970s. In the end, we must replace the whole concept of prison abolition, as valid and urgent as it is, with abolishing global capitalism. This social transformation is a genuine revolutionary rallying cry and one that we cannot pursue further here, other than to note that the counter-hegemonic forces needed to abolish the criminal (in)justice system are still weak. There is currently an upsurge of counter-hegemonic movements worldwide. We must organize a transnational hegemonic movement against global capitalism that is not state-centered but organized transnationally (Robinson and Soto, 2019).

What *barrio criminology* is pushing forward is abolitionist points of systemic change with the end goal of changing the system that contributes to vast amounts of social, political, and economic inequalities. As supporters of barrio criminology, we believe the following points are critical to dismantling the current system of polarization between the haves and have-nots, the 1% and the 99%, the bourgeoisie and the proletariat. First, it is vital to have an anti-imperial and decolonial agenda that dismantles, defunds, and abolishes the global militarization and invasion of poor racialized communities on a global scale. Part of the anti-imperial and anticolonial agenda, is to find an alternative system other than capitalism which continues to reproduce political, social, and economic inequalities. With that said, the second point is to have an anticapitalist framework. As we know it today, capitalism continues to perpetuate different forms of division of labor, racism, and other oppressive mechanisms that contribute to social, political, and economic inequality. Third, the nation-state that contributes to the social control of poor communities must be abolished.

Opening up borders will dismantle the social control mechanism created by borders and protection of private property, including militarized death squads all across the globe, immigrant detention centers, border patrol, and immigrant customs enforcements. Fourth, we must allow communities to dictate alternative new possibilities of resistance and autonomy for people in the barrios and the world –a resistant and autonomous barrio that includes all social sectors that struggle against global capitalism and for liberty and justice for all. Fifth, it is necessary to abolish all industrial complexes, including, but not limited to, the military industrial complex, the immigration industrial complex, the prison industrial complex, and the non-profit industrial complex. In addition, the more significant abolitionist movement must also include eliminating police and private security that is vested in protecting private property: Sixth, political and revolutionary education in organic and autonomous community spaces is crucial. Organic spaces, lead by the mantra *for the people, by the people* will deter co-optation by capital, major corporations, and the global elite. Seventh, there must be an alternative media that includes working-class communities instead of mainstream media that incorporates left-oriented opinions. Finally, we must create repositories of knowledge managed by poor working-class communities of color. This will allow people from oppressed communities to create their own curricula and promote autonomy from the existing global capitalist agenda.

We suggest the implementation of fully developed spaces that include more barrio criminologists. This group seeks to abolish social control agendas, as interrupters of the larger global capitalist scheme.

To conclude, our abolitionist agenda encourages systemic change to liberate people pushed into barrios, but also for those who want to see an alternate system where poverty, exclusion, and marginalization become transformed.

We argue here that even when we leave the barrio, the barrio continues to be part of our identities, phenotypically and ideologically. As we navigate social institutions, in this case, education, prison, and our communities, we proudly embody our culture, heritage, and honor our ancestors. This proud embodiment comes at a cost, as we continue to suffer from exclusion, criminalization, and super-policing at the hand of the state, institutions, and our communities. Why should it be up to us to raise awareness about our situation? It is critical for educational institutions, prisons, and dominant communities to speak up and tell us why they're so invested and threatened that people from the barrios should be the prime targets of policing, caging, and militarization. We call for these institutions and others to reflect on how their spaces can contribute to the exclusion of voices from the barrio. Rather than seeing barrios and, more specifically, people from the barrios as enemies, the dominant society needs to respect abolitionists and systemic and institutional change. We must move beyond assimilation. We argue that social institutions, including education, prisons, and communities, need to take responsibility for the continued marginalization of certain classes, racialized groups, and gender and sex-based inequalities. Our exclusion should not be our responsibility; there must be a total systemic change with barrio voices at the center as they are mostly affected by state violence, the prison industrial complex, and mass incarceration.

Short of an overthrow of the system and moving towards abolition of the whole system of global capitalism, the only way out of the crisis is a reversal of global inequalities, which will then shift race and class relations. We must simultaneously change the consciousness of millions of people who continue to see capitalism as a viable system of equality; we must have a revolutionary organization coupled with revolutionary ideology and praxis.

Notes

1 An inclusive, gender-neutral lexicon term that denotes a community or person from Mexican, Latin America, and/or Indigenous cultures. This term is an alternative to Chicana or Chicano.
2 An inclusive, gender-neutral lexicon term that denotes a community or person of Latin American culture. This term is an alternative to Latina or Latino.
3 We use *Brown* as an ethnic term, as it is used in the barrio, to describe Chicanx and Latinx persons.
4 In the United States, redlining is the systematic denial of various services by federal, state, and local government agencies either directly or through the selective raising of prices in the community. For a full analysis of the segregation of neighborhoods as it is manifested through unscrupulous real estate agents, unethical mortgage lenders, and exclusionary

covenants working outside the law, including redlining, see Rothstein (2017) and Smith (1996).

5 Spanish term for "ice cream vendor." This street vendor sometimes sells other miscellaneous food items such as chips and sodas. We applied the *x* in *paleterxs* as a gender-neutral lexicon term to denote an ice cream vendor of Mexican, Latin America, and Indigenous cultures.

6 Spanish term for "corn vendor." We applied the *x* in *eloterxs* as a gender-neutral lexicon term to denote a corn vendor of Mexican, Latin America, and Indigenous cultures.

7 Spanish lexicon term for "murals." Beautiful art murals can be seen throughout the barrios of Los Angeles, San Diego, and Santa Barbara, where the authors grew up.

8 A full list of gang injunctions in San Diego can be found at www.sdcda.org/preventing/gangs/injunctions.html

9 This framework suggests that human behavior, in this case, criminal behavior, is chosen, and the benefits to committing crime outweigh the consequences.

10 A means by which people, in this case, incarcerated persons, get absorbed by the prison system. This process involves the acceptance of rational choices and rejecting structural arrangements that push people to commit crimes. The criminal injustice system, correctional staff, and administrators embrace an assimilation agenda.

11 I.e., cultural lexicon, "streetwear" such as Adidas Superstars, Ben Davis pants, and Pendletons, and nonverbal communication cues.

12 Chicanx lexicon term meaning penitentiary.

13 Similar to the ways that Black communities experience ghettoization in American society, barrios emerged as Latinx people migrated to the global north. "Barrioization" involves concentrated poverty, unequal access to U.S. resources, and societal pacts that exacerbate super-segregation. In this article, we use this term to describe subordination in prison education, academia, and the barrio.

14 Derald Wing Sue defines this term as the everyday verbal, nonverbal, and environmental slights, snubs, or insults, whether intentional or unintentional, which communicate hostile, derogatory, or negative messages to target persons (people of color, women, LGBTQ+) based solely upon their marginalized-group membership.

15 This is a culmination of system-wide practices and ideologies that seek to exclude or limit a person of color, woman, or formerly incarcerated or system-impacted person's life chances. Macroaggressions can be intersectional by promoting multiple layers of discriminatory practices.

16 The term sCHOLAr represents a working-class resistance term that's a play on letters. The term sCHOLAr highlights the word *chola*, which means female gang member. Here we use the term to describe a male or female academic who is often disproportionately underrepresented in academia as both student and faculty,

17 This concept refers to Latinx convict criminology scholars' second-class citizenship status within the larger "New School of Convict Criminology."

18 People of color also include American-Indians and Asians, with each group constituting 1% of the inmate population.

19 Erving Goffman argues that total institutions may be defined as a place of residence and work where many like-situated individuals cut off from the broader society for an appreciable period of time together lead an enclosed, formally administered round of life (p. 11). Examples of total institutions may be an asylum or prison.

20 We are pro-Black, and we are in solidarity with Black Liberation among other struggles. We suggest here as a future proposition to fully develop elsewhere that the literature focuses only on the Black-white binary.

21 For a complete list of corporate donors, see https://money.yahoo.com/here-are-the-companies-donating-to-racial-justice-causes-191413371.html

Bibliography

Alexander, M. (2012). *The New Jim Crow: Mass Incarceration in the Age of Colorblindness*. New York: The New Press.

American Federation of Labor & Congress of Industrial Organizations. (2018). *Death on the Job: Toll of Neglect, 2018*. Washington, DC: AFL-CIO. Retrieved from https://aflcio.org/reports/death-job-toll-neglect-2018. (2018, April 26).

Anzaldúa, G. (2012). *Borderlands/La: The New Mestiza Frontera*, 4th edition. San Francisco: Aunt Lute Books.

Armstrong, G. and Seidman, D. (2020). "Corporate Backers of the Blue: How Corporations Bankroll US Police Foundations." *SLUDGE*. Retrieved from https://readsludge.com/2020/06/19/corporate-backers-of-the-blue-how-corporations-bankroll-u-s-police-foundations/. (2020, June 19).

Baldwin, J., F. R. Standley, and L. H. Pratt. (1989). *Conversations with James Baldwin*, 1st edition. MS Oxford: University Press of Mississippi.

Barajas, F. P. (2007). "An Invading Army: A Civil Gang Injunction in A Southern California Chicana/o Community." *Latino Studies*, vol. 5, no. 4, pp. 393–417.

Bickel, C. (2010). "From Child to Captive: Constructing Captivity in a Juvenile Institution." *Western Criminology Review*, vol. 11, no. 1, pp. 37–49.

Bonilla-Silva, E. (2018). *Racism without Racists: Color-blind Racism, and the Persistence of Racial Inequality in America*. Lanham: Rowman & Littlefield Publishing Group, Inc.

California Community Colleges. (2020). "Currently and Formally Incarcerated Students." Retrieved February 24, 2020, from www.cccco.edu/About-Us/Chancellors-Office/Divisions/Educational-Services-and-Support/What-we-do/Currently-and-Formerly-Incarcerated-Students.

Castañeda, E. (2019). "Latin Neighborhoods in the U.S." Retrieved May 1, 2020, from www.american.edu/centers/latin-american-latino studies/upload/castanedalatinneighborhood-spresentation.pdf.

CDCR. (2020). "Fall 2019: Population Projections." Retrieved February 24, 2020, from www.cdcr.ca.gov/research/wp-content/uploads/sites/174/2020/01/Fall-2019-Population-Projections.pdf.

Collins, P. H. (2009). *Black Feminist Thought*. New York: Routledge.

Combahee River Collective. (1979). "Combahee River Collective: A Black Feminist Statement." Off Our Backs, vol. 1, no. 1, pp. 6–8.

Corrections to College California. (2020). "Don't Stop Now." Retrieved April 1, 2020, from https://correctionstocollegeca.org/resources/dont-stop-now.

Correia, D. and T. Wall. (2018). *Police: A Field Guide*. Brooklyn: Verso.

Davis, A. (1972). "Reflections on the Black Woman's Role in the Community of Slaves." *The Massachusetts Review*, vol. 13, no. 1–2, pp. 81–100.

Davis, A. (1995). "Hell Factories in the Field: A Prison-Industrial Complex." *The Nation*, vol. 260, no. 7, pp. 229–234.

Davis, A. (1998). 'Masked Racism: Reflections on the Prison Industrial Complex.' *Colorlines*. Retrieved from www.colorlines.com/articles/masked-racism-reflections-prison-industrial-complex. (1998, September 10).

Davis, A. (2003). *Are Prisons Obsolete?* New York: Seven Stories Press.

Druery, D. M., J. L. Young, and C. D. Elbert. (2018). "Microaggressions and Civil Disobedience." *Women, Gender, and Families of Color*, vol. 6, no. 1, pp. 73–78.

Equal Justice Initiative. (2020). "Banning Books in Prisons." Retrieved February 24, 2020, from https://eji.org/news/banning-books-in-prisons/.

Forrest-Bank, S. and J. M. Jenson. (2015). "Differences in Experiences of Racial Ethnic Microaggression among Asian, Latino/Hispanic, Black, and White Young Adults." *Journal of Sociology & Social Welfare*, vol. XLII, no. 1, pp. 141–161.

Gilmore, R. W. (2007). *The Golden Gulag: Prisons, Surplus, Crisis, and Opposition in Globalizing California*. Berkeley: University of California Press.

Goffman, E. (1968). *Asylums*. New York: Penguin.

Gramsci, A. (1971). *Selections from the Prison Notebooks*. Edited and Translated by Quintin Hoare and Geoffrey Nowell Smith. New York: International Publishers.

Harvey, D. (2005). *A Brief History of Neoliberalism*. New York: Oxford University Press.

Hernandez, K. L. (2017). *City of Inmates: Conquest, Rebellion, and the Rise of Human Caging in Los Angeles, 1771–1965*. Chapel Hill: The University of North Carolina Press.

hooks, b. (1994). *Teaching to Transgress: Education as a Practice of Freedom*. New York: Routledge.

International Labour Organization. (1998). *International Labour Organization World Employment Report 1998-99*. No. 27. Geneva: ILO. Retrieved from https://www.ilo.org/wcmsp5/groups/public/---dgreports/---dcomm/documents/publication/dwcms_080628.pdf. (2020, June 1).

International Labour Organization. (2018). *More than 60 Percent of the World's Employed Population are in the Informal Economy*. Geneva: ILO. Retrieved from https://www.ilo.org/global/about-the-ilo/newsroom/news/WCMS_627189/lang–en/index.htm. (2018, April 30).

KCET. (2020). "Highland Park: White Flight." Retrieved January 12, 2020, from www.kcet.org/shows/departures/white-flight.

Kim, C. Y., D. J. Losen, and D. T. Hewitt. (2010). *The School-to-Prison Pipeline: Structuring Legal Reform*. New York: New York University Press.

Laguerre, M. (1999). *Minoritized Space: An Inquiry into the Spatial Order of Things*. Berkeley: Institute for Governmental Studies.

Latina/o/x Criminology. (2020). "Latina/o/x Criminology." Retrieved, June 1, 2020, from www.latcrim.org/.

Ledwith, Sean. (2020). "Fred Hampton: Black Panther and Red Revolutionary." *Monthly Review*. New York, NY. Retrieved from https://mronline.org/2020/06/11/fred-hampton-black-panther-and-red-revolutionary/. (2020, June 8).

Leyva, M. J. (2018). "From Prison Towers to Ivory Towers: Education as a Means of Reentry." Unpublished thesis, scholarworks, California State University San Marcos.

Loomis, D. and D. Richardson. (1998). "Race and the Risk of Fatal Injury at Work." *American Journal of Public Health*, vol. 88, no. 1, pp. 40–44.

Martinez, C. M. (2016). *The Neighborhood Has its Own Rules: Latinos and African Americans in South Los Angeles*. New York: New York University Press.

Moore, J. (1991). *Going Down to the Barrio: Homeboys and Homegirls*. Philadelphia: Temple University Press.

Muñiz, A. (2015). *Police, Power, and the Production of Racial Boundaries*. New Brunswick: Rutgers University Press.

NietoGomez, A. (1997) "Sexism in the Movimiento." Pp. 97–100 in *Chicana Feminist Thought: The Basic Historical Writings*, edited by Alma Garcia. New York: New Routledge.

Osanloo, A. F., C. Boske, and W. S. Newcomb. (2016). "Deconstructing Macroaggressions, Microaggressions, and Structural Racism in Education: Developing a Conceptual Model for the Intersection of Social Justice Practice and Intercultural Education." *International Journal of Organizational Theory and Development*, vol. 4, no. 1, pp 1–18.

PBS. (2017). *City Rising: Gentrification and Displacement.* Retrieved from https://www.kcet.org/shows/city-rising/episodes/city-rising-gentrification-and-displacement. (January 12, 2020).

Pérez, G. M. (2017). "Barrio." Pp. 18–20 in *Keywords for Latina/o Studies,* edited by Deborah R. Vargas, Lawrence La Fauntain-Stokes, and Nancy Raquel Mirabal. New York: New York University Press.

Prison Policy Initiative. (2020). "Mass Incarceration: The Whole Pie 2020." Retrieved January 12, 2020, from www.prisonpolicy.org/reports/pie2020.html.

Ramirez, R. (2002). *Latino Homicide: Immigration, Violence, and Community.* New York: Routledge.

Raza, A. E. (2011). "Legacies of the Racialization of Incarceration: From Convict-Lease to the Prison Industrial Complex." *Journal of the Institute of Justice and International Studies,* vol. 11, pp. 159–170.

Richards, S. C. (2013). "The New School of Convict Criminology Thrives and Matures." *Critical Criminology,* vol. 21, no. 1, pp. 375–387.

Richards, S. C. and J. I. Ross. (2001). "The New School of Convict Criminology." *Social t Justice,* vol. 28, no. 1, pp. 177–190.

Robinson, W. I. (2004). *A Theory of Global Capitalism: Production, Class, and State in a Transnational World.* Baltimore: Johns Hopkins University Press.

Robinson, W. I. (2008). *Latin America and Global Capitalism: A Critical Globalization Perspective.* Baltimore: The Johns Hopkins University Press.

Robinson, W. I. (2014). *Global Capitalism and the Crisis of Humanity.* New York: Cambridge University Press.

Robinson, W. I. (2018). "Accumulation Crisis and the Global Police State." *Critical Sociology,* pp. 1–14.

Robinson, W. I. and O. F. Soto. (2019). "Passive Revolution and the Movement against Mass Incarceration: From Prison Abolition to Redemption Scripts." *Social Justice: A Journal of Crime, Conflict & World Order.* Retrieved from www.socialjusticejournal.org/from-prison-abolition-to-redemption- script/. (2019, May 9).

Rothstein, R. (2017). *The Color of Law: A Forgotten History of How Our Government Segregated America.* New York: Liveright Publishing Corporation.

Sanchez, G. J. (1995). *Becoming Mexican American: Ethnicity, Culture, and Identity in Chicano Los Angeles, 1900–1945.* New York: Oxford University Press, Inc.

Santos, X. and C. Bickel. (2017). "Apartheid Justice: Gang Injunctions and the New Black Codes." *Sociology of Crime, Law and Deviance,* vol. 22, pp. 27–38.

The Sentencing Project. (2020). "Trends in U.S. Corrections." Retrieved January 12, 2020, from www.sentencingproject.org/wp-content/uploads/2016/01/Trends-in-US-Corrections.pdf.

Smith, N. (1996). *The New Urban Frontier: Gentrification and the Revanchist City.* New York: Routledge.

Solorzano, D., M. Ceja, and T. Yosso. (2000). "Critical Race Theory, Racial Microaggressions, and Campus Racial Climate: The Experiences of African-American College Students." *Journal of Negro Education,* vol. 69, no. 1/2, pp. 60–74.

Sue, D. W. (2010). "Microaggressions, Marginality, and Oppressions: An Introduction." Pp. 3–22 in *Microaggressions and Marginality Manifestation, Dynamics, and Impact,* edited by Derald Wing Sue. Hoboken: John Wiley and Sons Inc.

Terry, C. M. (2003). "From C-Block to Academia: You Can't Get There from Here." Pp. 95–199 in *Convict Criminology,* edited by Jeffrey Ian Ross and Stephen C. Richards. Belmont: Wadsworth/Thompson.

Thomas, J. M. (2013). "Mass Incarceration of Minority Males: A Critical Look at its Historical Roots and How Educational Policies Encourage its Existence." *Race, Gender & Class*, vol. 20, no. 1–2, pp. 177–190.

Tucker, R. B. Jr. (2017). "The Color of Mass Incarceration." *Ethnic Studies Review*, vol. 37–38, no. 1, pp. 135–149.

Vera Institute. (2019). "Incarceration Trends in California." Retrieved March 1, 2020, from www.vera.org/downloads/pdfdownloads/state-incarceration-trends- california.pdf.

Villa, R. H. (2000). *Barrio Logos: Space and Place in Urban Chicano Literature and Culture*. Austin: University of Texas Press.

Wacquant, L. (2001). "Deadly Symbiosis: When Ghetto and Prison Meet and Mesh." *SAGE Publications*, vol. 1, no. 3, pp. 95–134.

Wacquant, L. (2002). "From Slavery to Mass Incarceration: Rethinking the 'Race Question' in the US." *New Left Review*, no.13, pp. 41–60.

Wacquant, L. (2009). *Punishing the Poor: The Neoliberal Government of Social Insecurity*. Durham: Duke University Press.

World Economic Forum. (2017). *More than 2 Million People Die at Work Each Year. Here's How to Prevent It*. Geneva, Switzerland: WEF. Retrieved from www.weforum.org/agenda/2017/03/workplace-death-health-safety-ilo- fluor/. (2017, March 23).

Re-mapping Criminology's Reach and Growing Visions for Abolition

9

BIOLOGY AND CRIMINOLOGY ENTANGLED

Education as a Meeting Point

Charlemya Erasme

Introduction

For some time, I have been searching for where matters of justice and science meet. Where and how do they overlap, if at all? Continual reflections on this question highlighted a dissonance that heightened throughout my educational experiences, particularly in science classrooms. It felt like I was being split in two: a scientist by day and a Black woman in need of justice by night. It was as if justice and science never intersected (e.g., Morales-Doyle, Vossoughi, Vakil, & Bang, 2020). Yet, whether I reflect on history, the present, or projections for the future, science and justice systems are entangled.

This entanglement requires a closer analysis than it has received. To begin, I wish to provide definitions. Science is the study of the natural, social, and physical world. Criminology is the study of crime (Saleh-Hanna, 2017; Anderson, 2019) – a social science. Biology is the study of living organisms and life – a natural or life science (McCulloch & Carr, 2016). I wish to note that:

> [i]n the K–12 context [and from my experiences, beyond 12th grade], science is generally taken to mean the traditional natural sciences: physics, chemistry, biology, and (more recently) earth, space, and environmental sciences.
> *(National Research Council, 2012, p. 11)*

For consistency, I use this definition throughout the chapter for the term "science." Next, I briefly reflect on the history of biology and criminology.

DOI: 10.4324/9780367817114-13

Reflections on the History of Biology

In many colonized lands, science "began" in Europe. This false narrative informs biology to this day (Medin & Bang, 2014). Western European ideologies and perspectives like positivism and Eurocentrism are central to biology. Positivism is a knowledge approach that values objectivity and neutrality (Willig, 2001). Eurocentrism is the prioritization of European ideas and knowledge. Applied to biology, Eurocentrism and positivism suggest that culture, politics, and identity do not influence biology. Eurocentrism and positivism are fundamental to modern conceptions of biology despite how they misrepresent reality. In reality, every scientific inquiry is filled with choices and values (Lemke, 1990). Likewise, people with authority make choices or conduct research that can preserve particular values (Nobles, Womack, Wonkam, & Wathuti, 2022). Therefore, biology cannot be without bias.

Eurocentric values center whiteness. Whiteness is membership in systems that prioritize Western European perspectives (Sammel, 2009; Delgado & Stefancic, 2001). Whiteness and Eurocentrism are linked because European ancestry, ideals, customs, and norms shape what it means to be white and who gets to be white (Harris, 1993; Sammel, 2009). Centering whiteness (or ideologies linked to whiteness) positions anything and everyone outside of whiteness as "other" (Kincheloe & Tobin, 2009; Sammel, 2009).

Labeling people and communities is not a recent phenomenon nor is attributing worth to these imposed labels. Historically, people have been ethnically and racially classified and reclassified (Parsons, 2014). The impacts heighten when intersections of race, class, ability, gender, and sexuality are considered. Ethnicity categorizes people and communities based on aspects they share, like location or culture, for example (Parsons, 2014; Smedley & Smedley, 2005; Nasir, Rowley, & Perez, 2015; Chapman & Feldman, 2017). Classifying and reclassifying people based on ethnicity is a construct that evolves arbitrarily. Eileen Carlton Parsons (2014, p. 169) writes:

> The White immigrants from southern and eastern Europe, the vast majority with free rather than indentured servitude status, were initially viewed upon their arrival as ethnically inferior individuals, but because they shared the phenotypes of the Anglo-Saxon settlers, the European immigrants were allotted various rights, given access to opportunities, and naturalized.

This quote reifies the affordances of whiteness and the proximity to whiteness; it highlights that there are social, political, and economic privileges to being classified as white.

Race is another form of classification with a definition that continues to evolve (Graves, 2009). Race is often defined by a single factor or a combination of a person's geography, skin color, physical features, and so forth. The US census reflects this fluctuating definition of race. For example, in the late 1700s, people were classified by enslavement (who was "free" and who was not "free") (Nobles, 2000). However, the U.S. Census Bureau (2022) now offers the following racial categories: American Indian or Alaska Native, Asian, Black or African American, Native Hawaiian or Other Pacific Islander, and white. Classifying people, especially racially, based on biology can have harmful implications (Yudell, Roberts, DeSalle, & Tishkoff, 2016).

Biologizing race suggests that there are genetic (biological) differences between racial groups and imposes hierarchies of worth on people and communities (Chadha, Lim, Kane, & Rowland, 2020; Duster, 2015). Researchers across fields such as anthropology (Smedley & Smedley, 2005), medicine (Fair & Johnson, 2021), and genetics (ASHG Executive Committee, 2018) challenge the belief that human differences are genetic or biological. Yet, some researchers still mention the "race effect" (i.e., Karter, 2003) to explain disparities. The "race effect" suggests that race is genetic and has measurable influences. Denouncing claims that position race as genetic does not mean that race − or more accurately, racism − can be ignored. Similarly,

> While race is not imaginary − it is a very real way our society categorizes people− its intrinsic origin in biology is. Race is not an illusion. Rather, the belief in intrinsic racial difference is a delusion.
>
> *(Roberts, 2012, p. 24)*

That is to say, the impacts of race as a construct are real. And more pointedly, the impacts of racism are real. For context, Audre Lorde (2007, p. 115) defines racism as "the belief in the inherent superiority of one race over all others and thereby the right to dominance." Science and racism connect whiteness with privilege and superiority (Nobles, Womack, Wonkam, & Wathuti, 2022). Like science, legal systems also justify racial hierarchies and prioritize whiteness (Harris, 1993).

Reflections on the History of Criminology

W. E. B. Du Bois (1901) writes:

> Two systems of controlling human labor which still flourish in the South are the direct children of slavery, and to all intents and purposes are slavery itself. These are the crop-lien system and the convict-lease system.
>
> *(p. 737)*

This quote highlights the evolution of crime and punishment from the perspective of the US South. I use it to illustrate how the same racist values that justified slavery inform and justify how crime is understood today (Alexander, 2020). Racism continues to shape perceptions of criminality (Roberts, 2007). For example, in 1705 the state of Virginia passed a law that justified slaveowners killing people who were enslaved in the name of "correction" (General Assembly, 1705), whereas people who were enslaved received violent punishment for reading or practicing customs of their cultures. These racial contradictions and hierarchies are foundational to modern criminology.

Modern criminology reflects criminology's roots in positivism and othering. Cesare Lombroso, credited as the founder of criminology, attempted to determine who is and who is not a criminal based on physical and genetic characteristics (Anderson, 2019). Lombroso's research involved phrenology – the pseudoscientific study of skulls and brains (Parsons, 2008; Anderson, 2019). To illustrate the positivist roots in Lombroso's work, I share two excerpts from "Physical Anomalies of the Born Criminal," a section in Lombroso's (1911)[1] final work, *Criminal Man*:

> Polymastia, or the presence of supernumerary nipples (which are generally placed symmetrically below the normal ones as in many mammals) is not an uncommon anomaly. Gynecomastia or hypertrophy of the mammæ is still more frequent in male criminals. In female criminals, on the contrary, we often find imperfect development or absence of the nipples, a characteristic of monotremata or lowest order of the mammals; or the breasts are flabby and pendent like those of Hottentot women.
>
> *(p. 19)*

> The Feet. Spaces between the toes like the interdigital spaces of the hand are very common, and in conjunction with the greater mobility of the toes and greater length of the big-toe, produce the prehensile foot, of the quadrumana, which is used for grasping. The foot is often flat, as in negroes.
>
> *(p. 21)*[2]

These two excerpts provide a glimpse into Lombroso's research. In the first excerpt, criminals are described as having characteristics "of monotremata or lowest order of the mammals" (p. 19). Also, criminals are said to share characteristics with "Hottentot women"[3] (p. 19). In the second excerpt, "the foot is often flat, as in negroes" (Lombroso, 1911, p. 21). These excerpts exemplify how people are labeled and then worth is assigned to said labels. Furthermore, in both excerpts there is the use of language like "common," "imperfect," "normal," "lowest," and "supernumerary," which creates a binary (normal vs. criminal) and a hierarchy of worth – an "othering."

In Lombroso's work, there are blatant associations of criminality with ethnic and racial groups; crime becomes racialized, genetic, and deemed an act of nature. Some argue that Lombroso's theories are no longer relevant (Mazzarello, 2011), or simply denounce the significance of race in Lombroso's theories (Musumeci, 2018).[4] However, Lombroso's theories cannot be removed from the construction of race or othering. Narratives that position human differences as biological are steppingstones to current constructions of race. Many of the values that uphold criminology rely on biology (Brewer & Heitzeg, 2008). Research with ideas like Lombroso's mold societal perceptions of justice through a colonizing lens – a lens that demands control over anything that is seen as a threat to whiteness.

Consider eugenics, a "late" quasi-scientific approach that categorized humans based on genetics. Eugenics perpetuates ideas of inferiority and othering by encouraging those deemed superior to have children (positive eugenics) and those deemed inferior to be sterilized (negative eugenics) (Parsons, 2008; Washington, 2006; Kevles, 2009). White people, people without disabilities, and people who had access to education were attributed to positive eugenics and were encouraged to have children. Conversely, Black people, Indigenous peoples, immigrants, people convicted of crimes, people with disabilities, and people in poverty were attributed to negative eugenics and were encouraged or forced to sterilize. The links between biology and criminality continue to perpetuate the racialization of crime centuries later.

Biology and Criminology: A Tangled Reality in Education

Biology and criminology preserve racist narratives about people, their lives, and their deaths. In this sense, biology and criminology are collaborators of the worst sort. Both disciplines legitimize claims about colonized people, even if these claims are not accurate (e.g., Benjamin, 2016a; Roberts, 2012). These claims are used to justify oppression in a variety of spaces, including education.

I draw on *Plessy v. Ferguson* (1896), a historic US case that deemed the separation of people by race constitutional – Black people were to be separated from white people. Justifications for segregation relied on arguments that promoted racial hierarchies and prioritized whiteness (Brown et al., 2017; Harris, 1993). The infamous notion that people can have "separate but equal" facilities was a product of this case. Narratives of racial superiority and inferiority materialized as a legal precedent. Ultimately, the *Plessy* decision led to *Brown v. Board of Education of Topeka* (1954). *Brown* was a series of cases taken to the US Supreme Court to combat inequality and segregation by race in public schools. In 1954, the Court deemed segregation by race in public schools unconstitutional (Bell, 1980). At its core, *Brown* demonstrates how legacies of racism in court rulings can emerge in education.

The US education system still grapples with injustice (Tate, Ladson-Billings, & Grant, 1993). The desegregation of schools did not eradicate the underlying beliefs that devalue Black students' educational experiences. This is evident in public schools across the US today. Currently, the education system is still unequal and inequitable (Moses, 2004). To illustrate, I use school funding. Funding is a powerful indicator of inequity across the education system (Lee, 2017) because worth becomes inscribed into monetary (and nonmonetary) investments. A 2019 report showed that "nonwhite"[5] schools receive $23 billion less than white school districts (EdBuild, 2019). The main differences? The demographics of students in the schools – their race and class.

Reflecting on Biology Education

Science classrooms reflect centuries-old critiques of racist ideologies in science (Sheth, 2019). Science education includes the teaching, instruction, and learning of the natural sciences through practices like questioning, interpreting, and more (National Research Council, 2012). Science education houses many branches of knowledge, so for specificity, and given my background, I will mainly reflect on biology education. Biology, the study of living organisms and life, includes topics of evolution, genetics, reproduction, and much more (National Research Council, 2012).

The history of racist ideologies in science education can be found in the curriculum. A curriculum is a body of work that varies in format, outlining teaching and learning expectations in a subject (Bergqvist & Bergqvist, 2016; National Research Council, 2012; Ladson-Billings, 2016). There are often unwritten or unspoken agendas or codes within the curriculum. As Ladson-Billings (2016) writes, "These invisible factors include those things that are learned but not openly taught" (p. 100). For instance, in *A Framework for K–12 Science Education: Practices, Crosscutting Concepts, and Core Ideas*, a guide for science teaching and learning, no explicit language is provided about teaching or learning about race or discussions about human differences in science education (National Research Council, 2012; Donovan, 2015). This absence highlights two positivist principles:[6] decontextualization and ahistoricity. In the case of decontextualization, any links between the construction of race and science are erased. Ahistoricity creates a narrative that history is insignificant to understanding and learning science; in other words, students are being taught to understand science without social or historical context. Current biology textbooks also employ narratives about the essentialism of race, which makes claims of sameness within racial groups and differences across racial groups (Donovan, 2014, 2017). Essentialism reduces differences in the community to a single thing: genetics. Ideas of inferiority and positivism can become inscribed in learners' classroom experiences.

Classrooms in various settings can subject learners to oppression. They are surveilled, punished, and tracked (e.g., Noguera, 2003; Basile & Lopez, 2018; Nasir, Rowley, & Perez, 2015). Their access to education is structurally hindered and stereotypes influence their experiences (Sheth, 2019). In science classrooms, such practices affect historically marginalized[7] learners' interactions with educators, peers, and the subject matter (Sheth, 2019; Mensah & Jackson, 2018; King & Pringle, 2019). Across the US, marginalized learners are by definition on the outskirts of science learning. Specifically, research shows that Black students are often excluded and denied access to adequate resources in STEM (e.g., King & Pringle, 2019). This exclusion can lead to the commodification of their experiences and cultures (Bancroft, 2018). For instance, to access STEM, Black students must show they are valuable to the economy. Thus, calls to diversify science turn learners from historically marginalized communities into tools for profit (Basile & Lopez, 2015). In this way, science becomes parasitic. For example, inclusion in science becomes a tool to benefit economic interests, while not always serving the interests of communities. Nonetheless, scholars are making efforts to address institutionalized racism and bias within the science education community (e.g., Sheth, 2019; Rivera Maulucci & Mensah, 2015).

Criminology Education

Likewise, researchers are studying and engaging with the racialization of crime in criminology education (e.g., Covington, 1995; Glover, 2019). Oftentimes, stereotypes treat Black people as a monolith and position them as inherent criminals (Robinson, 2000). These representations of Black people become inscribed in criminology education and have lasting impacts. In a discussion about how schools are agents of socialization, Glover (2019) writes,

> students and educators of criminology transfer their understandings of law, crime, and justice in their everyday discourses and actions, which becomes particularly important for those who go on to careers in the criminal legal system.
>
> *(p. 374)*

This quote highlights why it is significant to address how criminality is represented in education. Teaching and learning influence how people interact and engage in the world. Thus, learning ideas that racialize criminality can influence justice systems today (and arguably already have). As with science education, positivist principles are present in criminology education – in this case, decontextualization.

To address the racialization of crime, criminology (and criminal justice) education cannot ignore race and racism (Rajah, Palmer, & Duggan, 2022; Brown, 2021). When the relationship between race and racism is not discussed, students are in effect being taught that it is nonexistent or irrelevant (Brown, 2021). Many students entering criminology classrooms are still introduced to positivist criminologists like Lombroso (Palmer, Rajah, & Wilson, 2022). These introductions must be carefully contextualized because they can contribute to curricular patterns that perpetuate positivist and racist ideologies.

Likewise, a study of racial images in 23 introductory textbooks for criminal justice and criminology revealed:

> The images presented in criminal justice and criminology textbooks that tend to present African-Americans as criminals and whites as professionals may impact the behavior of criminal justice personnel toward one of punishing instead of serving. The other troubling image presented according to this study is that of African-Americans as victims and whites as professionals. This image foments a view of inequality and helplessness among African-Americans by presenting them as needing to be rescued by whites.
>
> *(Park et al., 2021, p. 853)*

This shows how the racialization of crime and criminality can become inscribed in textbooks – educational tools. Thus, education becomes a means to perpetuate particular values and biases.

Personal Experiences

Medin and Bang (2014) write, "Although there are new scientific discoveries every day, science itself is now treated as 'settled'" (p. 15). That is, the values and ideals that drive scientific discoveries and science itself have been established for some time. These "settled" values and ideals in science are rooted in whiteness and Eurocentricity and are preserved by positivist approaches and perspectives. This link to whiteness is in science education too (Ridgeway, 2019).

I vividly remember feeling like I had to drop my identity before stepping into my science courses. There was no room for me. Rarely, if ever, was race a topic in my courses. It was as if science was absent from my everyday reality. It was as if Black people did not exist. Eurocentric and positivist assumptions were valued. Most, if not all, scientists introduced to me were European and white. Moreover, science was nonexistent beyond the US and European geographic borders, as if science started and ended in the US and Europe.

In many ways, exams illustrated the idea that science was "settled" because they typically depended on how well I could memorize. There was little room for me to go beyond the multiple-choice options presented, and little room to question. The result of my exams relied heavily on my ability to memorize and recite information as given. In my academic science experiences, rote memorization was the primary means to obtain knowledge and succeed – I was expected to receive and recite information as given. This model of thinking was reflected in labs too. Learning and engaging with science in the lab meant completing rigid, predefined steps – receive and learn as instructed. Labs in no way mirrored the collaboration, team building, critical thinking, or creativity I yearned for. It seemed like there was only one way to conduct science. My lab reports were to reflect a "scientific method," be objective, and be matter of fact. All of these represented a positivistic ideology, which was that science and science practices were one-dimensional (e.g., Kincheloe & Tobin, 2009). Some of the values I was learning about science were that there was only one way to learn, there was only one way to communicate science, and there was only one way to conduct scientific inquiry. Much of the learning was focused on what was considered the "right" way to obtain and show knowledge. There were rewards and consequences based on how well I could assimilate to the constructed realities of science. Likewise, it was not uncommon for some required courses to be referred to as "weeding-out" classes – a *survival of the fittest* practice, if you will.

My experiences present only a glimpse into a structural matter. Science education is often presented as ahistorical, apolitical, and established. My educational experiences exemplify presentism.[8] Science ignores the realities and histories that center Black people. Positivist approaches give way to the emergence of carceral approaches – values, actions, and practices that transcend the physical to demand control, punishment, and isolation (e.g., Noguera, 2003; Ali & Buenavista, 2018) – and in some cases, control of learning (e.g., rote memorization) or communication (e.g., prioritize scientific language).

Projections for the Future

Education becomes an ideal space to spread and weaponize the convergence of science and criminology. At a macro level, the convergence of criminology and science requires attention because it continues to evolve. For example, technology (e.g., digital and virtual) comprises modern ways to reinforce human differences (Benjamin, 2016b; Roberts, 2012). In the 21st century, Lombroso's experimental notions of who is a criminal and who is not a criminal become coded into machines. People can embed technology with the same values and belief systems that uphold racialized science and criminology (Roberts, 2012; Duster, 2015). Unfortunately, the impacts of such technology have already begun to surface, like wrongful accusations made by AI machines (Hill, 2020). Claims that biologize race and human difference fortify legacies of genocide, racial segregation, and medical exploitation (Chadha, Lim, Kane, & Rowland, 2020). Furthermore, beliefs that link racial disparities to biology are maintained, despite overwhelming research that racial disparities are a product of many factors – social, economic, and environmental (Donovan, 2014; Graves, 2011; Roberts, 2012; Duster, 2015).

Conclusion

To end, I propose a continual reflection on how the convergence of biology and criminology can begin to be addressed. First, I propose a historical perspective. History provides context; it acts as a reminder of the past, present, and future. History continues to remind society about the value of Black people, Black intellect, Black thought, and Black lives. It is important to understand history to not repeat it and to envision possibilities. To imagine possibilities, there must be detachment from positivist ideologies: what does an abolitionist view of science or criminology (and the convergence) look like? Does it already exist? In addition, whiteness and Eurocentrism need to be decentered. Biology and criminology do not start and end with (western) Europe or whiteness. So what are the global realities and possibilities? And finally, what could education look like beyond the gaze of carcerality, oppression, and social control?

There is much (more) to reflect on, process, and act on. I hope that this chapter can add to the conversation to disrupt racist and carceral ideologies in science, criminology, and education. This chapter only scratches the surface; there are levels to how such entanglements exclude.

Notes

1 The book includes a summary of Cesare Lombroso's work by Gina Lombroso-Ferrero, Cesare Lombroso's daughter (Lombroso, 1911).
2 "Quadrumana" is used to refer to non-human primates. For example, in an 1841 book by W. C. L. (William Charles Linnaeus) Martin, Linnaeus writes: "Of all the lower Mammalia, the Quadrumana (and among them the Orang and Chimpanzee) . . ." (p. 28). It is

important to note that Linnaeus is considered an originator of "scientific racism" (Pontén, Burnett, & Hulth, 2021).

3 A derogatory racial term used towards particular populations in South Africa in the early 1600s (Saleh-Hanna, 2017).

4 Musumeci (2018) notes that Lombroso's work has been used by the FBI in an attempt to link criminality and biology; Musumeci also notes that the blame for how the work has been used cannot be ascribed to Lombroso.

5 This classification of "non-white" vs. "white" reinforces white as the default and identifies anyone who is not white as "other" (Rivera Maulucci & Mensah, 2015).

6 Kincheloe & Tobin, 2009.

7 Historically marginalized by gender, race, sexuality, and socioeconomic status, etc.

8 "A view that often detaches systemic group-level, structural conditions from history and treats them as isolated, individual occurrences that emerge in the present-day moment in which they are being considered" (Parsons & Turner, 2014, p. 101).

References

Alexander, M. (2020) *The new Jim Crow: Mass incarceration in the age of colorblindness*, New York, The New Press [Online].

Ali, A.I. & Buenavista, T.L. (2018) 'Introduction: Toward an antiwar pedagogy: Challenging materialism, militarism, and racism in education', in Ali, A.I. & Buenavista, T.L. (eds.) *Education at war*, New York, Fordham University Press, 1st ed., pp. 1–28.

Anderson, G. (2019) *Biological influences on criminal behavior*, Boca Raton, FL, CRC Press [Online].

ASHG Executive Committee. (2018) 'ASHG denounces attempts to link genetics and racial supremacy', *The American Journal of Human Genetics*, vol. 103, no. 5, p. 636 [Online].

Bancroft, S.F. (2018) 'Toward a critical theory of science, technology, engineering, and mathematics doctoral persistence: Critical capital theory', *Science Education*, vol. 102, no. 6, pp. 1319–1335 [Online].

Basile, V. & Lopez, E.J. (2015) 'And still I see no changes: Enduring views of students of color in science and mathematics education policy reports,' *Science Education*, vol. 99, no. 3, pp. 519–548 [Online].

Basile, V. & Lopez, E.J. (2018) 'Assuming brilliance: A decriminalizing approach to educating African American and Latino boys in elementary school STEM setting's', *Journal of Women and Minorities in Science and Engineering*, vol. 24, no. 4, pp. 361–379 [Online].

Bell, D.A. (1980) 'Brown v. board of education and the interest-convergence dilemma', *Harvard Law Review*, vol. 93, no. 3, pp. 518–533 [Online].

Benjamin, R. (2016a) 'Catching our breath: Critical race STS and the carceral imagination', *Engaging Science, Technology, and Society*, vol. 2, pp. 145–156.

Benjamin, R. (2016b) 'Innovating inequity: If race is a technology, postracialism is the genius bar', *Ethnic and Racial Studies*, vol. 39, no. 13, pp. 2227–2234 [Online].

Bergqvist, E. & Bergqvist, T. (2016) 'The role of the formal written curriculum in standards-based reform', *Journal of Curriculum Studies*, vol. 49, no. 2, pp. 149–168 [Online].

Brewer, R.M. & Heitzeg, N.A. (2008) 'The racialization of crime and punishment: Criminal justice, color-blind racism, and the political economy of the prison industrial complex', *American Behavioral Scientist*, vol. 51, no. 5, pp. 625–644 [Online].

Brown, A.F., Bloome, D., Morris, J.E., Power-Carter, S. & Willis, A.I. (2017) 'Classroom conversations in the study of race and the disruption of social and educational inequalities: A review of research', *Review of Research in Education*, vol. 41, no. 1, pp. 453–476 [Online].

Brown, R.A. (2021) 'There can be more than one: A Black man's journey through the academy', *Race and Justice*, vol. 11, no. 3, pp. 276–287 [Online].

Brown v. Board of Education of Topeka, 347 U.S. 483 (1954).

Chadha, N., Lim, B., Kane, M. & Rowland, B. (2020) *Toward the abolition of biological race in medicine: Transforming clinical education, research, and practice, institute for healing and justice in medicine: And othering & belonging institute*. www.crg.berkeley.edu/wp-content/uploads/2020/07/TowardtheAbolitionofBiologicalRaceinMedicineFINAL.pdf [Online].

Chapman, A. & Feldman, A. (2017) 'Cultivation of science identity through authentic science in an urban high school classroom', *Cultural Studies of Science Education*, vol. 12, no. 2, 469–491 [Online].

Covington, J. (1995) 'Racial classification in criminology: The reproduction of racialized crime', *Sociological Forum*, vol. 10, no. 4, pp. 547–568 [Online].

Delgado, R. & Stefancic, J. (2001) *Critical race theory*, New York, New York University Press.

Donovan, B.M. (2014) 'Playing with fire? The impact of the hidden curriculum in school genetics on essentialist conceptions of race', *Journal of Research in Science Teaching*, vol. 51, no. 4, pp. 462–496 [Online].

Donovan, B.M. (2015) 'Reclaiming race as a topic of the US biology textbook curriculum', *Science Education*, vol. 99, no. 6, pp. 1092–1117 [Online].

Donovan, B.M. (2017) 'Learned inequality: Racial labels in the biology curriculum can affect the development of racial prejudice', *Journal of Research in Science Teaching*, vol. 54, no. 3, pp. 379–411 [Online].

Du Bois, W.E.B. (1901) 'The spawn of slavery: The convict-lease system in the South', in Pierson, A.T., Gracey, J.T., Leonard, D.L., Meyer, F.B. & Pierson, D.L. (eds.) *The missionary review of the world*, New York, Funk & Wagnalls, pp. 737–745 [Online].

Duster, T. (2015) 'A post-genomic surprise. The molecular reinscription of race in science, law and medicine', *The British Journal of Sociology*, vol. 66, no. 1, pp. 1–27 [Online].

EdBuild. (2019) *23 Billion*, viewed June 2022. https://edbuild.org/content/23-billion.

Fair, M.A. & Johnson, S.B. (2021) 'Addressing racial inequities in medicine', *Science*, vol. 372, no. 6540, pp. 348–349 [Online].

General Assembly. (1705) 'An act concerning servants and slaves', *Encyclopedia Virginia*, 2021, June 1. https://encyclopediavirginia.org/entries/an-act-concerning-servants-and-slaves-1705 [Online].

Glover, K.S. (2019) 'Identifying racialized knowledge through a critical race studies lens: Theory and principles for the criminology textbook realm', *Contemporary Justice Review*, vol. 22, no. 4, pp. 371–388 [Online].

Graves, J.L. (2009) 'Biological v. social definitions of race: Implications for modern biomedical research', *The Review of Black Political Economy*, vol. 37, pp. 43–60 [Online].

Graves, J.L. (2011) 'Evolutionary versus racial medicine', in Krimsky, S. & Sloan, K. (eds.) *Race and the genetic revolution*, New York, Columbia University Press, pp. 142–170.

Harris, C.I. (1993) 'Whiteness as property', *Harvard Law Review*, vol. 106, no. 8, pp. 1707–1791 [Online].

Hill, K. (2020) 'Wrongfully accused by an algorithm', *Nytimes.com*. www.nytimes.com/2020/06/24/technology/facial-recognition-arrest.html [Online].

Karter, A.J. (2003) 'Commentary: Race, genetics, and disease – in search of a middle ground', *International Journal of Epidemiology*, vol. 32, no. 1, pp. 26–28 [Online].

Kevles, D.J. (2009) 'Eugenics, the genome, and human rights', *Medicine Studies*, vol. 1, pp. 85–93 [Online].

Kincheloe, J.L. & Tobin, K. (2009) 'The much exaggerated death of positivism', *Cultural Studies of Science Education*, vol. 4, pp. 513–528 [Online].

King, N.S. & Pringle, R.M. (2019) 'Black girls speak STEM: Counterstories of informal and formal learning experiences', *Journal of Research in Science Teaching*, vol. 56, no. 5, pp. 539–569 [Online].

Ladson-Billings, G. (2016) 'And then there is this thing called the curriculum: Organization, imagination, and mind', *Educational Researcher*, vol. 45, no. 2, pp. 100–104 [Online].

Lee, C.D. (2017) 'Integrating research on how people learn and learning across settings as a window of opportunity to address inequality in educational processes and outcomes', *Review of Research in Education*, vol. 41, no. 1, pp. 88–111 [Online].

Lemke, J.L. (1990) *Talking science: Language, learning, and values*, Norwood, NJ, Ablex.

Lombroso, G.F. (1911) *Criminal man, according to the classification of Cesare Lombroso*, New York, G P Putnam's Sons.

Lorde, A. (2007) 'Age, race, class, and sex: Women redefining difference', in *Sister outsider essays and speeches*, Berkeley, CA, Crossing Press, pp. 114–123.

Martin, W.C.L. (1841) *A general introduction to the natural history of mammiferous animals,* London, Wright and Co. Printers, doi: 10.5962/bhl.title.32451.

Mazzarello, P. (2011) 'Cesare Lombroso: An anthropologist between evolution and degeneration', *Functional Neurology*, vol. 26, no. 2, pp. 97–101 [Online].

McCulloch, E. & Carr, J.P. (2016) *Biological innovation: Benefits of federal investments in biology.* www.aibs.org/assets/pages/policy/AIBS-Biological-Innovation-Report.pdf [Online].

Medin, D.L. & Bang, M. (2014) *Who's asking? Native science, western science, and science education.* Cambridge, MA, MIT Press [Online].

Mensah, F. & Jackson, I. (2018) 'Whiteness as property in science teacher education', *Teachers College Record*, vol. 120, pp. 1–38 [Online].

Morales-Doyle, D., Vossoughi, S., Vakil, S. & Bang, M.T. (2020) 'In an era of pandemic and protest, STEM education can't pretend to be apolitical', *Truthout.* https://truthout.org/articles/in-an-era-of-pandemic-and-protest-stem-education-cant-pretend-to-be-apolitical/.

Moses, Y.T. (2004) 'Commentary: The continuing power of the concept of "race"', *Anthropology & Education Quarterly*, vol. 35, no. 1, pp. 146–148 [Online].

Musumeci, E. (2018) 'Against the rising tide of crime: Cesare Lombroso and control of the "dangerous classes" in Italy, 1861–1940', *Crime, Histoire & Sociétés/Crime, History & Societies*, vol. 22, no. 2, pp. 83–106 [Online].

Nasir, N.S., Rowley, S.J. & Perez, W. (2015) 'Cultural, racial/ethnic, and linguistic diversity and identity', in Corno, L. & Anderman, E.M. (eds.) *Handbook of educational psychology: Third edition*, New York, Routledge, pp. 186–198 [Online].

National Research Council. (2012) *A framework for K-12 science education: Practices, crosscutting concepts, and core ideas*, Washington, DC, The National Academies Press [Online].

Nobles, M. (2000) 'History counts: A comparative analysis of racial/color categorization in US and Brazilian censuses', *American Journal of Public Health*, vol. 90, no. 11, pp. 1738–1745 [Online].

Nobles, M., Womack, C., Wonkam, A. & Wathuti, E. (2022) 'Science must overcome its racist legacy: Nature's guest editors speak', *Nature*, vol. 606, no. 7913, pp. 225–227 [Online].

Noguera, P.A. (2003) 'Schools, prisons, and social implications of punishment: Rethinking disciplinary practices', *Theory into Practice*, vol. 42, no. 4, pp. 341–350 [Online].

Palmer, J.E., Rajah, V. & Wilson, S.K. (2022) 'Anti-racism in criminology: An oxymoron or the way forward?,' *Race and Justice*, vol. 12, no. 3, pp. 531–547 [Online].

Park, S-M., Kim, J.L., Park, H., Kim, Y. & Cuadrado, M. (2021) 'Social constructions of racial images in introductory criminal justice and criminology textbooks: A content analysis', *Race Ethnicity and Education*, vol. 24, no. 6, pp. 842–855 [Online].

Parsons, E.R.C. (2008) 'Positionality of African Americans and a theoretical accommodation of it: Rethinking science education research', *Science Education*, vol. 92, no. 6, pp. 1127–1144 [Online].

Parsons, E.R.C. (2014) 'Unpacking and critically synthesizing the literature on race and ethnicity in science education', in Lederman, N.G. & Abell, S. (eds.) *Handbook of research on science education, volume II*, New York, Routledge, pp. 181–200.

Parsons, E.R.C. and Turner, K. (2014) 'The importance of history in the racial inequality and racial inequity in education: New Orleans as a case example', *Negro Educational Review*, vol. 65, no. 1–4, pp. 99–113 [Online].

Plessy v. Ferguson, 163 U.S. 537 (1896).

Pontén, A.W., Burnett, L.A. & Hulth, A. (2021) *Linnaeus' complicated relationship with racism*, Uppsala University. https://www.uu.se/en/news/article/?id=16894&typ=artikel [Online].

Rajah, V., Palmer, J.E. & Duggan, M. (2022) 'The personal is political and so is discomfort: Intersectional, anti-racist praxis in feminist criminology', *Race and Justice*, vol. 12, no. 3, pp. 548–568 [Online].

Ridgeway, M.L. (2019) 'Against the grain: Science education researchers and social justice agendas', *Cultural Studies of Science Education*, vol. 14, pp. 283–292 [Online].

Rivera Maulucci, M.S. and Mensah, F.M. (2015) 'Naming ourselves and others', *Journal of Research in Science Teaching*, vol. 52, no. 1, pp. 1–5 [Online].

Roberts, D.E. (2007) 'Constructing a criminal justice system free of racial bias: An abolitionist framework', *Columbia Human Rights Law Review*, vol. 39, no. 261, pp. 261–285 [Online].

Roberts, D.E. (2012) *Fatal invention: How science, politics, and big business re-create race in the twenty-first century*, New York, New Press/ORIM.

Robinson, M. (2000) 'The construction and reinforcement of myths of race and crime', *Journal of Contemporary Criminal Justice*, vol. 16, no. 2, pp. 133–156 [Online].

Saleh-Hanna, V. (2017) 'Reversing criminology's white gaze: As Lombroso's disembodied head peers through a glass jar in a museum foreshadowed by Sara Baartman's ghost', in Wilson, J., Hodgkinson, S., Piché, J. & Walby, K. (eds.) *The Palgrave handbook of prison tourism*, London, Palgrave Macmillan, pp. 689–711.

Sammel, A. (2009) 'Turning the focus from 'other'to science education: Exploring the invisibility of whiteness', *Cultural Studies of Science Education*, vol. 4, no. 3, pp. 649–656 [Online].

Sheth, M.J. (2019) 'Grappling with racism as foundational practice of science teaching', *Science Education*, vol. 103, no. 1, pp. 37–60 [Online].

Smedley, A. & Smedley, B.D. (2005) 'Race as biology is fiction, racism as a social problem is real: Anthropological and historical perspectives on the social construction of race', *American Psychologist*, vol. 60, no. 1, pp. 16–26 [Online].

Tate, W.F., Ladson-Billings, G. & Grant, C.A. (1993) 'The Brown decision revisited: Mathematizing social problems', *Educational Policy*, vol. 7, no. 3, pp. 255–275 [Online].

U.S. Census Bureau. (2022) 'About the topic of race', *census.gov*. www.census.gov/topics/population/race/about.html [Online].

Washington, H.A. (2006) *Medical apartheid: The dark history of medical experimentation on Black Americans from colonial times to the present*, New York, Doubleday Books.

Willig, C. (2001) *Introducing qualitative research in psychology: Adventures in theory and method*, Buckingham, Open University Press, pp. 50–69.

Yudell, M., Roberts, D., DeSalle, R. and Tishkoff, S. (2016) 'Taking race out of human genetics', *Science*, vol. 351, no. 6273, pp. 564–565 [Online].

10

ABOLISH THE COURTHOUSE

Uncovering the Space of "Justice" in a Black Feminist Criminal Trial

Vanessa Lynn Lovelace

Introduction

Criminology's central concern is to understand the root causes of criminal behavior, whether they be biological or social. A Black Feminist abolitionist lens of criminology "critiques dominant, White supremacist constructions of colonized/colonizing, enslaved/enslaving and imprisoned/imprisoning bodies, lives, deaths, and histories" (Saleh-Hanna, 2015). This analysis critiques the notion that Black, Brown, and Indigenous people are simply objects for studying. Much like the process of colonization, criminology necessitates the transformation of BIPOC (Black, Indigenous, and people of color) into being seen as things to be eradicated (Césaire, 2000). Through this framework, Blackness is criminal and whiteness is power. This power translates into maintaining control over how each piece of the criminal justice system is constructed, maintained, renewed, and legitimized. Whiteness sets the parameters of what is right/moral, just, and legal, and Blackness its opposite. As such, a Black Feminist abolitionist lens necessitates the formation of multiple ways of eradicating the carceral state.

Abolitionist practitioners and scholars have emphasized that criminology's goal of establishing a theory of crime does not address the fact that what counts as crime relies on (neo)colonial-imperial violences (Saleh-Hanna, 2017a; Carrier and Piché, 2015; Agozino, 2004). This chapter examines criminology above and beyond theories. It assesses the architecture of criminality by analyzing courthouse and courtroom design and praxis. For the purposes of this chapter, the following definitions are used: *courthouse* means the building containing the administrative offices of a municipality which houses courtrooms; *courtroom* refers to the individual rooms within a courthouse where a court of law meets; while *court* references a court of law, which is a tribunal presided over by a judge, judges, or magistrate (civil and criminal cases).

DOI: 10.4324/9780367817114-14

Much work has been done to analyze the colonial – white supremacist, hetero-patriarchal – nature of the criminal justice system. Concurrently, much has been done to analyze the physical landscape and geography of the legal system as it exists outside of the courthouse – from policing policies (Dillon and Sze, 2016), to redistricting (Forest, 2004), to the physical space of jails and prisons (Gilmore, 2007) to racial segregation (Shabazz, 2015). There has been minimal work, however, on analyzing the physical landscape, architecture, and architectural style of the courthouse and courtroom. The proper functioning of the courthouse and courtroom relies on the proper placement of spaces of confinement and access. The courthouse's and its individual courtrooms' designs put into action criminological theories of how crime defines a location, allowing criminality to come from place (Gilmore, 2007; Tyner, 2012). The entirety of the legal process adheres to these violent frameworks. The physicality of the courthouse and courtroom provides a site for understanding a key relationship between how coloniality informs these two separate yet interconnected spaces, and the possibilities for abolitionary justice to inhabit space. Courthouses and courtrooms are the perfect representation of the lack of access the nonlegal professional public has to the law's creation, implementation, and process.

I articulate a Black Feminist abolitionist analysis of U.S. courthouses and courtrooms to resituate how we read Assata Shakur's New Jersey criminal trials. This chapter proceeds in four parts. First, I provide a review of legal architectural literature. Here I highlight the two analytical strands – symbolic, and physical structure analysis – while focusing on the latter. Second, I examine how Black Feminist conceive of carceral power, and how this establishes the conditions for surveilling Blackness. Third, I apply Black Feminist Geographies in the viewing of Middlesex County (New Jersey) Courthouse, and its high modern style. While focusing on Shakur's New Jersey criminal trials, I am attentive to two architectural by-products: access and criminology. Lastly, I provide a conclusion that considers how the question (and methods) of accessing the courthouse and courtroom is an abolitionary project.

The Visage of Justice: Designing Courthouses

This chapter explores what, if any, justice can be found in U.S. courthouses and courtrooms, and explores the bodies that travel in, out, and through them. Legal architecture is the representational and symbolic analysis of the architectural design and structure of courthouses. There are two analytical strands: one that studies the influence of symbols of justice, and another that focuses specifically on the history of courthouse construction and design (Tait, 2012, p. 4). Legal architecture contributes to abolitionary research by examining how criminology, architecture, and geography combine to construct the courthouse as a building uniquely designed to surveil and contain.

The history of the courthouse follows the progression of public life in relation to the law. Resnik and Curtis (2012) argue that the democratization of societies is linked particularly with the public nature of court proceedings. Symbols of justice (especially those displayed in courthouses and civic buildings) went from being purely abstract to representative of actual people. In particular, these symbols promoted white supremacist, hetero-patriarchal values, thus endorsing a vision of justice that privileged these values and the bodies they represent and protect. Modern courthouses, however, are not just representative of expanding protections of privileged elite. The public nature also represents further societal democratization, as "open access, . . . equal and dignified treatment of all participants – are outgrowths of social movements that transformed the meaning of legal 'personhood,' the idea of justice, and the obligations of government" (Resnik and Curtis, 2012, p. 27). Social movements have forced the changing of who is considered to be a member of the public. This expansion, however, has not found its way into what is represented within the courthouse.

While Resnik and Curtis address the representational and symbolic artifacts found in courthouses, Martha J. McNamara explores how architectural design plays into the performance of the law. Examining the evolution, rebuilding, and relocation of "the physical spaces that enclosed commercial, legal, and social transactions in colonial Boston, we can begin to understand the interplay between market and court and between performance and exchange" (McNamara, 2004, p. 126). Colonial courthouses existed in multiple different types of buildings, but their purpose was to house all manner of public business. U.S. courthouses come out of this history. Thus, modern courthouses centralize legal control as spaces where all manner of legal business is resolved. Each iteration of the courthouse was thought to be a social, political, democratic, and architectural improvement on legal proceedings themselves (McNamara, 2004).

Linda Mulcahy combines structural and symbolic analysis to argue that the architectural history of courthouses influences courtroom identities. Mulcahy has concerns for how the public "participates" in the courthouse, noting that "the principle of open justice is in serious danger of being undermined when the public are first searched, then channeled through space, and finally positioned within tightly controlled zones within the courtroom" (Mulcahy, 2010, p. 10). For Mulcahy, the architecture of the courthouse (much like its representational figures) is complicit in ensuring that those who do not have the privilege of being experts in the law and the legal arena are excluded from equal access to justice. She points out "the complicity of architecture in classifying and containing participants in the trial in ways [that] are problematic to those of us interested in the delivery of equal access to justice" (Mulcahy, 2010, p. 5). Space within the courthouse is deliberately designed to control and surveil public participation in the administration of justice, specifically in the courtroom. This design sets up the conditions for hierarchy, exclusion, and criminality, making apparent who belongs ("occupants"), and who does not ("intruders").

Norman W. Spaulding is particularly concerned with how justice is connected to the structure of a space. While it was once the case that courthouses lay open for more public use, Spaulding argues that they became more enclosed as common law progressed to more adversarial confrontation. Indeed, "[e]nclosure offers control, efficiency, and rationality in the administration of justice. By specializing the use of space and restricting access, disruption and surprise can be avoided, deference can be enforced in participants and observers" (Spaulding, 2012, p. 340). The manipulation of space is not necessarily a bad thing for Spaulding, as he finds control over the courthouse to be important to the productivity of courtroom activities. The courtroom's further partitioning, creating clear divisions and hierarchies, allows for better containment of the adversarial confrontations within the courtroom. Spaulding goes on, arguing that "[o]n a symbolic level, elevation, ornamentation, and partitions, specialized boxes, benches, bars, and tables serve to fix and hierarchically segment lay and expert role players. At the visual and aural level, however, the division of space accentuates accessibility" (Spaulding, 2012, p. 330). The public is continuously controlled by the landscape of the courthouse because they lack the knowledge to properly navigate the building and the clearance to be able to do so. Additionally, the confinement of trials and legal procedures within the walls of a courtroom has contributed to the further ease in surveillance of bodies in space, and bodies and space.

X-Ray Machines and Metal Detectors: Disrupting Carceral Power

This section expands upon Mulcahy and Spaulding's arguments about the confining nature of courthouse design by arguing that race and racism play an important role in designing surveillance and access. Using Black Feminist Geographies, I analyze how courthouse and courtroom architecture specifically surveils and disciplines Black, Brown, and Indigenous bodies in a way that readily marks them as criminal/deviant. Black Feminist Geographies links anti-oppressive feminists' frameworks – which are built through the histories, theories, and movements of Black, Third World, Indigenous, Queer, Postcolonial, Women of Color, and transnational feminisms (Lovelace and Turcotte, 2020) – with an exploration of how "Black matters are spatial matters" (McKittrick, 2006, p. xii). Black Feminist Geographies theorize that carceral power is mobilized to create spaces of easy confinement and surveillance.

The administration of justice inside courthouses and courtrooms is racially biased (Davis, 2011; Alexander, 2010; Spade, 2015). The geography of courthouses and courtrooms exists within the logics of carceral power. This power necessitates that there are zones of and for surveillance as a means of restricting and containing "criminal" bodies. Carceral power draws upon Foucault's premise that the modern prison taught other institutions – schools, home life, military, urban planning, etc. – how to punish through everyday disciplinary and spatial practices (Foucault, 1995). Carceral power is mobilized through internal regulation, and people are disciplined via external punishment (Davis, 2003). Black Feminist Geographies expands upon Foucault's premise, arguing that the power and punishment of the prison is uniquely racialized, and expands into all places associated with Black life (McKittrick, 2006; Shabazz 2015; Gilmore, 2007). As a result, the courthouse and courtroom spatializes blackness – puts Blackness in its place. Rashad Shabazz states, "The term 'spatializing blackness' underscores how mechanisms of constraint built into architecture, urban planning, and systems of control that functioned through policing and the establishment of borders literally and figuratively created a prison-like environment" (2015, p. 2). The courthouse and courtroom, like all other spaces in the dominant culture where Black life exists, operate within the disciplinary logics of the prison – thus have carceral power. This set-up situates defendants (and Black, Brown, and Indigenous people in whatever dominant-culture spaces they occupy) as bodies that need to be policed – monitored, surveilled, and contained (Story, 2019).

Intruders and Occupiers: How to View Shakur Through the Courthouse and Courtroom

Middlesex County, New Jersey, exists on Lenape land. Located within New York City's metropolitan area, Middlesex County was developed by colonialism and slavery, which emphasizes racism, violence, and white supremacy. Understood as a moderate county, Middlesex has a history of supporting freedoms with "compromises", as a means of not upsetting the status quo. In fact, after Lincoln's Emancipation Proclamation, a *New Brunswick Times* writer felt that Abolitionists were "insulting to those who, 'support the Constitution and the Laws and don't yet think the [racial epithet for African-American deleted] is better than the white man" (Jackson, p. 142). Middlesex County is representative of mid-Atlantic U.S. life, one that takes its name from colonizers and denies its role in Indigenous genocide and Black enslavement.

On Interstate 95, the New York State Thruway joins the New Jersey Turnpike, and passes directly through Middlesex County. One of the most heavily traveled highways in the U.S., the New Jersey Turnpike is funded by state agencies and secured by state troopers. On May 2, 1973, three members of the Black Liberation Army (BLA), Assata Shakur, Sundiata Acoli, and Zayd Malik Shakur, were pulled over by New Jersey State Trooper James Harper for a faulty headlight, a "reason consistent with the FBI COINTELPRO guidelines, which directed that activists be arrested for minor traffic violations" (Hinds, 1987, p. xiv). At the time, Shakur was already a fugitive because of the FBI and the New York City Police Department's media and law enforcement campaign to name her a violent, kidnapping, bank-robbing, murdering terrorist (Shakur, 1987). The traffic stop turned into a turnpike shootout, and Zayd and Werner Forester (another New Jersey State Trooper, who Harper called for backup) were killed. Shakur was wounded, taken to Middlesex General Hospital, later held in Middlesex County Workhouse, and was eventually held at the Middlesex County Correctional Center for Men as she awaited her multiple trials. She was convicted on seven charges, including being an accomplice to the murder of Werner Forester. One of Shakur's lawyers, Lennox S. Hinds, argues that Shakur did not and could not have received a fair trial in Middlesex County. He states the trial was "fueled by biased, inflammatory publicity in the local press before and throughout the trial" (1987, p. xvi). This was further "fanned by the documented government lawlessness that made it possible for the white jury to convict Shakur on the uncorroborated, contradictory, and generally incredible testimony of Trooper Harper, the only other witness to the events on the turnpike" (1987, p. xvi). Harper in fact admitted to lying during both Acoli and Shakur's trials. Hinds' statement is supported by newspaper articles at the time. For example, a January 18, 1977, *New York Times* article states, "A defense poll shows that 70 percent of the people surveyed in the Middlesex County area were already convinced Mrs. Chesimard was guilty" (Sullivan, para. 4). Shakur changed her name in 1971, finding that the name JoAnne did not fit her Africanness, and Chesimard was a master's name. She states in her autobiography, "[m]y mind, heart, and soul had gone back to Africa, but my name was still stranded in Europe somewhere" (Shakur, 1987, p. 185). Middlesex County Courthouse is a product of the county's racist, colonialist history, and its architecture contributes to the fast and easy criminalization of defendants even before their trials.

Built in 1958, Middlesex County Courthouse is located in New Brunswick's Civic Square, a testament to the midcentury urban planning style of high modernism.[1] The court's entrance has two sets of connecting doors, which are surrounded by silver paneling. There is a small overhang, presumably to protect those who

FIGURE 10.1 "Middlesex County Courthouse New Brunswick NJ."

Source: Photo credit Hudconja, distributed under CC-BY-SA-4.0.

enter and leave from rain or snow. The entire building is paneled in the same way as the doors, except they are colored mahogany brown. On the right-hand side of the building there are two columns of windows, while two mature trees block the lower-level windows from public view. Simple metallic or metal lettering marks the building as MIDDLESEX COUNTY COURTHOUSE. My focus on the exterior of the building is related to access. I never gained access to Shakur's trial records, and a deeper online search for pictures, blueprints, or descriptions of the inside of the courthouse came up empty. I cannot gain access to the interior of the building to see what it looks like, but I have multiple images of the flat, straight-lined, and uniform exterior. The courthouse design and access (not just physical but the visual archive) is representative of the high modernism architectural philosophy used to design it: it is regimented, restricted, and organized.

U.S. courthouses tend to follow two distinct architectural styles and philosophies: neoclassicism and high modernism.[2] While these architectural styles present different visuals, they draw from an ideological philosophy which views architecture as a discipline and practice for controlling and organizing bodies. Middlesex County Courthouse is built in the architectural style of high modernism. High modernism produces "symmetric, somber, imponent" buildings, "and much like a classic revivalist courthouse, the intention [is] to accentuate the state's presence pervaded by social hierarchy" (Blumetti et al., 2020). The goal of high modernism is to institute order – by establishing hierarchies and control – through the use of space and design. Middlesex County Courthouse accomplishes this through a straight-lined, paneled exterior, and an obscured interior.

Loos' *Ornament and Crime* (1909–10), a foundational text of high modernist architecture, claims ornament – both on one's person and in buildings – is not only criminal but linked to crime. A common definition of "ornament" is something that is used to improve the attractiveness of an object. It has no functional purpose. Loos uses the practice of tattooing and those who are tattooed to substantiate his claim. He argues tattooing is an uncivilized practice performed by "primitive" Indigenous people around the world and criminals in prisons: "Ornaments . . . were physical manifestations of unmodernity, for among other things 'they are markers of place,' of ethnic identity" (Purdy, 2006, p. 50). Tattooing represents criminality through a childlike, animal-like, and unmodern interest in decoration. Loos' architectural philosophy of high modernism is premised on taming nature through rationality, order, and science. Designers of high-modern houses, government buildings, cities, and manufacturing facilities view ornament as representative of criminality (Schwartz, 2012; Scott, 1998; Colomina, 1990; Shabazz, 2015). This architectural philosophy believes the careful designing of space will discipline, contain, and order criminals and their criminality.

Loos' architectural "vision" is important, not just to understanding the outside of the Middlesex County Courthouse, but also for interpreting the elusiveness of the interior as well. For the "house does not have to tell anything on the exterior; instead all its richness must be manifest in the interior" (Loos, 2002, p. 106). He argues that in order to "secret vice the law courts must seem to make a threatening gesture" (Loos, 2002, p. 84). The architectural practice of *Raumplan*, a Loosian creation, endeavors to design rooms and interior spaces in a way that allows for easy monitoring of the "Other" (Colomina, 1990). An ideal room would have windows that let in light but preclude viewing outward. The interior is made intimate by its nonobviousness, and by its ability to invite the gaze of "the intruder," while simultaneously facilitating the viewing of "the intruder" by "the occupant" (Colomina, 1990). The outside of the courthouse is composed, its goal to blend in and provide cover, the inside available for controlled occupation. Each room, hallway, painting, symbol, staircase, and item of furniture is carefully selected and positioned to allow for "intruders" (Black, Brown, and Indigenous people, and those marked as "Other," deviant, and criminal) to be gazed upon and put on display. This allows their movements and visual, social, political, and cultural presentations to be easily controlled. "Intruders" cannot occupy space – they go through it to be surveilled.

Given the architectural history and philosophy that inspires the creation of the high-modern courthouse, how can we interpret the influence of courthouse and courtroom architecture on Shakur's criminal trials? The courthouse and courtroom demarcate criminality through their very design. If Loos' ornament as criminal is a theory of crime, then Shakur's ornamentality, her body as excessive decor with no purpose, situates her as criminal. Her body is on display to be disciplined and punished (Foucault, 1995).

Figures 10.2–10.5 are courtroom sketches of Assata Shakur's New Jersey criminal trials, illustrated by Ida Libby Dengrove. In the sketches, Shakur is illustrated with an airbrush border in white, which classically portrays angel-like figures. Shakur wears a light-colored headscarf, a sign of her Black Muslim femininity. The complexity of her identity is not played with in either color variance or blending, thus rendering a flat, one-dimensional idea of her. What is important about these images, in the context of Loos' theory of ornamentality as criminality, is that because Shakur stands out in sharp contrast to her surroundings, she is on full display for intense scrutiny (Apter, 2002). The viewer is forced to look directly at Shakur, and this gazing is itself a form of surveillance through forced monitoring. Surveillance is used to enact social control measures for determining Black and white space. Simone Browne argues that this is a form of "racializing surveillance" (2015). Browne explains that this technology of social control allows "surveillance practices, policies and performances [that] concern the production of norms pertaining to race and exercise a 'power to define what is in or out of place'. . . signaling those moments when enactments of surveillance reify boundaries, borders, and bodies along racial lines" (2015, p. 16). Browne's articulation of racializing surveillance provides the framework by which we can analyze how courthouses and courtrooms criminalize Black, Brown, and Indigenous people in their very design, and Shakur's courtroom in particular.

In an article written for *CONTRAST*, Ontario, Canada's Black community paper, Edwin B. Hogan comments on the visual image of Shakur's presence in the courtroom. He posits her trial as a "tragicomedy" of a "media event . . . complete

FIGURE 10.2   "Chesimard & Jury, 1973 NBC–TV."

Source: Photo credit Ida Libby Dengrove.

when a petite, diminutive woman with handcuffs, leg irons, and chains, emerge from her towering, rifle-toting escorts, as the subject for electrifying security and precautions" (Hogan, 1977). Criminology necessitates securing criminal bodies, and the best way to do so is by highlighting their criminality through ornamentality – excess (Agozino, 2003, 2004). Shakur in her very makeup is a criminal. Indeed, criminology understands Shakur, born a Black woman in the United States, to be predisposed to criminal behavior, precisely because of her locations – her race, sex, ethnicity, class, and place (Saleh-Hanna, 2017a). Every security and policing measure put into place is because Shakur is a criminal, and every measure communicates Shakur's criminality as a fact.

The "securing" of the courtroom requires that Blackness/"the intruder"/the "Other" be made into a spectacle for observation and containment – surveillance. Dengroves' sketches and a few *New York Times* newspaper articles are the only access I have to the inside of the courthouse and courtroom. An analysis of these articles explores further how "securing" the courtroom presented jurors, and all others who entered, with the presumed criminality of the defendant and her defense team. Hogan (1977) argues, "No longer is it uncommon to view a political trial through

FIGURE 10.3   "Security Bringing in Mrs. Chesimard."

Source: Photo credit Ida Libby Dengrove.

a thick, bullet-proof glass shield, while being viewed over closed-circuit television." In order to even get there, one must pass "through exotic metal detector devices where the public and press are formally fingerprinted and photographed for future reference" (Hogan, 1977). At the same time, it is not uncommon "for the defendant to arrive amidst an entourage of sirens wailing, a kaleidoscope of flashing red and white lights, motorcycle escorts, and procession of police vehicles" (Hogan, 1977). Further, in the *Times* article published on the opening day of the trial, Sullivan states, "Mr. Kunstler [Shakur's attorney] complained about the tight security around the courtroom that he said would give prospective jurors the impression that Mrs. Chesimard was a 'wild animal'" (Sullivan, 1977, para 13).

In a *Times* article published on October 9, 1973, entitled "Security Is Tight for the Chesimard Trial" we are given the full extent of the security measures employed to contain Black radicalism and deviance, in the form of Shakur, Acoli, and their supporters. Shakur and Acoli were kept in the jail next to the courthouse, and shuttled into the courthouse underground. The entire policing force of the city of New Brunswick was placed on high alert as Black radicals were expected to disrupt the proceedings. The trial was thought to be so high risk that an 850-person police

FIGURE 10.4   "Chesimard."

Source: Photo credit Ida Libby Dengrove.

reserve, made up of the New Brunswick Police Department, the Middlesex County Sheriff's Police, and the Rutgers University campus patrol, was kept on standby (Johnston, 1973). The prosecution team, jurors, trial judge, and their families had around-the-clock security. Rutgers University security was told to prepare for a large influx of visiting students who would be joining the campus to participate in demonstrations in support of Shakur and Acoli. Johnston (1973) reports that "[o]fficials confirmed no unusual influx of visitors had been found."

Johnston (1973) continues, explaining the exhaustive measures taken as a means of controlling, surveilling, and containing "intruders" to the courthouse, as if it were not a public place. Members of the press had to apply in advance for photo credentials provided by the Sheriff's Department. Only 20 spectators (including press) were allowed in the courtroom at a time. Additionally, all parking around the courthouse was available only to police vehicles. A ten-man team comprised of state and city police officers was a hand-picked reactionary force stationed at City Hall, and a special plan was devised to address any bomb scares throughout the entire city that might occur during the trial. The police headquarters – located six blocks from the courthouse – established additional protocols for a potential raid on the headquarters

FIGURE 10.5   "Chesimard, Jury."

Source: Photo credit Ida Libby Dengrove.

meant to procure firearms that would presumably be used to free the defendants. These security measures exhibit the role the city of New Brunswick, Middlesex County, and criminal trials play in state making. Indeed, "State-making requires the securitization of borders, maximization of profits, regulation of population, and increasing positions of power within global affairs" (Lovelace and Turcotte, 2020). The excess of security hides state violence – the violence in the structure of the courthouse and its individual courtrooms, and the deployment of mass numbers of law enforcement – by making violence endemic to these two figures of radical Blackness, Shakur and Acoli (Turcotte, 2014). Shakur's trials, and the "security" they "necessitated," makes visually and structurally explicit the fact that Middlesex County is, and has always been, an occupied territory.

Coda: Basement Readings

Through the process of researching Shakur's court case, it became clear that learning how to access the courthouse and courtroom are an important part of the project of abolishing criminology. Since 2018 I have attempted to gain access to the records of even one of Assata Shakur's criminal trials. I still do not have access. I have contacted court records offices via email, phone, and mail. I have visited the Schomburg Center archives in New York City, and been in contact with Stanford University's Special Collections. I have enlisted the help of university and law school librarians. All of this is in order to gain access to court records that are said to be public. It is an expensive process in time, money, and mobility. I still do not have access.

The formalization of the court process – from the ritualistic procedures, to the professionalization of legal personnel, to the establishment of designated buildings meant only for legal proceedings – has indeed placed barriers on access to state-sanctioned "justice." As an academic my job is to sift through archives and records to piece together histories and, I argue, the politics surrounding them, but as many researchers have shown, access is neither cheap nor easy. When access to the archives is achieved, it reveals narratives of violence against, and the death of, Black, Brown, Indigenous, queer, and poor people. Each of these results is needed to broaden the scope of what we are looking for, and indeed to read in what is "left out" or "missing" from the formalized archives that exist (Arondekar, 2009). And to "read against the grain" of the narratives offered by those in power (Hartman, 1997). Black Feminist Abolitionists scholars have continuously done the work of grappling with archival material in order to assemble historical and literary narratives of those like them. Indeed, what we access in the archives is not just the lives of the authors, recorders, or artists who produced particular images and texts, but more importantly we access traces of resistance and freedom-making of enslaved people and colonial subjects (Spivak, 1988; Hartman, 1997, 2007; Arondekar, 2009; Fuentes, 2016).

My archival goal, however, was not to access items from hundreds of years in the past. I was not looking to "read against the grain," or to analyze the power present in reading the archives. I simply sought access to one of the most infamous criminal trials in 20th-century Black history, and I could not. The courthouse is designed in this way, to limit access. It is designed to create and hold on to presumed criminality and guilt, and to reinforce this with every person who seeks to "intrude" on its well-designed security. I still do not have access.

Notes

1 New Brunswick's Civic Square holds multiple city and federal public buildings, including Middlesex County Courthouse, New Brunswick's main post office, and the New Brunswick Free Public Library.
2 In February 2020 the Trump administration drafted an Executive Order titled, "Making Federal Buildings Beautiful Again," or MFBBA, which draws upon his campaign slogan of "Make America Great Again" as a means of linking his political inclination to seek a perceived past American glory (usually via racist, sexist, homophobic, and xenophobic rhetoric, laws, and personal actions) to returning American architecture to a style of the past. The MFBBA Executive Order would mandate that all future government buildings, and all future government building renovations, be (re)designed in the neoclassicist style. This would effectively force a rewriting of *Guiding Principles for Federal Architecture*, in place since 1962, which dictated there should be no universal architectural style for federal buildings, and that they should instead be built in the style of the time. The Executive Order draft asserts that many government buildings do not embody the country's "self-governing ideals."

Bibliography

Agozino, B. (2003) *Counter-Colonial Criminology: A Critique of Imperialist Reason*, London, Pluto Press.

Agozino, B. (2004) 'Imperialism, Crime and Criminology: Toward the Decolonisation of Criminology', *Crime, Law and Social Change*, vol. 41, pp. 343–58.

Alexander, M. (2010) *The New Jim Crow: Mass Incareration in the Age of Colorblindness*, New York, The New Press.

Apter, A. (2002) 'On Imperial Spectacle: The Dialectics of Seeing in Colonial Nigeria', *Comparative Studies in Society and History*, vol. 44, no. 3, pp. 564–96.

Arondekar, A. (2009) *For the Record: On Sexuality and the Colonial Archive in India*, Durham, Duke University Press.

Blumetti, D., Rodrigues, P. and Januario, P. (2020) 'Courthouse Architecture and Power Performances in the 20th Century'.

Brown, M. and Schept, J. (2017) 'New Abolition, Criminology and a Critical Carceral Studies', *Punishment & Society*, vol. 19, no. 4, pp. 440–62.

Browne, S. (2015) *Dark Matters: On the Surveillance of Blackness*, Durham, Duke University Press.

Carlton, B. and Russell, E. (2018) 'We Will Be Written Out of History: Feminist Challenges to Carceral Violence and the Activist Archive', *Oñati Socio-Legal Series*, vol. 8, no. 4, pp. 267–87.

Carrier, N. and Piché, J. (2015) 'The State of Abolitionism', *Champ pénal/Penal Field*, vol. 12.

Césaire, A. (2000) *Discourse on Colonialism*, New York, NYU Press.

Colomina, B. (1990) 'Intimacy and Spectacle: The Interiors of Adolf Loos', *AA Files. Architectural Association School of Architecture*, no. 20, pp. 5–15.

Davis, A. (2003) 'Race and Criminalization: Black Americans and the Punishment Industry', in McLaughlin, E. and Muncie, J. (eds.) *Criminological Perspectives: Essential Readings*, Thousand Oaks, Sage, pp. 301–10.

Davis, A. (2011) *Are Prisons Obsolete*, New York, Seven Stories Press.

De Angelo, W. A. 'The History Buff's Guide to Middlesex County'.

Dillon, L. and Sze, J. (2016) 'Police Power and Particulate Matters: Environmental Justice and the Spatialities of In/Securities in US Cities', *English Language Notes*, vol. 54, no. 2, pp. 13–23.

Franklin, S. (2020, February 4) '[Updated] Potential Executive Order Might Force Neoclassical Style on Federal Buildings', *The Architect's Newspaper*. Available at: www.archpaper.com/2020/02/trump-draft-executive-order-neoclassical-style/ (Accessed: 29 June 2020).

Forest, B. (2004) 'The Legal (de)construction of Geography: Race and Political Community in Supreme Court Redistricting Decisions', *Social & Cultural Geography*, vol. 5, no. 1, pp. 55–73.

Foucault, M. (1995) *Discipline and Punish: The Birth of the Prison*, New York, Vintage.

Fuentes, M. J. (2016) *Dispossessed Lives: Enslaved Women, Violence and the Archive*, Philadelphia, University of Pennsylvania Press.

Gilmore, R. W. (2007) *Golden Gulags: Prisons, Surplus, Crisis, and Opposition in Globalizing California*, Berkeley, University of California Press.

Hartman, S. (1997) *Scenes of Subjection: Terror, Slavery, and Self-Making in Nineteenth-Century America*, New York, Oxford University Press.

Hartman, S. (2007) *Lose Your Mother: A Journey Along the Atlantic Slave Route*, New York, Farrar, Straus and Giroux.

Hinds, L. S. (1987) 'Foreward', in *Assata: An Autobiography*, Chicago, Lawrence Hill Books, pp. xi–xiii.

Hogan, E. B. (1977) 'Why Is Assata on Trial?' *"Contrast"*, Ontario.

Johnston, R. J. H. (1973, October 8) 'Security Is Tight for Chesimard Trial', *New York Times*.

Long, C. (2009) 'The Origins and Context of Adolf Loos's "'Ornament and Crime'"', *Journal of the Society of Architectural Historians*, vol. 68, no. 2, pp. 200–23.

Loos, A. (2002) *On Architecture*, Riverside, Ariadne Press.

Lovelace, V. L. and Turcotte, H. M. (2020) 'Immobolizing Bodies of Surveillance: Anti-Oppressive Feminisms and the Decolonization of Violence', in Caliskan, G. (ed.) *Gendering Globalization, Globalizing Gender: Post-Colonial Perspectives*, Oxford, Oxford University Press, pp. 196–209.

McKittrick, K. (2006) *Demonic Grounds: Black Women and The Cartographies of Struggle*, Minneapolis, University of Minnesota Press.

McNamara, M. J. (2004) *From Tavern to Courthouse: Architecture & Ritual in American Law, 1658–1860*, Baltimore, John Hopkins University Press.

Mulcahy, L. (2010) *Legal Architecture: Justice, Due Process and the Place of Law*, New York, Routledge.

Purdy, D. (2006) 'The Cosmopolitan Geography of Adolf Loos', *New German Critique*, no. 99, pp. 41–62.

Resnik, J. and Curtis, D. (2012) 'Re-presenting Justice: Visual Narratives of Judgment and the Invention of Democratic Courts Representing and Contesting Ideologies of the Public Spheres', *Yale Journal of Law & the Humanities*, vol. 24, no. 1, pp. 19–96.

Richardson, L. S. (2016) 'Systemic Triage: Implicit Racial Bias in the Criminal Courtroom Review', *Yale Law Journal*, vol. 126, no. 3, pp. 862–93.

Richardson, L. S. and Goff, P. A. (2012) 'Implicit Racial Bias in Public Defender Triage', *Yale Law Journal*, vol. 122, no. 8, pp. 2626–49.

Saleh-Hanna, V. (2015) 'Black Feminist Hauntology: Rememory the Ghosts of Abolition', *Champ Pénal/Penal Field*, vol. 12, pp. 1–28.

Saleh-Hanna, V. (2017a) 'An Abolitionist Theory on Crime: Ending the Abusive Relationship with Racist-Imperialist-Patriarchy [R.I.P]', *Contemporary Justice Review*, vol. 20, no. 4, pp. 419–40.

Saleh-Hanna, V. (2017b) 'Reversing Criminology's White Gaze: As Lombroso's Disembodied Head Peers Through a Glass Jar in a Museum Foreshadowed by Sara Baartman's Ghost', in Wilson, J. Z. et al. (eds.) *The Palgrave Handbook of Prison Tourism*, London, Palgrave Macmillan, pp. 689–711.

Schwartz, F. J. (2012) 'Architecture and Crime: Adolf Loos and the Culture of the "Case"', *The Art Bulletin*, vol. 94, no. 3, pp. 437–57.

Scott, J. C. (1998) *Seeing Like a State: How Certain Schemes to Improve the Human Condition have Failed*, New Haven, Yale University Press.

Shabazz, R. (2015) *Spatializing Blackness: Architects of Confinement and Black Masculinity in Chicago*, Chicago, University of Illinois Press.

Shakur, A. (1987) *Assata: An Autobiography*, Chicago, Lawrence Hill Books.

Spade, D. (2015) *Normal Life: Administrative Violence, Critical Trans Politics, and the Limits of Law*, Durham, Duke University Press.

Spaulding, N. W. (2012) 'The Enclosure of Justice: Courthouse Architecture, Due Process, and the Dead Metaphor of Trial Representing and Contesting Ideologies of the Public Spheres', *Yale Journal of Law & the Humanities*, vol. 24, no. 1, pp. 311–44.

Spivak, G. (1988) 'Can the Subaltern Speak?' in Nelson, C. and Grossberg, L. (eds.) *Marxism and the Interpretation of Culture*, Urbana, University of Illinois Press.

Story, B. (2019) *Prison Land: Mapping Carceral Power across Neoliberal America,* Minneapolis, University of Minnesota Press.

Sullivan, J. F. (1977 January 18) 'Courthouse is Picketed as Chesimard Trial Starts', *New York Times*.

Tait, A. A. (2012) 'What We Didn't See Before Representing and Contesting Ideologies of the Public Spheres', *Yale Journal of Law & the Humanities*, vol. 24, no. 1, pp. 3–18.

Turcotte, H. M. (2014) 'Feminist Asylums and Acts of Dreaming', *Feminist Theory*, vol. 15, no. 2, pp. 141–60.

Tyner, J. A. (2012) *Space, Place, and Violence: Violence and the Embodied Geographies of Race, Sex, and Gender*, New York, Routledge Press.

11

MARXIST CRIMINOLOGY ABOLISHES LOMBROSO, MARXIST CRIMINOLOGY ABOLISHES ITSELF

Erin Katherine Krafft

Introduction

Nadezhda Mandelstam, wife of the Russian poet Osip Mandelstam and a writer in her own right, recalls in her memoirs:

> We never asked, on hearing about the latest arrest, "What was he arrested for?" but we were exceptional. Most people, crazed by fear, asked this question just to give themselves a little hope: if others were arrested for some reason, then they wouldn't be arrested, because they hadn't done anything wrong. [. . .] "What was he arrested for?" "*What for?*" Akhmatova would cry indignantly whenever, infected by the prevailing climate, anyone of our circle asked this question. "What do you mean, *what for*? It's time you understood that people are arrested *for nothing!*"
>
> *(1970, pp. 10–11)*

This empty what-for had caught Osip Mandelstam, had deemed a poem that he wrote criminal or counter-revolutionary, but by the time he was taken from his home in 1938, during the reign of Joseph Stalin and at the height of the Great Purges of the late 1930s, no legal justification was necessary for someone to be criminalized and taken in this way. By that point, Article 58 – the section of the Soviet criminal code regarding "counter-revolutionary criminal activity"– had become the arbitrary law of the land, and there was a widespread understanding that accusations of crime were simply tools for totalitarian control.

It had been only twenty years since the Russian Revolution of 1917 and the rise of Bolshevism, a communist ideology based on the theories of German theorist Karl Marx and Russian revolutionary politician Vladimir Lenin; within this ideology,

DOI: 10.4324/9780367817114-15

both the production and wealth of the nation would be centralized, and differences in economic class would cease to exist. The bourgeoisie – or the wealthy, land-owning class – would no longer wield power over the proletariat – the working class. Bolshevism evolved to become the Communist Party of the Soviet Union, and the consolidation of power by the party – and ultimately by Stalin himself – led to a period of dictatorship known as Stalinism. A part of this evolution was the growth, transformation, and manipulation of Marxist-Leninist notions of crime and justice; forced into an orthodox adherence to Marxism-Leninism, criminology became a snake eating its own tail until, eventually, consuming itself.

Marx himself wrote next to nothing on crime. Marxist criminology, then, is an interpretative creation of later theorists. In the U.S. and Western Europe, Marxist criminological theory grew most visibly throughout the 1970s. Taylor, Walton, and Young (1975) summarize its basic approach: "Insofar as the crime-producing features of contemporary capitalism are bound up with the inequities and divisions within material production and ownership, then it must be possible via social transformations to create social and productive arrangements that would abolish crime" (p. 20), and they propose the establishment of "a criminology which is normatively committed to the abolition of inequalities in wealth and power" (p. 44). The criminologists of the U.S. and Western Europe, however, approached Marxist criminology as theory, while Soviet Marxist criminology approached it as practice; Marxist-Leninist studies of "crime" and "deviance" were put to use as the Soviet state attempted to build a society free of social problems and class inequities. In their historical practice, we find that abolishing capitalism in favor of communism does not, in itself, abolish violence, social divisions, or inequalities in wealth and power.

As criminologist Louise Shelley (1979a) writes: "The history of early Soviet criminology raises serious questions concerning contemporary Marxist claims that socialism leads to a progressive legal system and improved criminology which better serves the interest of the masses" (p. 396). Shelley leaves her argument on those questions; this is where we begin. The aim of this chapter is to deconstruct Marxist criminology by observing Marxist criminology deconstruct itself.

Early Criminology in Russia: Enter Lombroso

Toward the end of the nineteenth century in Russia, the social sciences became an object of focus for both the intelligentsia and the revolutionary working class.[1] The modernization of Russian social, political, and legal structures, alongside growing anti-imperialist movements, created a chaotic and dynamic environment for social scientists and revolutionaries. Particularly in the cities, questions of morality, sexuality, and acts deemed criminal became central to visions of alternatives to imperialism and capitalism.

Historian Sharon Kowalsky (2009) has detailed efforts to standardize the administration of criminal law and the growth of three distinct schools of criminology in Russia during this period: the anthropological school (or what would be more commonly referred to now as biological criminology), the sociological school, and what Kowalsky describes as the "left wing," which included the Marxist-Leninist school (pp. 23–40). As historian Laura Engelstein (1992) has demonstrated, though Russian philosophical trends tended to take a primarily sociological approach to examining behaviors considered criminal or deviant, from the 1880s onward, Russian psychologists and medical doctors began to turn toward biological and psychological explanations (pp. 131–33). Russian physician Praskov'ia Tarnovskaia's 1889 *Anthropometric Study on Female Prostitutes and Thieves*[2] was, in fact, a source text for Cesare Lombroso's 1893 book *The Female Criminal and the Prostitute*,[3] and by the mid-1890s, Lombroso's work was in turn becoming influential in Russian criminology. This era of reform and impending revolution, however, was premised on the belief that both society and individuals could be fundamentally transformed, and so even those researchers and doctors who incorporated Lombroso into their work were reluctant to eliminate sociological considerations (Engelstein 1992, pp. 139–43). Even Tarnovskaia, who had taken measurements of the bodies of prostitutes to argue for a correlation between biology and behavior, argued that poverty, lack of employment opportunities, and poor health care were likely to have an impact on both behavior and biology (cited in Engelstein 1992, pp. 138–39). Similarly, D.A. Dril', a jurist and law professor, wrote in 1904: "We do not know man outside of society, and we do not know society without man and the surrounding cosmic environment. Therefore science, in its totality . . . cannot study crime and criminality as a result of only anthropological or sociological or cosmic factors" (cited in Kowalsky 2009, p. 30). Nevertheless, the prerevolutionary period was marked by a rise in everyday acts of violence and anti-imperialist terrorism, and biological criminology in particular "provided a justification for the removal of criminals from society" (Kowalsky 2009, p. 28), which was useful to an imperialist state struggling for survival.

Eliminating crime was one of the grand visions of Marxism-Leninism, and so the biological "born criminal" framework was seen as defeatist and unacceptable. Revolution-era Marxist-Leninist criminologist M.N. Gernet (1906) argued that economic factors were surely the key, and that the legal system had an obligation to represent the mostly impoverished masses, rather than act as a foot-soldier for the wealthy. Between 1905 and 1917, as the triumph of Bolshevism over imperialism began to appear increasingly imminent, Marxist-Leninist frameworks for analyzing everything from politics to gender roles to basic social norms became ever more common.

During the first several years after the 1917 revolution, conceptions of crime largely framed it as a remnant of the imperial past, and by the early 1920s, new criminal codes were being created and adopted by the new Bolshevik government (Kowalsky 2009, pp. 9–12). Shelley (1979a) has demonstrated that criminology from the revolution through the mid-1920s was a very robust field, and that researchers from across disciplines and practices examined acts classified as criminal from multiple approaches, from individual motivations to the effects of new social, political, economic, and family and gender norms, taking into account everything from age, region, education, employment, childhood experiences, biology, and psychology to alcoholism, artistic and cultural practices, and more. The constant changes in social, political, and economic structures meant that criminological studies were also pressed to define and account for these changes. In other words, a new and shifting post-revolutionary society called for new and shifting post-revolutionary understandings of society. This became dangerous, however, to both Bolshevik rule and to criminologists themselves.

Marxist Criminology Abolishes Lombroso . . .

Friedrich Engels wrote in 1845: "We eliminate the contradiction between the individual man and all others, we counter-pose social peace to social war, we put the axe to the root of crime – and thereby render the greatest, by far the greatest, part of the present activity of the administrative and judicial bodies superfluous" (p. 248). In the Soviet case, this is not what happened. After the revolution, the Bolsheviks began to put ample resources into criminological research. In 1918, a research center was built in Petrograd (now St. Petersburg), with several research centers and publications appearing within the next few years (Shelley 1979b). From the first years following the revolution, new administrative bodies focused on surveillance and social control were created, and the Cheka – the infamous Soviet secret police – materialized just a few months after the revolution (Juviler 1976, pp. 18–24). These bodies conscripted criminologists to support their work. As Kowalsky (2009) writes, "[B]ecause the state supported the discipline and had a specific purpose for it, namely, to understand the causes of crime and to develop methods to hasten its elimination, criminology remained bound by the state's needs and dependent on the state for its existence" (p. 51). As such, the promise of post-imperial egalitarianism gave way to State-centered control.

The implications of this for criminology – and for criminologists themselves – were profound. The State, ostensibly Marxist-Leninist, demanded the elimination of all non-Marxist frameworks, and so allowable approaches to the development of criminological theory were slowly but definitively reduced throughout the 1920s. By 1929, this meant a clear condemnation of what was termed "neo-Lombrosianism", as well as explicit accusations that criminology up until that point had focused on individualist, rather than social and economic, causes, and was therefore fundamentally bourgeois and anti-Marxist. S.Ya. Bulatov (1929) was one of the first people to articulate these accusations clearly, in his essay "Revival of Lombroso in Soviet Criminology." Here, Bulatov writes that Lombroso's theories represent a fundamental misunderstanding of the socioeconomic and historical foundations of crime (p. 43). According to Marx, Bulatov argues, individuals are fully formed by their social relations and class position, and so "neo-Lombrosian" theories that support individualist understandings of crime threaten social cohesion with their bourgeois understandings of society; he openly challenges the "neo-Lombrosian" criminologists to disprove the accusation that Lombroso's theories contradict

Marxism-Leninism (pp. 53–57). Biological criminology, in essence, was positioned as dangerous to the Soviet vision.

These condemnations of "neo-Lombrosian" criminology reached the Communist Academy, a Marxist-Leninist think tank and research center in Moscow, and in 1929, discussions at the academy made it clear that previous approaches to criminology were to be eliminated. Marxist-Leninist ideology had led the academy to the conclusion that, as crime was a result of social and socioeconomic conflicts, the establishment of Soviet socialism would naturally result in the decrease or disappearance of crime, rendering useless any theories and disciplines that did not study and reveal further methods for molding the properly Soviet citizen. Within a year of the Communist Academy's dismissal of all but Marxist-Leninist criminology, most criminological centers were shuttered (Shelley 1979b, pp. 624–5). According to their ideologies, this was sensible: with the conflicts of capitalism abolished, crime would cease, and the only remaining conflicts would be those between counter-revolutionaries and the (revolutionary) State.

. . . Marxist Criminology Abolishes Itself

Crime did not cease. On the contrary, millions of people over the next decade were arrested and imprisoned during the most aggressively punitive phase of Soviet history. And here we split for a moment from the historical narrative to follow a fork in the road and look more closely at Marxist criminology, as it was partially the limits of Marxist criminology itself that gave authoritarianism this opportunity. The Soviet approach to Marxist-Leninist criminology was clearly directed by the State, so it may be obvious that it was molded to fit the needs of Stalin and his party, but even in non-Soviet Marxist criminology, we may find the seeds for this tyranny.

Early Marxist criminologist Willem A. Bonger, in his influential book *Criminality and Economic Conditions* (1916), lays the foundations for critical Marxist criminology. Biology and anthropology cannot tell us anything about crime, he argues – only sociology can, as crime is inherently a social act bound by the morality of the society within which it takes place (pp. 378–9). On a structural level, he recognizes that it is the ruling class which has the ability to "class a certain act as a crime," and also that "punishment is still in great part a manifestation of the desire for vengeance (although regulated)" (pp. 379–80). One of his central questions is why a person acts against the larger interests of the social group, and he rejects the conclusion that these acts are simply due to the "innate egoism" of the individual (p. 381). This idea, he argues, rests on the faulty belief that egoistic acts are isolated holdovers from more "primitive," "less-developed" societies, while people of more advanced societies have become less egoistic. Instead, he says, it only *looks* like modern society is less egoistic and violent, and that the business of capitalism hides all the same forms of violence behind a veneer of trade and regulation: the capitalist who exploits workers and low-wage consumers is no less egoistic or violent than medieval robber-barons, and colonizers who force the colonized into the capitalist fold are no less violent than their murderous forebears (pp. 389–90). Further, he argues, these capitalists and colonizers are the ones writing the criminal codes.

On the other hand, he argues, the most altruistic social groups, where acts of egoism and crime are fewer, are groups where things are held in common (in a sort of "state of communism"), where there is no stratification of wealthy/poor, and where collective effort guarantees survival (pp. 395–97). Ultimately, he writes, their peace was found

> in *the mode of production, which brought about a uniformity of interest in the persons united in a single group, obliged them to aid one another in the difficult and uninterrupted struggle for existence, and made men free and equal, since there was neither poverty nor riches, and consequently no possibility of oppression.*
>
> *(p. 397; the italics are his)*

When the mode of production became capitalist, however, and when labor became an item for exchange and personal savings rather than a collective effort toward survival, "the mode of production begins to run counter to the social instincts of man instead of favoring it as heretofore" (pp. 398–9). This is where the Marxist really comes out: capitalist modes of production are the root of criminal transgression. He is arguing, then, that crime is created, not simply by economic conditions, but by a moral corruption caused by capitalism that leads to an environment where "man has become very egoistic and hence more capable of crime" (p. 402). The reliance on exchange rather than collaboration; the focus on individual survival and profit-seeking; the fact that profit, rather than people's needs, drives social relations; the exploitation and competition upon which this is all built; and the relationship between state power and the ruling classes: all of these lead to both moral and material poverty (pp. 402–7). Social cohesion becomes an impossibility, and at this point, "the economic interests of all are in eternal conflict among themselves, compassion for the misfortunes of others inevitably becomes blunted, and a great part of morality consequently disappears" (p. 532). In this scenario, both lawful and unlawful transgressions are bound to occur.

Bonger divides crime into four categories: economic, sexual, political, and vengeance-based, with the first and fourth being most prevalent (pp. 536–44). He eventually concludes that each of the categories is either fully created or exacerbated by capitalist economic conditions. And ultimately, he argues that "where crime is the consequence of economic and social conditions, we can combat it by changing those conditions" (pp. 667–9). Essentially, if society were to move toward communistic production, in which cultural and real wealth were shared by all, acts born of poverty and greed, moral debasement, and even prostitution and alcoholism would all be curbed. He concludes: "These crimes will not totally disappear so long as there has not been a redistribution of property according to the maxim, 'to each according to his needs'" (p. 671). The Soviet Marxist-Leninist criminologists would certainly concur with Bonger's arguments.

It was not until the late 1960s and 1970s that critical Marxist criminology would emerge again with any prominence, at which point both activist and academic engagement with Marx became more common. William Chambliss, for instance, in "Toward a Political Economy of Crime" (1975), rejects cultural and psychological explanations and argues that an analysis of the social relations within capitalism reveals "that crime becomes a rational response of some social classes to the realities of their lives" and that "[t]he state becomes an instrument of the ruling class enforcing laws here but not there, according to the realities of political power and economic conditions" (p. 168). Chambliss, like Bonger, pays particular attention to the idea that the State and hence the laws are on the side of the bourgeoisie:

> As capitalism develops and conflicts between social classes continue or become more frequent or more violent (as a result, for example, of increasing proletarianization), more and more acts will be defined as criminal.
> The criminal law is thus not a reflection of custom (as other theorists have argued), but is a set of rules laid down by the state in the interests of the ruling class, and resulting from the conflicts that inhere in class structured societies; criminal behavior is, then, the inevitable expression of class conflict resulting from the inherently exploitative nature of the economic relations.
>
> *(p. 151)*

Chambliss also points out that, due to the preferential treatment shown to the ruling classes by any system of crime and punishment within capitalism, it will always appear that the working classes commit more crimes (p. 166). Finally, like Bonger, he concludes that crime creates competition among the proletariat, distracting them from their exploitation, and that "socialist societies should have much lower rates of crime because the less intense class struggle should reduce the forces leading to and the functions of crime" (pp. 152–3). And again: the Soviet Marxist-Leninist criminologists would certainly concur.

Central to this later wave was Richard Quinney, whose development as a Marxist criminologist is visible in a chronological examination of his theories. Early on, Quinney (1964) recognizes that "[c]riminal law in a society is related to the success of certain groups to influence the agencies that formulate and enforce the criminal law, the values and norms of these groups, and shifts in the structure of power" and that, as a result of this politicization of how criminal codes are created and enforced, "[c]riminal behavior, thus, is a product of political behavior" (pp. 20–21). Quinney's (1970) book *The Social Reality of Crime* furthered his argument that it was not just those deemed criminal, but those who have the power to determine what is criminal, who play a part in the overall creation of crime, and thus the nature of that power must be interrogated. Quinney's argument increasingly molded around a Marxist framework, and by the end of the 1970s, he even saw the field of criminology as culpable in this capitalist cycle: the bourgeoisie exploits the proletariat, and to maintain order even in light of the class divisions, particular classes are created to perform this maintenance, including criminologists. He writes: criminology "has been, and continues in large measure to be, a body of thought and practice that seeks to control anything that threatens the capitalist system of production and its social relations" (1979, p. 447). And Quinney, again like the others, sees socialism as the only way out: "Only with a different society (for me, a socialist one, a classless society) could there be a good society with little crime. This also means that criminology . . . must locate the source of class and power, and make possible a form of practice" (quoted in Wozniak, Cullen, and Platt 2015, p. 212). And again: the Soviet Marxist-Leninist criminologists would certainly concur.

Why, then, did the installation of Marxism-Leninism lead not to a decrease or disappearance of crime but to a surge? In order to answer this question, we return to the fork in the road where theory and the historical narrative split; this time, we take the path of the historical narrative, until the two paths converge.

Journalist and activist Masha Gessen (2017) describes an onslaught against the social sciences that began in the early 1920s under the leadership of V.I. Lenin, pointing to Lenin's deportation of hundreds of researchers and intellectuals; to the shutting down of all social science and humanities departments and institutes at Moscow State University between the mid-1920s and the early 1930s; and to Lenin's derision of both the word and the concept of sociology and his targeting of those who supported it (pp. 17–30). The field of criminology was among those abolished. Shelley (1979a) has demonstrated that, at the point that criminology began to disappear, it had already become the foot-soldier of a regime aiming to find ways to scientifically classify what it framed as the dangerous and counter-revolutionary impulse of kulaks (wealthy peasants), speculators (capitalists), and Caucasian and Central Asian peoples, and "by discussing these politically motivated arrests in scholarly terms, [criminologists] helped legitimize repressive policies" (p. 395).[4]

State structures of surveillance and punishment had become more pervasive throughout the 1920s, and by the mid-1930s, any behavior or person deemed undesirable by Stalin was criminalized, labeled as counter-revolutionary. Shelley (1979b) points out that among the last remaining criminologists in the later 1930s, some "justified the worst of the society's repressions as the appropriate answer to the threatening problem of class crimes" (p. 628). Ultimately, under Stalin's thirty-year reign, millions of people were "purged" (imprisoned or executed) by a robust and intricate network of bureaucrats and secret police. In the first wave of purges, known as the Great Terror, 1937–38, nearly 1.4 million people were arrested for Article 58's "counter-revolutionary crimes,"[5] which included the broad criminalization of any propaganda or agitation that threatened or undermined the Soviet project. The rate of persecution decreased until the second wave of purges, 1942–46, during which time nearly 525,000 people were arrested under Article 58 (Vert, Mironenko, and Ziuzina, 2004, pp. 608–9).[6] Osip Mandelstam was among these millions, disappearing alongside poets, painters, farmworkers, doctors, students, politicians, and even former allies of Stalin – no one was exempt.

Persecution based on ethnicity and nationality also occurred on a widespread level. Musial (2013) has demonstrated that through the 1930s, ethnic and national minorities in the USSR were persecuted because they were perceived as anti-Soviet and inherently counter-revolutionary. Hundreds of thousands of Poles and Ukrainians[7] were forcibly resettled, deported, arrested, or executed, as well as smaller but still significant numbers of people of German, Romanian, Bulgarian, Czech, Latvian, Lithuanian, Estonian, Greek, Iranian, Armenian, Uzbek, Tatar, Chechen, Chinese, and Korean descent. This persecution was ostensibly based on the perception that these ethnic and national minorities were insufficiently committed to Soviet ideology, but as Musial argues, "[f]oreign relations only played a role in so far that many victims were accused of crimes (such as sabotage and espionage) in the name of foreign powers," and in reality, "they were only scapegoats for the massive and obvious deficiencies in all areas of the Soviet economy" (p. 123). Additionally, targeted deportations, forced migrations, constructed famines, and executions of ethnic minorities were part of a larger project of creating what philosopher Hannah Arendt (1951) would refer to as the "objective enemy." This vilification of ethnic minorities allowed for the strengthening of systems of surveillance, policing, and persecution. In fact, the Soviet practice of targeted deportations and forced migrations – as well as Soviet financial backing – were explicitly acknowledged as key supports for the (notably non-Marxist) State of Israel's violent expulsion of Palestinians in the late 1940s (Otto Pohl 2006).

Notably, persecution of ethnic minorities did not occur within a binary framework in which whiteness is positioned against people of color, largely because, as Roman (2012) has demonstrated, official Soviet policy did not recognize race as a category at all; this was an explicit move to position the USSR as more advanced, anti-racist, and egalitarian than the U.S., where anti-Black racism was known to be rampant. Clearly, however, the Soviet insistence that the USSR was free of racial and ethnic discrimination does not reflect the persecution that was carried out, and it is also clear that its Marxist-Leninist framework allowed no examination of racial or gendered oppression. Criticisms of these omissions within Marxist theory more generally have been and continue to be common. Indigenous scholar Vine Deloria Jr., for example, notes that Marxism's Eurocentric worldview means that the social problems it identifies, as well as the solutions it offers, are inapplicable and unable to deal with other worldviews, experiences, and power dynamics; instead, the narrow Eurocentric frame is simply a new version of colonialist "saviors," or as he puts it, "yet another group of cowboys riding around the same old rock" (1983, p. 135), deciding that their understanding of the world is the only valid understanding of the world. Similarly, committed Black feminist Communist Claudia Jones pointed to "the gross neglect of the special problems of Negro women" and insisted that Marxist-Leninist theory must develop an understanding of intersecting forms of oppression in order to be truly relevant (1949, p. 3). Jones saw Marxist-Leninist theory as a necessary component of breaking down gendered, racial, and class-based oppressions, but was also not naively under the impression that focusing only on class exploitation would magically eliminate racism or sexism.

And indeed, violence against women in the Soviet era suffered a similar erasure as violence against ethnic minorities. Official statistics on the incidence of violence against women do not exist through most of the Soviet period, as it was generally lumped with "hooliganism"; however, narratives on violence against women in the private sphere make it clear that, despite the fact that the state declared that it had officially "solved" gender inequality, violence against women was still rampant (Attwood 1999, pp. 4–15; Fitzpatrick 2000). As legal studies scholar Marianna Muravyeva (2014) notes, this suppression of statistics and state discourse on gendered violence was designed "in order not to reveal the existence of trends similar to those in capitalist countries. . . . In view of official gender equality and the new model of the Soviet family based on true communist morals, to admit that women were being beaten or killed by their husbands meant admitting that the whole project had failed" (p. 93). By the time the state began to examine family violence and sexual assault in the 1970s and 1980s, officials estimated that the majority of murders actually occurred in the domestic space (Sperling 1990). Within Marxist theory and the Soviet Marxist-Leninist state framework, class differences were the sole root of social conflict and harm, so there is no explanation for nor analytical framework to even begin to address the reasons for racial or gendered violence. Clearly, power dynamics other than class are at play, but the Marxist-Leninist insistence on the primacy of class reveals its own frailty when it lacks the language to examine these other power dynamics or the forms of violence they entail. That precise lack, in fact, allowed these harms not only to persist but also effectively rendered them invisible.

The central reason that criminology came under fire was that, in its ability to expose social problems uneradicated by communism, it held the potential to undermine the political imaginary of the increasingly totalitarian regime. As Kowalsky (2009) writes, the structures that were built around criminology in the 1920s indicated its legitimization as a field, but ultimately, it was determined that criminology was "a potentially dangerous and subversive discipline for the state to sponsor" (p. 75), and criminology itself was deemed unforgivably un–Marxist and counter-revolutionary. By the 1930s, criminology itself – even Marxist-Leninist criminology – had become undesirable for the State, and it was not only the research that was eradicated; many criminologists were themselves arrested and imprisoned, criminalized by the new (anti-criminology) criminology (p. 190). Political scientist and criminologist Peter Solomon's (1970) selected bibliography of Soviet criminology shows clearly that aside from a handful of stragglers, writings on criminology all but stopped between the late 1920s and the late 1950s (after the death of Stalin). As Solomon writes, "Conformity and contribution replaced debate and speculation as the norms for academic and intellectual behavior," and Soviet leaders determined that "criminology was neither Marxist (especially the biological research), nor did it square with a penal policy which had become punitive in word as well as in deed" (p. 393).

Here, then, the paths converge. The historical narrative meets critical Marxist criminology, and we find that in their meeting in the Soviet Union, criminology overall was deemed not Marxist at the point that the Terrors began. And here, where the paths converge, Arendt can act as a guide to our final analysis. As Arendt (1951) has noted, the key features of totalitarianism are isolation, terror, a firm but fickle ideology, and a fictional reality, and under Stalin, Soviet Russia collapsed into this framework. Criminology as a field was employed to aid in the installation of isolation and terror, to cover millions of people with the blanket of "counter-revolutionary," but when it became perceived as a threat to the glorification of Marxist-Leninist ideology and to the fictional reality of revolutionary utopianism, it had to be eliminated, and Marxist-Leninist criminology itself laid the groundwork for its own elimination.

Bonger argues that economic, sexual, political, and vengeful conflicts and harm would be curbed by state socialism, and that communistic living allows for altruism, morality, and social harmony to develop. Chambliss argues that political power is uniquely skewed under capitalism, and that state socialism would prevent that imbalance of power and relieve the pressures of the class struggle, which give rise to crime. Quinney argues that under capitalism, all crime is political, and that even criminology itself props up crime; like the others, he sees state socialism as the antidote to crime. Stalin and his party agreed with each of these points, and ultimately used all of these points to further build the fictional reality that was key to their consolidation of power: if state socialism has been installed, then crime should cease, and any remaining crime is counter-revolutionary in nature, as it disrupts the achieved harmony. At its worst, Marxist criminology does not acknowledge the possibility of corruption within the political and economic structures of state socialism nor other roots of violence and harm, and Stalin exploited this blind spot to its fullest extent.

By taking such a narrow view of the causes and solutions for acts deemed unlawful, Marxist-Leninist Soviet criminology offered justification for political persecution, and in a fatal twist, even justified persecution of itself. It described the world in which its own existence was counter-revolutionary by pure merit of suggesting that crime needs any analysis at all. Rather than a tool for analysis or explanation, it became a tool for dismissing analyses and explanations. It eliminated the need for the now-empty question: "what for?"

As Arendt (1951) writes, "Through the constant zigzag of the Communist Party lines, and the constant reinterpretation and application of Marxism which voided the doctrine of all its content because it was no longer possible to predict what course or action it would inspire," Stalin achieved a form of totalitarianism in which "the most perfect education in Marxism and Leninism was no guide whatsoever for political behavior – that, on the contrary, one could follow the party line only if one repeated each morning what Stalin had announced the night before" (p. 324). Political behavior, economic behavior, and social solidarity and harmony are not as closely intertwined as Marxist criminologists would have us believe. Each can transform independent of the others, and a theory which does not allow for this dynamism can no more help us account for what is considered crime within a Marxist-Leninist economic system than in a capitalist one.

Conclusion

Arendt (1951) argues that "the totalitarian ruler proceeds like a man who persistently insults another man until everybody knows that the latter is his enemy, so that he can, with some plausibility, go and kill him in self-defense" (p. 424). This is the logic that Marxist-Leninist criminology handed to Stalin: he imagined a scourge of criminals and counter-revolutionaries, imagined so completely that he built bureaucracies to ferret them out, and used his own persecution of these imagined enemies to justify very real and pervasive surveillance and punishment. The core theory that crime would be solved by the revolution, and hence that crime and counter-revolutionary acts were synonymous, laid the groundwork for the cruel and arbitrary and profoundly far-reaching Terrors.

Returning to Nadezhda Mandelstam (1970), she wrote: "The members of the exterminating profession had a little saying: 'Give us a man, and we'll make a case'" (p. 14). In a cruel and dizzying cycle, the persecution was itself the reason for the persecution. This would not have been possible without the development and weaponization of Marxist-Leninist criminological theory, which was first used against other forms of criminology and then against itself, ultimately leaving in its wake a malleable and manipulation-ready blueprint for a large-scale campaign of political persecution. It abolished its own "what for?" and was in turn abolished.

Notes

1 For an overview of prominent figures and trends of this era, see Isaiah Berlin, (1978) *Russian Thinkers*, London and New York, Penguin Books.
2 As Pauline Tarnowsky, (1889) *Étude anthropométrique sur les prostituées et les voleuses,* Paris, Lecrosnier.
3 With Guglielmo Ferrero, (1896) *La Femme criminelle et la prostituée,* Paris, Félix Alcan.
4 "Caucasian" here refers to those from the Caucasus, and Central Asian tends to refer to those from Kazakhstan, Kyrgyzstan, Tajikistan, Turkmenistan, and Uzbekistan; all of these areas were absorbed into the USSR.
5 The text (in Russian) is available here: ru.wikisource.org/wiki/Уголовный_кодекс_РСФСР_1926_года/Редакция_05.03.1926#Глава_I._Контр_._РЕВОЛЮЦИОННЫЕ_ПРЕСТУПЛЕНИЯ
6 The text (in Russian) is available online through the Russian state archives at http://statearchive.ru/459, and the numbers in question may be accessed at http://opisi.garf.su/pdf/gulag1/08-0-pril.pdf (Accessed 1 May 2020).
7 While the history of persecution of Ukrainians in the USSR is beyond the scope of this chapter, it continues to play a role in Russia-Ukraine relations. See, for instance, Lina Klymenko, (2016) "The Holodomor Law and National Trauma Construction in Ukraine," *Canadian Slavonic Papers*, vol. 58, no. 4, pp. 341–61.

References

Arendt, H. (1951) *Origins of Totalitarianism*, New York, Harcourt (1973).

Attwood, L. (1999) *Creating the New Soviet Woman: Women's Magazines as Engineers of Female Identity*, Houndmills, Macmillan.

Bonger, W.A. (1916) *Criminality and Economic Conditions* (trans. Henry P. Horton), Boston, Little, Brown, and Company.

Bulatov, S.Y. (1929) "Vozrozhdenie Lombrozo v Sovetskoi kriminologii" [Revival of Lombroso in Soviet Criminology], *Revoliutsiia prava* [Revolution of law], vol. 1, pp. 42–61.

Chambliss, W.J. (1975) "Toward a Political Economy of Crime", *Theory and Society*, vol. 2, no. 2, pp. 149–70.

Deloria, Jr., V. (1983) "Circling the Same Old Rock", in *Marxism and Native Americans*, Boston, MA, South End Press, pp. 113–36.

Engels, F. (1845) "Speech in Elberfeld", in Karl Marx and Frederick Engels, eds., *Collected Works*, vol. 4, London, Lawrence and Wishert (1975).

Engelstein, L. (1992) *The Keys to Happiness: Sex and the Search for Modernity in Fin-de-Siècle Russia*, Ithaca, Cornell University Press.

Fitzpatrick, S. (2000) "Lives and Times", in Sheila Fitzpatrick and Yurii Slezkine, eds., *In the Shadows of Revolution: Life Stories of Russian Women from 1917 to the Second World War*, Princeton, NJ, Princeton University Press, pp. 3–17.

Gernet, M.N. (1906) "Sotsial'nye faktory prestupnosti" [Social Factors of Crime], *Ezhenedel'naia iuridicheskaia gazeta* [Weekly Legal Newspaper], no. 26, pp. 2278–2283.

Gessen, M. (2017) *The Future Is History: How Totalitarianism Reclaimed Russia*, New York, Riverhead Books.

Jones, C. (1949) "An End to the Neglect of the Problems of the Negro Woman!" *PRISM: Political & Rights Issues & Social Movements*, 467, https://stars.library.ucf.edu/prism/467.

Juviler, P.H. (1976) *Revolutionary Law and Order: Politics and Social Change in the USSR*, New York, The Free Press.

Kowalsky, S. (2009) *Deviant Women: Female Crime and Criminology in Revolutionary Russia, 1880–1930*, DeKalb, IL, Northern Illinois University Press.

Mandelstam, N. (1970) *Hope Against Hope: A Memoir* (trans. Max Hayward), New York, Atheneum.

Muravyeva, M. (2014) "Bytovukha: Family Violence in Soviet Russia", *Aspasia*, vol. 8, no. 1, pp. 90–124.

Musial, B. (2013) "The 'Polish Operation' of the NKVD: The Climax of the Terror Against the Polish Minority in the Soviet Union", *Journal of Contemporary History*, vol. 48, no. 1, pp. 98–124.

Otto Pohl, J. (2006) "Socialist Racism: Ethnic Cleansing and Racial Exclusion in the USSR and Israel", *Human Rights Review*, vol. 7, no. 3, pp. 60–80.

Quinney, R. (1964) "Crime in Political Perspective", *The American Behavioral Scientist (pre-1986)*, vol. 8, no. 4, pp. 19–22.

Quinney, R. (1970) *The Social Reality of Crime*, New Brunswick and London, Transaction Publishers.

Quinney, R. (1979) "The Production of Criminology", *Criminology*, vol. 16, no. 4, pp. 445–58.

Roman, Meredith L. (2012) *Opposing Jim Crow: African Americans and the Soviet Indictment of U.S. Racism, 1928–1937*, Lincoln, NE, University of Nebraska Press.

Shelley, L. (1979a) "Soviet Criminology After the Revolution", *The Journal of Criminal Law and Criminology*, vol. 70, no. 3, pp. 391–6.

Shelley, Louise (1979b) "Soviet Criminology: Its Birth and Demise, 1917–1936", *Slavic Review* vol. 38, no. 4, pp. 614–28.

Solomon, P.H. Jr (1970) "A Selected Bibliography of Soviet Criminology", *Journal of Criminal Law and Criminology*, vol. 61, no. 3, pp. 393–431.

Sperling, V. (1990) "Rape and Domestic Violence in the USSR", *Response to the Victimization of Women & Children*, vol. 13, no. 3, pp. 16–22.

Taylor, I., P. Walton, and J. Young, eds. (1975) *Critical Criminology*, London, Routledge & Kegan Paul.

Vert, N., S.V. Mironenko, and I.A. Ziuzina, eds. (2004) *Istoriia stalinskogo Gulaga: Konets 1920-kh – pervaia polovina 1950-kh godov, 1: Massovye repressii v SSSR* [History of Stalin's Gulag: End of the 1920s to the First Half of the 1950s, 1: Mass Repression in the USSR], Moscow, Rosspen.

Wozniak, J.F., F.T. Cullen, and T. Platt (2015) "Richard Quinney's *The Social Reality of Crime*: A Marked Departure from and Reinterpretation of Traditional Criminology", *Social Justice*, vol. 41, no. 3, pp. 197–215.

12

ABOLITION NOW

Counter-Images and Visual Criminology

Michelle Brown

Abolition Envisioning and Criminology

In 2013, in the aftermath of Trayvon Martin's death and the acquittal of his killer, George Zimmerman, the most important social movement to emerge in decades took shape around a viral tweet that became #BlackLivesMatter. Alicia Garza, Patrisse Cullors, and Opal Tometi's call to action and Black love became the organizing platform of the Movement For Black Lives (M4BL), a global network of longstanding and emergent organizers with a decentralized platform and hierarchy dedicated to building Black power (Garza et al. 2014; Taylor 2016). Organizers, like Ash-Lee Woodard Henderson, Highlander Research and Education Center's first Black woman codirector, recount how the M4BL platform became an abolitionist document in which the word *abolition* does not appear, a vision that "came out of a moment in which everyone was saying there was no vision" (Chamseddine and Salehi 2017).

Yet the images, artwork, performances, protests, and visual iconography of abolition that accompany this moment have transformed the political terrain of reform and struggle in the public sphere surrounding criminal justice. The M4BL speaks to the manner in which an "image-event" can generate temporal oscillations, pulling a moment out of time, in such a manner as to invoke historical reckonings, tethered to the deeply visual scene of state crime, in this case, police killings (Smith 2020). Strassler defines the image-event as "a political process set in motion when a specific image or set of images erupts onto and intervenes in a social field, becoming a focal point of discursive and affective engagement across diverse publics" (2020: 9–10). These images take on a kind of iconic form. Shared millions of times, they are the flagship visuals of movements, simultaneously carrying a sacred, affective life for movement work and intensely contested by counterinsurgent and opposing forces.

DOI: 10.4324/9780367817114-16

As one exemplar, activist and artist Ricardo Levins Morales' deep blue image of Trayvon Martin in his hoodie, an object imbued after his death with racist fears and desires for violence, envisions a future without the killing of Black children through the repetition of historical demands (see Figure 12.1). It at once echoes the placement in his coffin, above his mutilated body, of photos of a smiling Emmett Till by his mother, Mamie Till-Mobley, as well as the pledge and aspiration of Ella Baker's Civil Rights–era words: "*Until the killing of black men, black mother's sons, becomes as important to the rest of the country as the killing of a white mother's son. We who believe in freedom cannot rest until this happens.*"

This image circulated widely, and continuously reappears when another state killing occurs, as a resurgent icon of the long struggle of Black mothers seeking justice for their murdered children and a related call for abolition via transformative justice, a movement that seeks to address harm with reduced reliance on the state (generationFive 2017; Smith et al. 2006; Dixon and Piepzna-Samarasinha 2020). This mobilization has taken shape among families and organizers whose communities have been radically and negatively reorganized around the carceral state. In opposition to mass criminalization and interpersonal, state, and structural violence, anti-violence organizers seek to generate community control, practices, and infrastructure by reducing, dismantling, and divesting from the major institutions of criminal justice (prisons, jails, police, money bail, immigrant detention, borders, etc.). These counterpublics, what Fraser names as "discursive arenas where members of subordinated social groups invent and circulate counterdiscourses," become key media justice spaces where Black women, sexual violence survivors, and queer people of color can be heard and seen (1990: 67; see also Highfield 2016; Powell 2015; Salter 2013, 2016; Dodge 2016; Fileborn 2017; Wood et al. 2019).

In many ways, abolitionists push back against the dominant frames of criminology, revealing the foundational and often problematic ways in which the visual operates in criminology. For instance, pioneering Italian criminal anthropologist Cesare Lombroso is most well known for his massive collection of photographs and drawings of prisoners that led him to theorize "the born criminal" as a biological predisposition, visualized through race, poverty, and ethnicity. Relatedly, criminologists have pointed to how photography's foundations are rooted in the identification of bodies designated as criminal, such as the mug shot. Efforts to catalog the "criminal man" through careful measurements and records of their bodies are found in the emergence of policing, in the vast collections of criminal photographs introduced by Francis Galton and Paris police clerk Alphonse Bertillon. In this manner, photography has been essential to criminology, with the camera a key technology through which to enhance systems of surveillance and control, from crime scenes to police stations, jails to border crossings, CCTV to drones and biometric recordings. Furthermore, the frequent circulation of images of handcuffs, badges, police officers, the racialized body behind bars, and people in orange jumpsuits and chains challenges us to rethink the supplemental, secondary, and thoughtless uses of images in reports, student papers, textbooks, and research.

FIGURE 12.1 "Trayvon Martin – Ella Baker."

Artist: Ricardo Levins Morales

Source: www.rlmartstudio.com/product/trayvon-martin-ella-baker.

Conversely, abolition images interrupt the public frames of safety and justice by interrogating the manner in which crime is linked to punishment and how both are linked to racialized bodies. It exposes the fetishization of the image or photograph as "proof" or evidence, frames that time after time have failed to address racialized violence, from lynchings to police killings, capital punishment to mass incarceration. These "scenes of subjection" (Hartman 1997), overly simplistic, capable of valorizing and reifying state violence, dominate the public field of vision. Here, as criminologists, we actively "subject the dead to new dangers and to a second order of violence" (Hartman 2008: 5), a reproduction and reification of the grammar of death. And whether mourning seeks to be public, as with Mamie Till Mobley's remarkable decision to display her son's mutilated body and her own grief, or private, as with Lesley McSpadden, clamoring in the August heat for her son's body to be removed from a Ferguson, Missouri, street, Black maternal rage is always a kind of counterpublic against the form of white liberal democracy in which these lives and deaths are considered ungrievable, vilified and disprized in fearful white imaginaries, rendered numbers in criminology. For Christina Sharpe, this counter-labor is an abolition project, as it is a question of how "we might continue to imagine new ways to live in the wake of slavery, in slavery's afterlives, to survive (and more) the afterlife of property" (18). As Sharpe insists, "We're all positioned by the wake, but positioned differently . . . it's a way to think about continued precarity and violence, and where you're positioned in relation to it. And it can give people across race a way to understand the visceral responses to this work" (Mitter 2017).

Like wake work, abolitionist visions carry a strategic focus on forms that generate visibility beyond Black death, by centering and humanizing the voices of those targeted by the state and challenging the official histories and master narratives of the carceral state and criminology. As Sharpe writes, the wake is also the space in which a particular kind of life through labor and impossible joy develops: Black social life insists, against all odds, its own existence. Critical elements of this anti-prison work defy universalizing white epistemologies through what Gilmore describes as a shared grief at the loss of children and one which makes no judgments about innocence. It practices hope by coding crisis as an opportunity where analysis and action allow those targeted for premature death to make visible the ways in which prisons and police negatively organize their families and communities (2007). Against the logic of criminal justice and prisons, they ask instead what might it look like to build around the unimaginable tasks of abolition in practices of everyday life. James writes similarly of the essential vantage points of those directly affected by mass criminalization and the carceral state, where "[l]ove and rage constitute the organizing force behind this gathering coordinated during expanding wars. Love for community, freedom, and justice, for the incarcerated and for the 'disappeared' – for those dying or surviving in war zones" (James 2013: 208; see also 2005).

This practice is evident in another widely shared graphic, by Jesus Barraza, Mazatl, and Melanie Cervantes of Justseeds.org. In it, "I am Trayvon Martin and My Life Matters" is printed beneath a colorful graphic rendition of another family photo of a smiling Trayvon. The artists encourage its distribution with "Download this graphic for free and share widely" (see https://justseeds.org/graphic/downloadable-i-am-trayvon-martin-posters/). The loving portraiture of Black lives taken by the state as well as the hashtag justice that follows – #HandsUpDontShoot; #IfThey-GunnedMeDown; #SayHerName; #FreeThemAll; #NoJusticeNoPeace; #NoN-ewJails; #DefundThePolice – continue as ongoing efforts to counter the deep criminalization and dehumanization of the carceral and white supremacist state.

For critical, radical, and Black revolutionary criminologists, criminology, as a project and discipline, is deeply implicated in this violence of the state, insepara-ble from its prosthetic institutions (policing, prisons, detention, etc.) and collusions with power. The empirical acknowledgment of criminal justice as foundational to the exercise of violence remains one of our largest obstacles in the pursuit of social change. An uneven history of radical and critical criminologies has pointed toward these structuring tensions, but it remains to be seen whether criminology can be a space for the work of abolition. The emergent study of visual criminology (Brown 2014; Brown and Carrabine 2017, 2019; Carrabine 2012) provides a fraught but potential space from which to better understand – and commit to – the project of abolition in its ongoing, urgent concern with the complexity of relationships between crime, law and the state, as well as the role of control, power, and resistance. From a critical visual and carceral perspective, crime and punishment are never neu-tral nor total in their representation, nor are they usefully coupled together. Only in rupturing the dyad of crime and punishment – in disturbing the assumptions that punishment meaningfully reduces crime or that mass incarceration is related to crime rates – do we get to rethink the terms of carceral reproduction, safety, and new ways of being. For an attuned visual criminology, scopic regimes – ways of seeing and understanding the world that dominate us – demand interrogation. In this sense, like abolition, visual criminology might point us toward insurrectionary images that challenge, coerce, constrain, transgress, and fail – in order to imagine an otherwise. Let us look at three ways in which this work of images and envisioning takes shape: the countervisual, material, and affective labor of abolition optics.

The Countervisual Work of Abolition Images

Abolitionists demand "the right to look" at what authority always seeks to conceal and control. This demand is situated against the long history of disappearances of largely queer, Indigenous, people of color into slavery, detention, prisons, and jails. In this way, the right to look is a plea to slow and halt the flow of systems of vio-lence and unmarked premature death – to not be disappeared. A key term for our purposes, visuality (Mirzoeff 2011; see also Schept 2017), captures the manner in which the control and containment of vision – and envisioning – is essential to the civilizational projects of empire and the state. It is a term that names the authorita-tive mobilization of specific forms of not just seeing but *ordering* the world. In this way, forms that prohibit questioning authority or challenging power are built into the fabric of societies. For abolitionists, visuality is the essential terrain of political struggle, as authority requires perpetual renewal and is therefore strategically open to chronic crises, contestation, and countervisual claims. Even as the broad set of social institutions and systems foundational to modernity – work, education, and family – are governed through the carceral capitalist state, where prisons, police, and law have become the normative "spatial fix" for *all* social problems (Gilmore 2007), abolition seeks to open up a space to contest these very configurations of power.

The countervisual practices of abolition attempt to expose and interrupt ideological sutures that have long reproduced and expanded the carceral: for instance, the racialization of criminality, the prison and a police/guard labor force as economic solution, punishment as related to crime, the police as safety, law as equal, criminal justice as progressive. In this disruption, countervisual tactics *also* simultaneously seek to open up and prefigure emancipatory spaces of possibility, not just through images, but through envisioning, which exceeds anything that could ever be made visible and is always a much larger affective and sensory project than looking – or the ocular – encompasses. This disturbance challenges the very terms, classifications, and methods of analysis we are given in order to open up the capacity to unsee, unimagine, and undo state violence – police and prisons – in an effort to make new worlds (Schept 2014; Story 2019). The right to look is the performative claim where none exists, and much of the work and iconography of abolition does just this. As those claims and demands enter the public sphere, they are quickly, once again, subject to counterinsurgent forces of the state that seek to weaken liberatory envisioning. This is the defining tension of abolition work. Urgent claims for Black life are met with counterinsurgent tweets, memes, and visuals characterising Black people as "thugs," "racists," "looters," and "terrorists." The "realism" of countervisuality is the means by which one tries to make sense of the unreality continuously coded by visuality's authority, while at the same time proposing viable alternatives. In this way, abolition animates refusals: No One Is Illegal. Public Health, Not Jails. Housing, Not Cops.

Much of the work of abolition, then, for those whose lives, families, and communities have been reordered by the carceral state, is to unsee, undiscipline, and undo technologies and forms of state violence by remembering, for instance, what land and life was – and looked like – before prisons and police (Schept 2014; Story 2019) and what it might look like after. It is an effort to mark how the oppressed have endured and survived the long *durée* of slavery, capital, and empire. As efforts at decolonization, abolitionists, like MPD150, an organization committed to ending policing on the 150-year anniversary of the founding of the Minneapolis Police Department, have created a report and a series of countervisuals dedicated to dismantling the police. As downloadable posters and prints on t-shirts, widely disseminated across social media, these images focus tightly on abolition as a necessary project of decolonization. One image reads: "There was a time before police and there will be a time after"(see Figure 12.2). Ghostly signs of life in the form of

FIGURE 12.2 "There was a time before police and there will be a time after."

Source: DeLesslin "Roo" George-Warren; www.mpd150.com/wp-content/uploads/2019/07/f27-time-before-and-time-after-1.jpg.

luminous Indigenous *thípis*, a Lakota term often reduced to "tipi" but originating from the verb *thí*, meaning "to dwell," materialize in the forefront of the frame while a state building recedes in the horizon. The artist, DeLesslin "Roo" George-Warren, a queer artist, researcher, and organizer from Catawba Indian Nation, writes:

> The reference image was taken in 2016/2017 at an Očhéthi Šakówiŋ Land Protection Event on the Lawn in Washington, DC in reaction to the threat to their land and water at Standing Rock. If you look closely, you can see the image of a Federal Building in the top left corner in light blue and yellow.
>
> *(Email correspondence with the Artist, June 30, 2020)*

In this indigenous and anti-colonial effort, abolishing the police becomes about marking temporal and spatial connections that open up past and future horizons. In their call for a police-free future, organizers write:

> Dream bigger: there was a time before police, and there will be a time after.
> Some of the solutions we need don't exist yet. There are some things we can do now, but this work is also about planting seeds. A vital first step toward a police-free future is simply being able to visualize what that future will look like. We must break out of the old mindset that police are this inevitable, irreplaceable part of society. They aren't. There are better ways for us to keep our communities healthy and safe, ways that do not include the violent, oppressive, unaccountable baggage of police forces. Check out the various sources mentioned here. Do more research, have more conversations, and help build the world in which you want to live.
>
> *(www.mpd150.com/10-action-ideas-for-building-a-police-free-future/)*

In another widely circulated image, organizers link the establishment of the Minneapolis Police Department to the protection of wealth, property, and whiteness of the entire city ("MinneaPOLICE") in the image of a surveillant weapon-wielding SWAT officer atop a police van (see Figure 12.3). Ricardo Levins Morales created the image in the aftermath of another Minneapolis police shooting, where Jamar Clark, a 24-year-old Black man, was killed.

Civilizational projects of empire and white supremacy – the border, the plantation, the reservation, the police, and the cage – are countered, in this work, through creative acts of community making. The histories of fugitive survival, revolt, and insurgency are replete with images that look directly at – and beyond – the production of state violence. They generate, by reappearing alternative ways of being – discussions, explanations, and alternatives – to the foundational violence of modernity. As Dillon writes, "The forms of culture created by fugitive activists are an index that makes visible connections, complicities, and ruptures that the discourses produced by the neoliberal-carceral state attempt to disappear." Writing and art," Dillon continues, become "sites for the creation of alternative epistemologies that the neoliberal-carceral state continually worked to erase and expunge from the knowable" (2018: 8).

The Material Work of Abolition Images

Many of the images selected for this chapter were chosen in part precisely because they are exemplars, subject to recirculation and repetition every time a new incident of state violence erupts into the public sphere – they have a long abolitionist life. What makes them so durable and prolific? Abolition spans an incredible time and space flow of global production. It arises out of the legacy of movements and organizers working to visualize the problems they face, the alternatives they might

FIGURE 12.3   "MinneaPOLICE: Protecting wealth and whiteness since 1867."

Source: MPD150 and Ricardo Levins Morales, www.RLMArtStudio.com.

imagine, and the information networks that can help build power. Material practices, from note boards to index cards, laptops to digital phones, point to how efforts to organize, store, and provide access in precarious spaces to abolitionist work is key to generating and sharing historically disappeared knowledge. This collective and banal labor – including the liking, sharing, posting, wearing of the everyday aesthetics of movement work – renders socially legible previously unimaginable futures. Spatially, abolition materializes as dialogic street art – graffiti in city streets, stencils on sidewalks, amateur videos, posters at direct actions, and flyers on neighborhood poles and windows across the world. It is the intentional swag of social justice: T-shirts to stickers, bookbag buttons and patches, mugs filled with coffee, intimately worn, promoted for fundraising, purchased to support. These artifacts carry a recognizable set of revolutionary aesthetic codes shared across borders, demanding the dismantling and destruction of prisons and police as institutions so that new worlds might arise, as in Figure 12.4, out of the flames.

While social justice art has a long legacy (Edelman 1995; Kauffman 2018; Milstein 2017; Reed 2005), as organizers Ejeris Dixon and Leah Lakshmi Piepzna-Samarasinha write, in the past few years, "transformative justice and community accountability strategies have become dramatically more visible" (2020: 8). Organizers, collectives, and activist scholars focused upon transformative justice have made intensive use of new and alternative media environments, providing free print and digital resources via action and outreach materials, flyers, posters, zines, legislative packets, newsletters, infographics, photos, online workshops and convergences,[1] podcasts,[2] webinars,[3] and digital toolkits and curricula,[4] that have produced a heightened public presence around abolition. Emergent modes and spaces of analysis have taken shape: from teach-ins to real-time idea mapping in movement spaces, archives to libraries to museums. The expressive use of media architecture – for instance, guerilla displays and projections on building facades – represents new cinematic sites for struggle within cities and increasingly privatized public spheres (www.pbs.org/newshour/arts/projection-light-artists-protest).

Spanning a range of demotic and horizontal media, the process of public envisioning is restless, viral, agonistic, ongoing. Abolitionist images move through intricate and unruly media ecologies – uncoordinated, rhizomatic, with fleeting monopolies on attention, seeking various and multitudinous channels of public address. This abolitionist mediascape generates important forms of vernacular, what Fleetwood calls "visual and haptic objects of love and belonging structured through the modern carceral system" (Fleetwood 2011; see also 2015: 490). Instead of looking at images, we are asked to watch them (Azoulay 2008) as they are constantly on the move and listen (Campt 2017) to them as they change the conversation and speak volumes about what has and has not been said. From Twitter to Instagram, Facebook to photographs, graphics to memes, images move in circuits of anonymous and authored production, digital permanence, viral proliferation, massive accumulation, and informal, new, alternative media channels. They produce a cumulative social

FIGURE 12.4 "Abolition, Not Reform: Burn the Prisons."

Source: Author's photograph, Melbourne, Australia.

and political effect that is challenging to measure empirically but vital to the transformation of public discourse. This happens, in part, because these images generate powerful, singular, intimate connections that become tangible material markers across neighborhoods and cities worldwide. We turn to this work of affect next.

The Affective Work of Abolition Images

Abolition images are cued to the possibility of an intrinsic affective connection. As Young writes, affect is not so much emotional or cognitive life but "the moment at which connection to something seen, heard, experienced or thought registers in the body and then demands that it be named or defined" (2014: 161; see also Young 2019). Abolition images seek to make the affective cut in the flow of information, to startle us long enough to ask other kinds of questions about the carceral state and the conventions of criminal justice. These images always materialize in interpretive and subjective spaces of desire, key spaces for "freedom dreams" and liberation study. As Hartman writes, overlooked images take form in an "archive of the exorbitant, a dream book for existing otherwise" (2019: xv), where, she argues, most people, including social scientists, have "fail(ed) to discern the beauty . . . they see only the disorder, missing all the ways black folks create life and make bare need into an arena of elaboration" (ibid: 5–6). Abolition has always been a space in which sites of intimacy, kinship, and futurity are visualized into existence.

As one contemporary example, Southerners on New Ground (SONG) have been instrumental in efforts across the US to end cash bail. Their Black Mamas National Bail Outs on the annual Mother's Day holiday in the US are intentional practices to create spaces of Black freedom, captured in the words and images that surround SONG cofounder Pat Hussain's declaration: "Money kept you in; Black love got you out" (www.scalawagmagazine.org/2020/01/song-combating-white-supremacy/). In sites of articulation, elaboration, and aspiration, abolition often visualizes the forms of emotional and intersectional labor that are dedicated to the emancipatory, with long legacies of producing visual and haptic objects of love. These include a massive but intimate archive of family photos from prison (Fleetwood 2015), as well as posters and photos at prison direct actions inscribed with "My son is not a paycheck" and "I am a mother" (Brown 2014), all affirmations of belonging and connection that reappear loved ones against the disappearance of relations by the carceral state. This affective life reverberates across new and social media as powerful communicative networks of emotions. Intensities of feeling search for new forms of expression and travel through mediated informational and sensory channels in a manner that often has an overwhelming cumulative dynamism and affective force, triggering trauma and pain for oppressed peoples – try following and analyzing a Twitter trend about state violence in real time. In all of this, abolition countervisual work offers modes of sensuous and aesthetic attunement, working as a conduit to focus attention, elicit public discourse, deepen community and intimate bonds, and shape cultural imaginaries as to how the world might be organized differently.

In these spaces, envisioning Black life is ceaselessly subject to white supremacist backlash. Charged signs of belonging work in complex ways – both insurgent and counterinsurgent – as mechanisms of identification and affective attachment that bind people to larger collectivities and histories. Affective investments that counter abolition, such as Blue Lives Matter or All Lives Matter, generate a desire for violence, both explicitly and implicitly, through erasure. They reveal the ways the carceral state produces a profound and dangerous psychic economy, resistant to any examination of its foundations and effects. The work of abolition exists always in relation to the perpetual tensions of white supremacy and racial capitalism – a tense field of utopian and dystopian, life-affirming and life-ending visions. In the visions produced by the carceral state, the ideas, feelings, and ideologies that police evoke are inseparable from "the structural privileges and marginalization that make some people desire state violence" (Seigel, loc 632), legacies imbued with whiteness (Seiler 2020; Hooker 2017). Moreover, these attachments to policing and prisons, undergirded by distant relations to those targeted by the state, refuse acknowledgment of histories of racial oppression, providing a moral infrastructure of support for intensive state violence.

Micah Bazant's graphic (see Figure 12.5) "I don't watch my neighbors. I see them. We make our community safer together"[5] counters this carceral dystopia. Instead, it reimagines community power and safety through an image that was designed for Justice For Families' "Night Out for Safety and Democracy" – an alternative to the National Night Out, a police and neighborhood watch–sponsored event.

The image is one of a lively, vibrant neighborhood block, where people of color across generations play, socialize, parent, and look out for one another. One can practically hear the voices, the music from the radio, the sounds of the city. The singular effect of the image is a refusal of policing: community replaces policing as safety, where people are *seen*, not surveilled and disappeared. Affectively charged, symbolic condensations of competing visions are always taking place in open-ended performances such as this – never fully exhausted, subject to repetition, transformation, and reactivation.

These counterpublics, "discursive arenas where members of subordinated social groups invent and circulate counterdiscourses" (Fraser 1990: 67), become key spaces where Black women, sexual violence survivors, and queer people of color can not only be heard but actively generate alternatives to the carceral state. Their efforts to highlight the gap between conflicting realities map the way in which fugitive ideas of hope are embedded and encoded in vexed but hopeful relationships. Public spheres are at once more participatory, more fractured, and more convulsive than ever before. The image is always happening, and always in the realm of the unpredictable. But as Tina Campt writes on the visual logics of fugitivity (see also Cobb 2015; Best and Hartman 2005; Neary 2016), in abolition work, "Something takes flight and escapes even as capture is always immanent" (2017: 18). Abolitionists look then to the "slippages, passages, undoings, proliferations and forms of flight that were impossible yesterday and might be impossible tomorrow" to "other ways of living, being, feeling, and thinking" (18). This is an "affective epistemology – a fugitive way of knowing that escapes articulation – that would give rise to a new ontology founded on collective becoming, not the singularity of being . . . to survive, thrive, and keep running in the space between escape and capture" (18).

FIGURE 12.5 "I don't watch my neighbors. I see them. We make our community safer together."

Source: Micah Bazant and Night Out for Safety and Democracy.

Conclusion

As a fugitive space, abolition and the cultural artifacts it produces interrupt the normative workings of criminal justice, exposing the violence of the carceral state. In doing this, they also teach movement work, provide modes of analysis, and point to how to live in uninhabitable spaces via new forms of relationality. Building from legacies of revolt and rebellion, they mobilize new and old kinds of skill-sharing and -building, tools and practices that criminological methods have often displaced and erased. As a shadow archive, abolition visions legitimate and center the intimate bonds, familial attachments, and solidarities of the most criminalized peoples of history. In doing so, they counter the official and criminological narratives that have sought to disappear them. Abolition, as an archive from the ground up, provides us a critical space for modes of visual and sensory study and engagement that work, instead, to dismantle systems of unfreedom and launch new legibilities and lexicons of emancipatory futures. Abolition now . . . and everywhere.

Notes

1 The 2018 theme for the Society for the Study of Social Problems was "Abolitionist Approaches to Social Problems"; the journal *Abolition* hosted a convergence in 2017 on abolishing border imperialism; and the International Conference on Penal Abolition annually engages these abolition-based themes.
2 See Beyond Prisons, Delete Your Account, and Rustbelt Abolition Radio.
3 For example, see Law for Black Lives' summer 2018 series: "This Is America: Lessons on Liberation"; Critical Resistance's donor webinars on abolition; Project South and Southern Assembly webinars.
4 See, for example: INCITE! Women of Color Against Violence's "Stop Law Enforcement Violence Against Women of Color & Trans People of Color!"; Creative Interventions Toolkit: A Practical Guide to Stop Interpersonal Violence; Project NIA's Transformative Justice curriculum guide; Popular Democracy, Law for Black Lives, and Black Youth Project 100's Freedom to Thrive: Reimagining Safety and Security in Our Communities; Critical Resistance's Abolition Toolkit; MPD150's Enough Is Enough.
5 https://justseeds.org/product/i-dont-watch-my-neighbors-i-see-them/

References

Azoulay, A. (2008). *The Civil Contract of Photography*. New York: Zone Books.
Best, S. and Hartman, S. (2005). Fugitive justice. *Representations* 92(1): 1–15.
Brown, M. (2014). Visual criminology and carceral studies: Counter-images in the carceral age. *Theoretical Criminology* 18(2): 176–197.
Brown, M. and Carrabine, E. (Eds.). (2017). *Routledge International Handbook of Visual Criminology*. London: Routledge.
Brown, M. and Carrabine, E. (2019). The critical foundations of visual criminology: The state, crisis, and the sensory. *Critical Criminology* 27(1): 191–205.
Campt, T. M. (2017). *Listening to Images*. Durham, NC: Duke University Press.
Carrabine, E. (2012). Just images: Aesthetics, ethics and visual criminology. *British Journal of Criminology* 52(3): 463–489.
Chamseddine, R. and Salehi, K. (2017, October 4). *Delete Your Account* (audio podcast). Retrieved from https://deleteyouraccount.libsyn.com/organize-the-south.

Cobb, J. N. (2015). *Picture Freedom: Remaking Black Visuality in the Early Nineteenth Century.* New York: NYU Press.

Dillon, S. (2018). *Fugitive Life: The Queer Politics of the Prison State.* Durham, NC: Duke University Press.

Dixon, E. and Piepzna-Samarasinha, L. L. (Eds.). (2020). *Beyond Survival: Strategies and Stories from the Transformative Justice Movement.* Chico, CA: AK Press.

Dodge, A. (2016). Digitizing rape culture: Online sexual violence and the power of the digital photograph. *Crime Media Culture* 12(1): 65–82.

Edelman, M. (1995). *Art to Politics: How Artistic Creations Shape Political Conceptions.* Chicago: University of Chicago Press.

Fileborn, B. (2017). Justice 2.0: Street harassment victims' use of social media and online activism as sites of informal justice. *British Journal of Criminology* 57(6): 1482–1501.

Fleetwood, N. R. (2011). *Troubling Vision: Performance, Visuality, and Blackness.* Chicago: University of Chicago Press.

Fleetwood, N. R. (2015). Posing in prison: Family photographs, emotional labor, and carceral intimacy. *Public Culture* 27(3 (77)): 487–511.

Fraser, N. (1990). Rethinking the public sphere: A contribution to the critique of actually existing democracy. *Social Text* 25/26: 56–80.

Garza, A., Tometi, O. and Cullors, P. (2014). A herstory of the# BlackLivesMatter movement. *Are All the Women Still White*: 23–28.

generationFIVE. (2017). *A Transformative Justice Handbook.* Retrieved May 15, 2018, from www.generationfive.org/wp-content/uploads/2017/06/Transformative-Justice-Handbook.pdf.

Gilmore, R. W. (2007). *Golden Gulag: Prisons, Surplus, Crisis, and Opposition in Globalizing California* (Vol. 21). Berkeley: University of California Press.

Hartman, S. V. (1997). *Scenes of Subjection: Terror, Slavery, and Self-Making in Nineteenth-Century America.* New York: Oxford University Press.

Hartman, S. V. (2008). Venus in two acts. *Small Axe: A Caribbean Journal of Criticism* 12(2): 1–14.

Hartman, S. V. (2019). *Wayward Lives, Beautiful Experiments: Intimate Histories of Social Upheaval.* New York: WW Norton & Company.

Highfield, T. (2016). *Social Media Everyday Politics.* Cambridge: Polity.

Hooker, J. (2017). Black protest/white grievance: On the problem of white political imaginations not shaped by loss. *South Atlantic Quarterly* 116(3): 483–504.

James, J. (2005). *New Abolitionists, the:(Neo) Slave Narratives and Contemporary Prison Writings.* Albany, NY: SUNY Press.

James, J. (2013). *Seeking the Beloved Community: A Feminist Race Reader.* Albany, NY: SUNY Press.

Kauffman, L. A. (2018). *How to Read a Protest: The Art of Organizing and Resistance.* Berkeley: University of California Press.

Milstein, C. (Ed.). (2017). *Rebellious Mourning: The Collective Work of Grief.* Chico, CA: AK Press.

Mirzoeff, N. (2011). *The Right to Look: A Counterhistory of Visuality.* Durham, NC: Duke University Press.

Mitter, S. (2017). What does it mean to be black and look at this? A scholar reflects on the dana schutz controversy. *Hyperallergic.* Retrieved June 1, 2019, from https://hyperallergic.com/368012/what-does-it-mean-to-be-black-and-look-at-this-a-scholar-reflects-on-the-dana-schutz-controversy/.

Neary, J. (2016). *Fugitive Testimony: On the Visual Logic of Slave Narratives.* New York: Fordham University Press.

Powell, A. (2015). Seeking rape justice: Formal and informal responses to sexual violence through technosocial counter-publics. *Theoretical Criminology* 19(4): 571–588.

Reed, T. V. (2005). *The Art of Protest: Culture and Activism from the Civil Rights Movement to the Streets of Seattle*. Minneapolis: University of Minnesota Press.

Salter, M. (2013). Justice and revenge in online counter-publics: Emerging responses to sexual violence in the age of social media. *Crime Media Culture* 9(3): 225–242.

Salter, M. (2016). *Crime, Justice and Social Media*. London: Routledge.

Schept, J. (2014). (Un) seeing like a prison: Counter-visual ethnography of the carceral state. *Theoretical Criminology* 18(2): 198–223.

Schept, J. (2017). Visuality and criminology. In *Oxford Research Encyclopedia of Crime, Media, and Popular Culture*. New York: Oxford University Press.

Seiler, C. (2020). The origins of white care. *Social Text* 38(1): 17–38.

Smith, A., Richie, B. E., Sudbury, J. and White, J. (2006). *The Color of Violence: INCITE! Anthology*. Cambridge, MA: South End.

Smith, S. M. (2020). *Photographic Returns: Racial Justice and the Time of Photography*. Durham, NC: Duke University Press.

Story, B. (2019). *Prison Land: Mapping Carceral Power Across Neoliberal America*. Minneapolis: University of Minnesota Press.

Strassler, K. (2020). *Demanding Images: Democracy, Mediation, and the Image-Event in Indonesia*. Durham, NC: Duke University Press.

Taylor, K. Y. (2016). *From# BlackLivesMatter to Black Liberation*. Chicago: Haymarket Books.

Wood, M., Rose, E. and Thompson, C. (2019). Viral justice? Online justice-seeking, intimate partner violence and affective contagion. *Theoretical Criminology* 23(3): 375–393.

Young, A. (2014). From object to encounter: Aesthetic politics and visual criminology. *Theoretical Criminology* 18(2): 159–175.

Young, A. (2019). Arrested mobilities: Affective encounters and crime scenes in the city. *Law, Culture and the Humanities*: 1743872119889824.

13

CIVIL LIES

Tatiana Lopes DosSantos

In Africa
The motherland
Her beauty stretches far and wide
The culture the colors so full of life
Her communities tight and full of love
People dance under the hot sun
People say the mountains sing
The land is rich with material things
Trees, gold, and silver took eons to make
But didn't take long for the colonizer to take
They ravage the fields for their precious cash crops
They take our oils, coffee, and tea
Mark up the price and sell it back
Our souls forced to be a means of production
Pay off the leaders
As a means of seduction
Of these riches, Africa sees not a sliver
They take their waste and dump it in our rivers
At this rate, the resources won't last
And all we'll have left is oceans of trash
Rubber, tobacco, ivory, and skin
How clever are they to disguise their sins?
Must be the best way to rebirth it again
Our label changes from slave to thug
Forced labor into a war on drugs

DOI: 10.4324/9780367817114-17

Because in fact it was never abolished
It was turned into something a little more polished
Flood the town with drugs and guns
Forced them to sell to feed little ones
We're kidnapped, arrested, for the problem you caused
Enslaved again under exploitative laws
Human? Or a criminal to whom no rights they gave
In America, a prisoner is synonymous with slave
What a coincidence, peculiar correlation
That following this, we saw mass incarceration
Doing their best to keep it subliminal
Dreaming up new ways to make Black people criminals
We're LGBT too, but get left behind
Are only white people allowed to have gay pride?
Will Black trans women always have to hide?
Under the guise of reform, we're on the same track
It's the American dream, what it's like to be Black
For hundreds of years, they have reigned
Millions of people enslaved
Of course, the mindset still remains
And they thought they were profound
But their minds were drowned
With greed, they were bound
But we still have our crowns
We still have our sound
we've risen from the burial grounds
They were mass, they were crass
A step up from the lash of the whip,
But now we're bloods, now we're crips
now we're libs smoking mids
All the labels are a trip
but they'll still steal our hair, and our clothes, and our lips
Now we're criminals, we're crazy liberals
a product of the time that we were 3/5
to be literal
They blame us for the shortcomings
They snuff out the Martin Kings
Drove a bus through our chains and links
But there will be a reckoning
They used white-out on what was once colorful
Laid thievery to ours that was cultural
Murdered mothers, fathers, aunts, uncles

Bodies cut up and put on display
Reduced to pseudo-science diagram, with no name
They said it was all in the name of God
They said they followed the rule of law
But your beloved bible told you what thou shalt not
So for each of these atrocities in hell, they will rot

INDEX